THE QUIET
REVOLUTION

THE QUIET REVOLUTION
The Story of a Small Miracle in American Life

&

Sara Harris
and
Robert F. Allen, Ph.D.

RAWSON ASSOCIATES PUBLISHERS, INC.
NEW YORK

Library of Congress Cataloging in Publication Data

Harris, Sara.
  The quiet revolution.

  1. Migrant agricultural laborers—Florida.
  2. Minute Maid Corporation.
  I. Allen, Robert Francis, 1928–   joint author. II. Title.
  HD1527.F6H37   1977   331.5′44′09759   77-17645

ISBN 0-89256-054-1

Copyright © 1978 by Sara Harris and Robert F. Allen
All rights reserved
Published simultaneously in Canada by McClelland and Stewart, Ltd.
Manufactured in the United States of America by
The Book Press, Inc., Brattleboro, Vermont

First Edition

This book is dedicated to the Minute Maid migrant workers and their families who, above everyone else, made the story happen. Their courageous crusade to help themselves—and all poor people in their vicinity—to a better life may well prove that the tragedy of migrancy in America is not unsolvable after all.

We lived and worked with them for two years off and on, and the experience, as we think and talk about it now, was miraculous, a time of joy for us both.

Contents

ACKNOWLEDGMENTS ix
A NOTE TO THE READER xi
INTRODUCTION xiii

Part I
Birth of a Vision 1

Part II
Two Women 189
    Saint Emanuela 192
    Johnnie Lou Atherton 226

Part III
Nine Years after the Beginning 247
INDEX 277

Acknowledgments

In writing this book we have incurred many obligations. For their assistance in all phases of the research project, but especially for their help in interpreting the life and feelings of poor black people—whether rural agricultural or city-bred—we are deeply grateful to our friends, Lily Haskins, able acting executive director of the Agricultural Labor Project, Inc. (ALPI), and Victoria Roberson, formerly a Minute Maid picker, now assistant director of the effective Fort Pierce–Indiantown branch of ALPI. Also Georgia Rushing, former picker, Outreach worker of the Frostproof-Wachula affiliate of ALPI and her son, Bobby, a college student on his way toward a career in engineering. And Herman Marshall and Dura Mae Everett, housing consultants during our time with ALPI.

To Pete and Marguerita Solano, and their wonderful children, we are grateful not alone for warm hospitality, but also diagnoses, anatomizing of migrant living.

We are indebted to William M. Kelly, now personnel director of Coca-Cola USA, and in our day vice-president in charge of the Florida citrus operation. He never interfered with our research among the workers and, in fact, encouraged them to be entirely open, even critical of the company, by assuring them that neither he nor any other executive would be privy to whatever information we should uncover. Also project managers, company-employed, Gerald Abell and Rudy Maxwell. And Kaye Clarke, the project's first registered nurse. And Mickey Roberts, the first child development coordinator.

We owe a special debt to supervisor Merle Albritton. He put us in touch with foremen and other supervisors who might never have allowed us into their lives without his intervention on our behalf.

We want to thank Arnold Harris, on-scene coordinator of consultants out of Human Relations Institute, (HRI), for clarifying many aspects of the program as he formulated and knew them.

⋞ A Note to the Reader

When this book was first conceived, we agreed that, although the events it relates are entirely true and accurate, it would be necessary to protect the privacy of most of the people involved, especially the agricultural workers, by turning them into symbols and giving them fictitious names. Further, they would not, could not, have shared with us their true feelings, thoughts, and life stories if they had not believed we valued their need for confidentiality as much as they themselves did.

There are, however, some people—mostly managers and company officials—whose true names and descriptions we do use. They are J. Paul Austin, C. Lucian Smith, Donald Keough, William M. Kelly, and Tom Cleveland, executives of The Coca-Cola Company. Gerald Abell, the first project manager; Kaye Clarke, first registered nurse and employed before the health center was established; Dr. Jerome Epstein, who screened migrants working for the company and their families for signs of pathology, also before the health center's beginning: Dudley Higgins, present director of the health centers; Mickey Roberts, first child development coordinator, Yvonne Patterson, present coordinator; Rudy Maxwell, project manager succeeding Gerald Abell; Ed Rouse, first trained accountant, and Ed Clark, present accountant; Lily Haskins, present acting executive director of the Agricultural Labor Project, Inc., and formerly its director of programs; Stanley Silverzweig, Arnold Harris, and the authors, of HRI-Human Resources Institute; members of governmental agencies who know and work with ALPI; Vernon Lee, director of a local Community Action Agency; Maynard Clayton of the Food Stamps Agency; Edward Ellsworth, regional director, Health and Rehabilitative Services, State of Florida, and president of the Council of Social Agencies at Fort Pierce and Indiantown; former pupils at the Central Region Child Development Center now in kindergarten and first grade in local public schools.

Also we, co-authors in every sense, decided that the story could be told best by concentrating on one person's view: Sara Harris's.

～§ Introduction

This is the story of the two most exciting, suspenseful, *emotional* years of our lives. We worked, lived, and participated in a quiet revolution of migrant orange pickers employed by Coca-Cola's Minute Maid operation within the existing order of conservative central Florida. A revolution sponsored, incredibly, by the conglomerate parent, which committed itself long-term to changing the appalling conditions under which its migrants lived and labored through *worker involvement* in policies and programs for change. They employed us members of the SRI-Human Resources Institute, management consultants to many large businesses and government agencies, as teachers and advisers to the newly named Agricultural Labor Project.

We went in 1968 to Auburndale, Florida, headquarters of Coca-Cola's Minute Maid operation, and began, almost immediately, to live, work, and mesh with the people, the migrants themselves. Some were beaten, defeated, hopeless; others, full of bootlicking "love" for their employers and, in fact, white people, most generally accepted the hard lives as their due. But this book must also stand as a testimonial to the ones, more than you'd expect, who'd managed, miraculously, to emerge from the quagmire of their lives—the shame, horror, poverty, knives, illegitimacy, brutality—as warm, dignified, capable human beings. We were, in the course of our changing relationship with them, to be constantly bowled over by some of their thinking and expressions.

"Well, when I first meet y'all . . . and a long time after, too," a migrant woman, later chairperson of one of the three effective child development centers, told Sara on a recent return trip to Florida, "I couldn' nohow figger you out, not y'all and not the company neither. And I says to everyones,

'Now, Coke, they must be have they reasons for saying all these great things they gon' help us do. And bring in the consultants put on this big act about how they cares so much about us people. They don't care, though. They's just here for the money, be all.'

"And once Coke decides it don't need to please us people no more . . . well, once the company do that, baby, this project were all gone and so was y'all. I used to talk about you all the time. I use to always say you has a long bunch of lies."

The book attempts to portray in its complexity the interaction between these migrant and agricultural workers, some of whom emerged as leaders, and the consultants, the company middle managers, and its executive suite. For all the conflict among us, and there was plenty, the resulting project managed to help the people achieve the organization of their own development corporations for pinpointing needs and taking the steps required to cope with them. They produced a list of successes that honestly went beyond our most fanciful hopes and dreams: a child *development,* not child care, program, staffed and administered ably by the people and open now to all of the poor; a people-run health center, presently funded to the tune of $590,000 annually by the Department of Health, Education and Welfare, governed by a community-wide board and serving, as does the child development center, not only Coca-Cola employees but all of the community's poor; a wonderfully equipped living-learning library whose minority-oriented books, films, recordings, etc., have to be the best in Florida and among the best in the country; people-owned low-income housing, *not* limited to Coca-Cola employees, financed by federally assisted low-cost mortgages, and built to the peoples' own specifications in place of the company shacks or sickening houses available for rent in the black or Mexican quarters; and migrancy in the Minute Maid groves on the way out, with nearly 40 percent of the groves and harvesting personnel regular company employees assured of both seniority rights and all fringe benefits enjoyed by other employees. Incidentally they are the best paid agricultural workers in America and the world.

What we think about most, though, discussing our experiences today, is the psychological result of the project that must be evident to anyone who knows the people now and knew them before it began. It's so clear, so wonderfully, excitingly clear, that some, more than we'd ever suspected could be, have been enabled to make an almost total break with their past and inbred feelings of inferiority based an pejorative ethnic and class labels. And even many, whose sense of dignity we'd believed to have been totally destroyed when we'd first met them, are slowly but, we believe, surely becoming less distorted about who they are, less filled with self-hate, less lowly in all their relationships. It is a matter of human dignity . . . and what is more important than that?

And the company's actions haven't been misconstrued, even if in some places its purpose has. Its harshest critics—some deeply inbred area and district supervisors who'd thought of themselves as highly placed "bossmen" and the workers as the lowest of the low before the project's beginning—have begun to admit, albeit reluctantly, it may be serving a good purpose after all.

To some of these bossmen before we and they came—finally, *finally*—to interact, we were "Commie furriners who come down here and brainwashed Coca-Cola and sold them a bill of goods till they're right in the migrants' pocket." A few of them, as would be expected, quit their jobs with open expressions of resentment, hate, and anger, soon after we came to Florida. The majority, however, predictably followed instructions to cooperate with us, though not only we but also the whole project went against their grain. They forced themselves, for instance, to participate in worker-management meetings where the workers' voices were for the first time as respected as theirs. But the fact is they did participate, often decently, too.

And, unbelievably to us, there were even a few out of that tight little world who developed, against all our so-called logic and odds, into project backers of total, obstinate devotion. This, in spite of the fact they had to confront—or live with and swallow—disapproval, dislike, and even sheer, blind hate, not from enemies as we occasionally had to do, but rather from their own neighbors, former friends, families. Certainly it took a lot more brave candor for them to speak out for the project than it did for us.

These men, and sometimes also their families, were the first people who, about six months or so after we had begun our work, put us face to face with our own warps and biases.

And the Coca-Cola executives completed the process. Having spent most of our lives among eastern liberals, we found it at first difficult to believe that the corporate commitment, strength of belief, and, if you will, idealism, where such a project was concerned, could be a lasting one.

And then we saw for ourselves.

We conducted, during the project's beginning, an executive orientation aimed at giving the officers their own glimpse of the migrants' world of total despair. They went into the shacks of some of the agricultural workers and those destined to become leaders, met their families, ate with them, and talked person to person about their lives and problems. And when, before leaving each shack, they apologized with a humility nobody in his right mind could characterize as false for their "former indifference," we could hardly remain unmoved or unimpressed. "We want to do our best to help change this situation, but we don't know how and so are asking you to tell us, please," they said.

The leaders told them, all right, and they listened.

Then, a week or so later, we held the first of many probing meetings with the area supervisors, and neither of us will ever forget Lucian Smith, President of The Coca-Cola Company, stressing and reemphasizing the company's and Board Chairman, Paul Austin's own commitment to the program.

"Paul Austin has asked me to speak to you for him, to tell you what he would tell you himself if he had the opportunity to be here. From this day on our groves' employees and seasonal workers are entitled to the same conditions through which they can live and work in human dignity and economic security as are all our co-workers." He went on to explain in very certain terms that could not possibly be misunderstood the "people power" aspects of the program and concluded his speech with the words, "I—all of us—hope you gentlemen as managers and supervisors can go with this new way because, you know, we want very much to keep you with the company."

We have experienced enough episodes in the years we worked in Florida to make us know the Agricultural Labor Program is unquestionably of capital importance to the Coca-Cola executive suite. We know they won't—can't, because their inner drives won't let them—give up on the project until it exhausts every opportunity for achieving all any of us ever dreamed it would. And if it does accomplish these things, it will have to affect governmental policies by spelling out the crucial role migrant and agricultural people—whose story this is more than anybody else's—can play in helping to resolve their problems. And perhaps it may even eventually generate many other such agribusiness programs, a giant step toward the abolition of migrancy countrywide.

PART I

Birth of a Vision

Chapter 1

This is a day I've been looking forward to since I arrived in Florida last week, my first visit to the orange groves. Bill G. Bennet, a longtime company supervising employee—his father and grandfather worked in these groves before him—is to be my escort for the day.

I've heard a lot about Bill Bennet from Bob, who's found him to be tough, capable, and very honest.

Bill's in his early forties, a slender figure with liquid, innocent blue eyes, a finely chiseled face, and a nice sort of grits-and-gravy voice. He is, however, quite uncommunicative despite my best efforts to bring him out.

I ask, "Do you like it here, Bill?"

"Yeh."

"Well, what do you like about it . . . particularly, I mean?"

"It's my home, ain't it?"

Bill says he forgot to bring ice from home and so has to stop at a gas station to buy enough to cool our drinking water and last us through the day. I ask what he *means* when he says he's got to buy ice for our drinking water. He says he means what he says.

"Well, where do the workers get ice to keep their water cool?"

"Gas station. Ice machine. A whole lots of places."

"They buy it?"

"Sure."

"Well, who pays for it?"

"They do."

"You are kidding," I say.

"I ain't, nope. Not only Coke but, well, no grower in the whole dolgone industry gon' give ice away to the workers."

"You mean it's a matter of principle in the citrus industry to expect workers to pay for ice water?"

Bill smiles with sunshine and smile sharing his face, as decent and straightforward-looking a person as I've seen in my life. He tells me, "See I ain't a northern psy-cho-lo-gist like y'all from HRI and I don't know all that much about human nature. But one thing I do know, simple as I am, and that is agricultural workers like this, nigras, Mexicans, and even white people of such a type, just do not appreciate nothing they would get for free."

I've never been in an orange grove before, and though I didn't ever believe oranges grew on bushes, I didn't know either they grew on trees up to twenty feet tall, the height of a two-story building. I can't imagine how the people—men, women, and children from thirteen and fourteen years old—ever manage to manipulate the huge, heavy ladders used for picking (Stan Silverzweig, executive vice-president of HRI and a strong, athletic man, told me recently he wanted to try out his strength during his first tour of this grove and tried to move a ladder but found he couldn't budge it). Or how they, especially the women and children, live through the long hours and days in the hot sun with the canvas sacks full to bursting with oranges over their shoulders.

When I ask Bill that question he answers unhesitatingly: "Women and kids of this class and type, or men either, for that matter, things just don't get to them like they do to the rest of us."

However, Bill's actions with the workers, especially the kids in the groves, belie his words. The relationship between them really interests me. He's got this way about him. Though no more talkative with them than he is with me, he nevertheless puts his hand on the head of a six- or seven-year-old boy who's helping his parents by picking oranges off the low-hanging branches and makes him squirm with the pleasure of being noticed. He whispers something in a little girl's ear to cause her to smile shyly up at him. And all the children stop their work long enough to wave at Bill as he goes by them and say conversationally, easily:

"Hiya, Bossman, sir, how you today?"

"Well, how you, Sam? Your cramps all cured now?"

Sam, a skinny kid of eight or nine, smiles and tells Bill,

"Yessuh, Mr. Bill, the medicine you done give me fix me up just fine."

"You know much medicine, Bill?" I ask.

He laughs. "More'n enough to treat these kids' headaches, bellyaches, and what have you."

"Bill," I ask, "what happens when these kids or their parents become seriously sick?"

"Depends on what you mean by serious."

I say, "Do the doctors here accept agricultural workers as patients?"

"Not can they help it."

"How about the hospitals?"

Bill stops to think. "Well, now, I can't rightly remember the last time one of mine was in a hospital. Seem like they wouldn't want to go even if they was to be welcome, not to no hospital and not to no doctor. Seem like they got a way of curing themself, sort of curling up and living through the thing till they get over it, more like a dog or cat."

I tell myself, remember you're supposed to be here as a participant-observer, not a missionary, so give it up and don't go banging your head and showing your face any more than is absolutely necessary this early in the game. And I change from the controversial subject of doctors and hospitals to one equally controversial. Though I'm trying to keep my voice controlled, I hear it emerging, despite myself, as sharp, very sharp:

"Do the school-attendance officers ever come to these groves?"

"What the Sam Hill for?"

"Lots of school-aged kids here."

"Yep."

"I just thought the attendance officers . . ."

Bill gives me a long, searching look and says, "You think it be a loss not having these kids in school, well, what they gon' learn in some school?"

"Well, what do any kids learn in school?"

"These kids ain't any kids, ma'am."

"Bill," I ask, "don't you think these kids ought to be going to school?"

Bill, a picture of the quiet moral strength and self-assurance that has built our nation, says, "I am not these kids' daddy and it ain't none of my damn business, if you'll pardon the profanity, what a man does with his own family. That is the American way, down here in Florida it is, anyways."

Well, who can top that? I think to myself and ask Bill about the Florida child labor laws and he answers:

"Law or no law . . . man, all that this company would need to do is to tell the parents their kids can't work in the groves no more and we be out of business so dolgone fast. These nigras and other migrants would run away from here so quick, man, you wouldn't see them for dust. Be gone to some other company'll let their kids work with them side by side so they'll make enough money."

I ask tentatively, and I hope inoffensively, whether Bill has ever thought, as I have, that agricultural workers' earnings, like those of other Americans, ought to be sufficient to cover their needs without the necessity for working their children. And his answer . . . admittedly, no one can claim to be able to read a man's thought in the look he gives you, but Bill's expression is so candid and meaningful that it clearly tells me: "You can't possibly be as stupid as you sound."

And it is in this climate I pluck up courage to bring up the subject that's been preying on my mind since Bob, as president of HRI, and the first person Coca-Cola contacted about the Agricultural Labor Project, discussed it with me before I ever came to Florida.

"Bill," I say, "what about the babies who have to stay all day in the groves while their parents work?"

"Well, what do you mean about the babies in the groves?" Bill's honestly puzzled at the question.

Walking along today we've seen several infants, some as young as a couple of weeks, lying either in their parents' hot cars or on blankets spread near the trees their parents are working. Most of them are perspiring wet in the heat; some, God knows how, sleeping profoundly in their pools of sweat. Others, though, have their eyes open and are rubbing wildly to avoid the bugs that are settling on them anyway.

One little girl makes sucking sounds through her heat-cracked lips as though needing water, and Bill, perceiving it faster than I do, runs to our car and comes back with a cup of ice water. Then, with infinite warmth, tenderness, even love, he picks the baby up and holds her close and comfortingly while feeding her the water drop by drop. I'll never forget my thoughts at the time: I'd never believe this if I weren't seeing it for myself. And, furthermore, no question about it, I'd feel a lot more comfortable with Bill if he would be all villain.

Partly in an attempt to return to my white-is-white and black-is-black attitude toward Bill, I ask him where the grove toilets are located, even though I know very well there aren't any.

"Sara, I'll drive you down to Millard's. They got the nicest bathrooms in town."

"No need to go to town, Bill, thanks anyway."

"No trouble to get you to town. I be glad to do it."

It's been a long time since I minored in dramatics at college but I figure my big, friendly, disarming grin would do my professors proud. "I don't mind using the grove toilets. Really."

"Well now, we don't have no bathroom in this or any grove." It's said without guile or shame.

"Say, you ever heard of an orange grove with bathrooms for the pickers? Bathrooms for pickers?"

He doubles up with laughter he can't control. This is one of the most hilarious things that's ever thrown him into convulsions, and he's heard many very funny things during his long life around these groves. If I don't mind, he's got to share my joke with his two colleagues, venerable, elderly Jarvis Liston, who's perhaps as hostile to us as any one here, and Old Red Wilson. Red's bright, charming, intelligent-looking and doesn't seem to dislike those of us from HRI as much as so many of the other foremen and supervisors do.

"I got somethin' to tell y'all. See, me and Sara was talking about, well, it don't matter what we was talking about, but she told me she got to go to the bathroom, and so, naturally, I offer to drive her down Millard's Restaurant and"—he wipes the tears of mirth—"she say . . . she really said she would use the field bathroom. The field bathroom."

"Bathroom?" Jarvis asks in a tone intimating he doubts my sanity.

"Bathroom?" Red, from whom I'd not expected it, echoes in a similar tone.

"Well, toilet, outhouse, whatever—"

Bill asks me solemnly:

"How'd you like to make a little bet—my one hundred

dollars against your twenty-five cents saying that if you was to talk with some of these nigras today—and I am personally gon' to see you get to talk to some—if you was to ask a dozen workers if they would want bathrooms in the groves, man, they would look at you and they wouldn't say it to you, but they'd think you was plumb crazy. And, well, you just do it, ask them yourself if they want bathrooms or not.

"And I'll tell you what they tell me when your back is turned, okay? And if they don't say you are crazy to ask such a question, well, you know I ain't rich, but you just earned youself one hundred dollars."

He adds with a superior smile, "I tell you our nigras and Mexicans . . . all of the migrants here or any other place rather just get behind a tree than any kind of toilet or even a outhouse. Man, it is what they used to and like best."

Jarvis announces:

"I am so sure about that that I will enter the pot with my own hundred dollars. As of now the bet be our two hundred against your twenty-five cents. Soon as lunchtime come we going to get your money away, though I never have liked to take anything off of ladies."

And now it's lunchtime, and the supervisors' chance to have me "hear it straight from the horse's mouth", as they put it. They're going to introduce me to ten of the "finest nigras in these groves" and let the people in this half hour have a friendly, heart-to-heart chat with me.

When I suggest the people might prefer to do other things with this precious little bit of free time, they dismiss the matter with light laughs and waves of the hand like lords and masters sure of their slaves. And Bill says:

"Nothing they like better than pleasing us, you know. They are like kids that way. Wait'll you see how happy they will be to talk to us."

I give it another try: I say, "Well, don't you think, Bill, that if you, Jarvis, and Old Red are around, the people'll tell you what they know you want to hear? When you say they'll be happy to talk to us . . ."

His eyelashes flicker in amazement. My God, what is this I'm telling him? Am I implying there isn't faith and trust between the supervisors and their workers? Am I sitting here and saying he, Red, and Jarvis have in any way, shape, or form intimidated the people? They confide all their deepest secrets to them, their innermost feelings. "Me, Red, and Jarvis, we've always been able to get along with colored people, they've always loved us."

But don't worry, he says. If I have the slightest feeling the supervisors' presence'll cramp my style or freedom, they'll leave me and the workers alone.

The scenario of what happened next may be summarized briefly as follows:

Bill, Red, and Jarvis dashing madly around here and there and managing, finally, to line up four women and three men. Bill, though, is the one to explain, with a proud paternal smile, that these "very good nigras" do not smoke, drink, or covet their neighbors' spouses. They're all one hundred percent pure saints out of the Holiness Church.

"This here's Ella, Saint Emanuela, a holy mother of the Bethlehem Star Church. And, Ella, this here's Miss Sara from New-York-City." The way he says New-York-City reveals he's got a lot of questions about "that place" and isn't shy about asking them. He, Jarvis, and Red want to know, as he's certain the Saints do, too: "Is New York really Sin City?" Just like that, straight from the hip.

Is New York Sin City? Well, I wouldn't go that far really; what's sinful in some people's eyes . . . Maybe someday the supervisors and the workers will come to New York themselves and so be in a position to make up their own minds. Hearing myself, I can't believe it's me talking this nonsense to these people at such a time.

Now, thankfully, Bill interrupts me. Miss Sara, she may be a resident of Sin City, ha-ha, but is nevertheless no sinner herself. Hell, if the Saints'll pardon the expression, a righteous company like Coca-Cola's not going to have anything to do with sinners "no matter if they be white, colored . . . or nigra." So do him a personal favor, and talk, you know, frankly to Miss Sara even if she will "shoot questions" that may seem, on their surface, to be critical of either the company or the supervisors.

He looks deep into the workers' faces. It is a moving moment. It's not every day, after all, that a bossman makes any kind of personal appeal to his workers, and don't believe for a minute these aren't touched and tremendously flattered as they wait for me to "shoot" my questions.

Instead of doing that, though, I take the opportunity to explain a bit about myself as a part of Bob and Stan's team. Most of the people I'm talking to may not know Bob is a behavioral scientist and president of Human Resources Institute, but they do know he comes from up north and is part of the Agricultural Labor Project and that he is *not* a Coca-Cola executive. Stan is quite familiar to them now. Two months ago he, as part of the HRI survey team, had brought his family including two babies, Amy, one, and Leslie, three, to live for a week in one of the shacks not far from this grove. Naturally, everyone here is very curious and has dozens of questions to ask me about him.

Is he from New York, too? Why does he have long hair? Do all New York men wear their hair long? Why did he drag such small babies all the way to Florida and force them to live in a "colored person's" shack. The company owns other houses occupied by white workers with screened windows and doors, indoor bathrooms, even playgrounds for the kids. Anyone would think Stan, if he had to bring his family to live in migrant housing, would at least have chosen a place in the white area, not alone for the conveniences, but also because they wouldn't have black neighbors.

Now Saint Emanuela rivets her eyes on my face.

Does she dare ask a question that has been and still is in the heads of everyone who's ever seen or even heard of Stan? Can I tell her . . . ? No, no, she shouldn't ask.

"Go on, ask me, you can ask me anything," I say over and over until it seems, finally, I really have convinced her, and, her face tight with excitement, she comes up with:

"Mr. Stan, miss, be he a Jew?"

"Yes."

"Oh," she says.

"Do you know what a Jew means?" I ask.

"No, ma'am."

"Well, what made you think Stan is one, then?"

She doesn't answer.

"I'll bet I know," I say.

She remains silent.

"Somebody told you."

She smiles shyly and nods.

"I'll bet I can guess who told you, too."

She keeps on nodding and smiling.

I say, "A supervisor told you."

She shakes her head and goes "ah-ah" with an expression of wonder at my perspicacity.

Bill, followed by Red and Jarvis, appears suddenly and catches Saint Emanuela and me red-handed. I say, "Bill, you've got a bet with me and I have one with Miss Emanuela. Somebody told her and the other folks Stan's a Jew, and I have a feeling the person who told them is . . ."

He breaks in:

"Well, me and Jarvis sure didn't mean nothing bad by it, Sara, now you know."

"Oh, I do know," I say.

Red says, "You ask the people the question? You ready to give up your quarter now?"

When I say no, Jarvis offers to take over and ask it for me. But he's tactful and leads into the subject with other relevant questions . . . Miss Sara wants to know: How do the workers rate The Coca-Cola Company as compared to other agricultural employers they've known.

Now the gentle-looking Saint Emanuela, a small, thin lady approaching sixty, says, smiling, "This company is the kindest, best and nicest peoples I ever work for in all my time of traveling up road and down. It be the nicest."

Hermit Smith, in his fifties, and a skinny man with a lugubrious face and voice, say The Coca-Cola Company's the best employer he ever came across in all his years of traveling.

The next innovator, a big man in his early twenties named Pepper Young, says, quite surprisingly, that in all his years of travel, "This here company, you know, it be the nicest, the best and the greatest. To tell you the truth, ma'am."

Every other person on that crew sits there and, with no seeming trace of self-consciousness, repeats Saint Emanuela's speech in more or less her words. And when Bill asks them about why The Coca-Cola Company's the best and the greatest, Saint Emanuela leads the chorus, telling me, "Well, a reason this company be nice is because our supervisors like Mr. Bill, Mr. Jarvis, all of them, really, be so good and kind to all of the workers. They will not have they hands in you little pie, and will never cheat you like some bossmen.

"And not only not have they fingers in your little pie by cheating you but also will take care of you, take care of they people like they do they own little kids, you know. White or color, it make no different with them."

She says, almost whispering, "To show you what I mean, ma'am, just one little bit of what I mean by how good they is, well, take the whole thing of money and you maybe running out of it before you week, you work week be up. So all you need to do when you get broke is go to one of them beautiful bossmen and say: 'Oh, Mr. Jarvis or Mr. Bill' . . . you can go to them both and say, 'Please, Bossman, I needs a li'l extry this week.' 'Why, sure, gal, how much you need?' They never ask question one about what you gon' do with the money. It don't make no different with them, you just do what you do.

"And they never worry about when will they get they money or will they get it back. They just trust you as good as anybody, and you know you got to love such men for that. And, talking to you now, ma'am, I just gotten so full up, and feel like crying, thinking about the way they just trust us people."

And there's such sincerity in her bootlicking voice and calm, resigned face that speaks silently of centuries of Christian forbearance and acceptance, I can't make up my mind. Is she giving one hell of a great performance in gaming whitey, conning the supervisors and perhaps also me, or is she really "full up and feel like crying" at their so-called goodness in maintaining their special moneylending services?

I mull it over, confused. And find myself fighting desperately to control my own urge—in case she's not conning—to tell her the sickening, vicious truth about these beloved supervisors and their kindly lending policies at 50, 75, 100 percent interest so workers, once they borrow from them, are in their debt all the rest of their lives.

Jarvis interrupts my inner conflict by asking Saint Emanuela suddenly, quietly:

"What do you feel about this company for not giving y'all no toilets away out here in the groves, Ella?"

Saint Emanuela stares at Jarvis and it's obvious she doesn't know how he wants the question answered.

"D'ya know what I'm asking you, Ella?"

"Why, no, sir," she whispers, humiliated to be so ignorant.

"Let me put it another way then," he says. "In your hearts do you get mad . . . you or your people . . . because we ain't got no toilets for y'all way out here?"

"Nossuh."

"Nossuh," the chorus repeats.

I know Jarvis is going to ask the next question before he does, and though I'm not a praying person, I find myself whispering, "O God, please don't let him ask her if she prefers the grove to an ordinary toilet facility."

"Listen, Ella, now you tell the truth and whole truth to my next question."

"I surely will, Mr. Jarvis." And says . . . Ella says she knows she's speaking for all of her people when she tells me that they wouldn't want to have toilet facilities in the groves because then the responsibility of keeping them clean would be too great. "Us'd only get them dirtied up and then, you know, we be feeling so bad over it."

I offered to pay my just debt but the supervisors wouldn't hear of it. All they hoped was that I'd found this day with them worthwhile and my conversation with the workers enlightening.

↭ Chapter 2

I remember with painful clarity the first time Bob took me through the company housing area known as Maxcy Quarters, where Saint Emanuela and other workers out of the groves lived. For all that we knew of the lushness of Florida landscape there were no trees, no flowers, no grass, no playground facilities for the children . . . just twenty-six institutional green, small, row shacks on a sand road littered with the kitchen carrion of poverty: chicken bones, watermelon rinds, decomposing animal and human offal. And last, though by no means least, empty Coca-Cola bottles, cans, and caps all over.

"It looks exactly like a slave quarter out of your history book, doesn't it?" Bob asks.

"Yeh."

Bob says then that the way he's managed to live through coming to this quarter all of the times he has is to see, in his mind's eye, not only the houses the company's going to help the people build to "their specifications" but also the dignity the people will develop as they keep moving further and further into the mainstream. "Sara, it's going to be so exciting to be around! Can you imagine the day the people see these houses actually take shape?" A hesitation, a sudden flicker of disbelief, of skepticism showing through the wild dream. "Well, once in a while I get to where I know you're at right now and begin to think this project'll never work out, we'll never be able to beat the system. But then I visualize . . ."

"You visualize, I hear you saying, and correct me if I'm wrong, that with a little patience, goodwill, and faith in The Coca-Cola Company above all, we *shall* overcome, right?"

"Let me tell you something," Bob says. "I wouldn't be here if I didn't believe that these people are really going to be able to pull this off, and that it really will make a difference in their lives."

Oh, Bob, I think to myself, here you go again, you crazy dreamer. You're unbeatable, a gold-medal winner when it comes to total dedication to an idea that cannot now or ever happen. Or can it? Can victims really become creators of their own environments? If only there were more lunatics such as he in this world!

This first visit to the Alpine Quarter occurred on a weekday afternoon when the only people around were those who were too old, too young, too sick, or too drunk to work.

We start out at the home of an elderly friend of Saint Emanuela's, her guide and mentor according to Bob. Granny May Lolly, in her late seventies, is a small, frail lady with burning eyes and is the quarter's midwife and witch doctor. Many of the babies she's delivered are themselves grandparents now and swear by her miracle cures with native roots and herbs.

She and her nine children and grandchildren live in a typical two-room shack with no sink or refrigeration, no indoor toilet, only an uninsulated, boxlike bedroom, and a so-called kitchen with a wood stove. It's immaculate, though, swept clean. Its three tightly made double beds more than fill both kitchen and bedroom. There are elegantly embroidered samplers all over—"Jesus Is Our Savior," "God Loves You"— and framed magazine pictures of John and Robert Kennedy. A toy Mickey Mouse wrapped in plastic is on one bed, a Minnie Mouse is on the other, and a Donald Duck is on the third.

Granny May, who some have dubbed the "Quarter Crepehanger," lights up at sight of us and begins immediately intoning, "Many bad, evil things taken place. Ol' death knock at Maisie Jones' door; you don't know Maisie, miss, but Mr. Bob knows what a fine lady she were."

"She was a fine lady, Miss May," Bob says.

"Now remember Johnny Rackley, Mr. Bob. Well, he done leave home and the family. First he beat up Annie Lou so bad, her face all swole and eyes black and blue. She come to me for medicine and tell me her man have fixed her up and then disappeared.

"Poor Annie Lou, that morning she come to me she still

think, you know, that maybe Johnny will find his way back sometime. But it been a week so far and he ain't come, and Annie Lou say someday she leave here, and go look for that crazy man, the way he always beat her up when he be drunk, but is so nice when he ain't."

"He was drunk a lot more often than not, wasn't he, Miss May?" Bob asks.

"Oh, Gawd, yeh, drunk all of the time."

She adds:

"It ain't no different than most of the men, Johnny being drunk; well, most men be that way unless they is saints, and you know youself, they ain't too many men Saints in the church."

I had been told a long time ago that drinking and violence were the ways of life in the groves, and that both men and women consume great quantities of cheap wine and beer, and then the fighting and killings happen. We all know that if only there were some way to combat the drinking, the violence might also be restrained. But unless and until circumstances change around here as utterly as Bob envisions they will, drinking will remain as it's been since people first began migrating on to these groves. It is their single form of entertainment, their only sport and recreation.

"Oh," Granny May tells Bob, "the other thing happen since you was here last week, terrible fire out to Joffe Green's house, whole place up in smoke and everything lost. He left the church, him and his wife. And Preacher done told them both, 'You two hearts gon' turn into the seats of Satan after you leave our little church. Then God, you know, gon' look down upon you in hate and vengefulness. And ain't no telling what gon' happen to y'all when he do—' "

Bob interrupts to ask, "Were any of the children in that house when it burned?" He turns to me, "My God, Joffe's got eleven kids."

"No, Gawd be that good to sinners. He not make the little ones suffer."

I ask, "How'd the fire happen, Granny?"

She starts all over again. "The seats of Satan. Ruin and damnation."

I look around her shack and see very well how a fire could occur here or in Joffe Green's similarly constructed house: exposed wiring.

I ask Bob where the quarter's fire-fighting equipment is and he says, practically whispering, "No, there isn't any."
I say, "The people must live in constant fear of fire."
He nods his assent.
Now, finally, Granny's got a piece of good news, well, partially good anyhow. Mary Green's had twins, strong, healthy little boys. The sad part of that good news, though, is that Mary's only a baby herself; thirteen going on fourteen. "And the daddy run away, nobody know where at."
Mary's shack, to which Granny May brings us, is exactly like hers except it is very dirty inside and out and contains one double bed, several scattered mattresses on the floor, and no other furniture except a kitchen table and a couple of straight chairs. Mary, a slender child who looks even younger than thirteen or fourteen, is lying on the bed on an unsheeted filthy mattress that smells of years of accumulated urine and decay, with a baby on either side. Her eyes are big and frightened, her forehead's glistening with sweat; the gnats and flies coming in through the unscreened windows and door are all over her and the babies.
"I feel terrible bad, Granny."
"What you done about it, gal?"
"Wait for you coming to bring my medicine."
"And ain't been praying to God meantime and thank Him for all of the good that He done you?"
"Tell me what good, Granny." It's really a cry from the heart; Mary doesn't know, and very much wants to, what actual good God has done her. And here's "all of the abundance of good as the Bible say," according to Granny May.
Mary's daddy does drink, true, but is living with the family all the same and works "oh, on many a day, really." And her mama's strong and willing and able to put in a good day's work in order to care for her kids. And she could have died in childbirth, as lots of girls' mothers have, but didn't. All of Mary's brothers and sisters are alive, too.
And the children have all gone to school, sometimes when it wasn't even raining and they could have worked in the groves as she'd always had to do when she was growing up. Neither Mary nor her brothers and sisters will ever have to sign their names with a humiliating X as Granny May must do. And they can, if they will, "read the Good book, the Bible, for youself."

"And now about you own babies. Little Sister, although you sinned in laying down under this boy was no husband to you, still good Gawd done pull you and them through healthy and strong."

I see Mary taking careful note of all Granny May's saying to her. There's a silence full of her weighing and considering. Then:

"Granny, why good Gawd make me bleed like a hog whilst having these twins?"

"Don't you talk about Him making you bleed."

"I nearly bleed to death."

"Shut you mouth, little Sister."

Mary impulsively touches her body and stares down at herself thinking about the blood and the pain. "How you say Gawd so good to me, making me bleed?"

No answer.

"How you say that?"

I hear Granny's voice finally:

"You lucky li'l gal, having your baby in you own bed, Little Sister. Gawd so good to let you do that."

"It is my daddy's and mama's bed," Mary whispers.

"It a bed, ain't it? And you have you two in you own little house and with you loving family all around you to help out any way they can. Oh, you is a lucky girl, Little Sister."

She shakes her head, smiles, and explains to Bob and me how it is that many migrant women and girls less fortunate than Mary—less "blessed" was the way she put it—have their babies "in a ditch to the side of the road. See, Mary herself been too little to remember when her last two sisters after her was born. The family were hitting the road when Lily, that is Mary's mama, and she and the family was migrating when her time come. So Mary's two li'l sisters, Lucy and Janie, they was born out in the open, in the ditch near the field of the bossman the family was picking for."

Granny May stops talking for a while, then resumes in a low tone, almost a whisper:

"Poor Lily, what scared her . . . The pain, you know, seemed like she hurt so bad she have to like cry out and scream out loud, and all of the time knowing that if the bossman or his lady was to hear her . . . Some bossmen and ladies find out a colored having a baby on their place they get so mad and call the cops to put them in jail.

"Look," she tells Mary grimly, "your little sisters could have been born in some jail, and how you like that."

Mary doesn't answer.

"How you like it?"

"I don't, Granny, no, I feel bad over it."

"Well, then, make sure you thank Him enough for letting yours be born in your bed and your little house."

I ask whether Granny or anyone had believed Mary ought to have gone to a hospital to have her baby.

"No ma'am."

"Why not?"

She studies me for a while, then smiles. She doesn't mean to boast about herself, but the fact is she herself, with God's help, has delivered many babies in the quarter and more than I'd suspect are alive today.

"And sometime, Gawd know what happens with some of them as do go to the hospital. Or they don't go exactly. They can't get in but they try, you know, and sometime die in the trying.

"Like this here friend I have by name of Billie Lee Hudgins. She have this one li'l gal named Honey Jean come out pregnant like Mary when she was just a little younger than her. And Billie Lee say, 'Well, Honey Jean ain't gon' have her baby in no ditch like I have her, she gon' go to a hospital.'

"And I tell her the same as I do to Mary today, 'Honey Jean having a baby in her own bed and your own little house ain't the same as in a ditch. Leave the hospital be, Sister.'

"But she won't, and I go along to the hospital with Honey and her. Well, this particular hospital, come to find out later, it were private, you know, what they calls a private hospital. And this nurse come on out asking, 'Has you got two hundred dollars to pay us with?' And that were more than I thought. Billie Lee done loaned fifty dollars off of her bossman, but two hundred . . . well, he might have give her that too excepting we didn't know to ask all of that, didn't know it be necessary.

"Anyway, Billie Lee offered up the fifty, saying. 'This be my only baby and my whole reason for living in the world anymore. So if you was to take this money on account, I would work and pay you all of the rest if it take me my whole life long.' "

She shakes her head. "That li'l ol' nurse was just the sweetest thing too, taking her time to smile at Billie Lee and say that, oh, she be truly sorry but this is a private hospital, you know, and you got to have all of the money to pay down, all.

"Well, she say, take Honey Jean on out to the other hospital and this was the county hospital. So I say to Billie Lee, 'Well, my friend, better you put your child in my keeping then drag her around from one hospital to another and her ready to pop.'

"Well, so we gotten Honey to county, and over there, they say, 'Who your doctor, auntie?' And Honey's mama offered the fifty dollars then. But the peoples say no, like the nurse at private say, the money ain't the thing at county. The thing there be that a person got to have her own doctor to get in it.

"And since Honey don't have none, they sorry, you know, but has got to send us away."

"Well," she says, with sadness but no censure, no trace of anger for anyone, "the child die on her way home. It was the saddest thing, really.

"And Billie Lee passed soon after Honey Jean, just passed away because she got nothing to live for no more and wouldn't take food nor water."

Her eyes fill with tears, of self-reproach, it turns out. "Sometime, oh, many a time, really, I lay awake in my bed and I can see her mouth right before the passing—Honey Jean's, not Billie Lee's—all stretched out so tight around her face like she locked it up. And I talking to myself, saying, 'Honey Jean, baby, you was such a good, sweet child and such a comfort to your mama.'

"And I know then and says it to myself that 'You, May Lolly, you be the one to blame for the angel's passing. Because you knowed she weren't ever gon' get in no private or county hospital and should have made her mama know the same. It is all your blame, May Lolly.'

"And that be why at night, sometime, I see her in my dreams. *Honey Jean, Honey Jean, Honey Jean.*"

The last quarter shack Granny brought us to belonged to a Mrs. Cranshaw and her five children and turned out to be odd even by the standards of the shack Mary's family occupied. A whole wall literally had been pushed in. Granny May said a car bumped and disabled it about four months earlier.

I say, "Well, did Mrs. Cranshaw report the accident?"

"She do, yes'm."

"And nothing was done, nobody came to fix it?"

"No, miss."

"What'd she do then?"

"Tell the man another time, her foreman, she tell him and he say, 'Okay, we gon' take care of it.' They never done, though. And sometime Amy get"—she smiles to take the onus out of her words—"sometime she get a li'l bit hot and say it's too bad about the wind blowing in at night and her children getting a cold seem like, you know, seem like they never git rid of it, if the wall don't be fixed."

One of the children, Cindiana, a skeletal child of six or so, is home now, lying on the bed, coughing and blowing her nose. She gets up suddenly, painfully and reaches for a large tin can behind another mattress. I see her vomiting into it, go to help her, and then, and then . . . I look into the can and catch my breath over what I see there: a live, wriggling foot-long worm. I'd read all the literature describing worms and rural low-country poor kids before I'd ever come here, but, oh, God, the most morbid, vivid, descriptive reading's a tepid business by comparison to yourself seeing a sight such as this.

Bob looks in the can and, "Oh, no," he says in a shocked tone over and over again, "Oh, no, oh, no." He says we've got to get to the doctor immediately and picks Cindiana up in his arms.

Granny May narrows her eyes a little, and smiles a half smile, a strange unfinished thing as she advises us, simply, not to trouble with Cindiana; there's little the doctor can do, while she herself knows a certain root that does, on occasion, help worm-ridden children.

Then; "I tell you one thing, that worm don't trouble Cindiana here like it does y'all, used as she be to 'em. Gawd, worms don't trouble her, does they, honey?"

"No'm, Granny." The forbearance and acceptance in her child's voice . . . Cindiana sounds unlike any flesh-and-blood kid I ever met in my life.

The doctor's virgin clean office is more crowded than any I've ever been to in New York or anywhere. There must be forty people here if there are ten. And we, obviously, have managed to capture the immediate and absolute attention of every person there. They all stare at us with intense, embarrassing concentration.

Bob seats Cindy and me before approaching a glassed-in counter behind which a large, middle-aged woman sat, dressed in a tight nurse's uniform accentuating her great, pendulous bosom and huge, sinewy arms. The conversation he repeated to me later goes:

"Excuse me, ma'am, we don't have an appointment, but this child . . ."

"That li'l colored girl y'all brought in here with you, you mean her?"

Bob nods.

"Well, how you all related to that nig— li'l colored girl?"

Bob doesn't answer her direct inquiry but says instead, "We'll take care of any charges, don't worry about it, please."

"Well, I got to fill her out a form since she's never been here before and who do I ask the questions of?"

"Me."

She asks Cindiana's age, address, telephone number.

"Oh, she doesn't have a phone."

"Well, yeh, I wouldn't think she'd have a phone." A long hesitation and flicker of a smile. "Well, you're not her parent or guardian, right?"

"Yeh, right."

"Could I ask you then why y'all are here with her, sir? Where you are from?"

"We're from Coca-Cola, Minute Maid. The child's parents work in the groves."

She jumps from her chair and says, "Well, excuse me and I'll go tell the doctor you're here." And adds, looking directly into Bob's eyes, "You mean the company is really doing that nig— colored folks' project after all?"

At this point, just before Bob comes to join us, an adorable seven-year-old boy with a fairy-tale blond look leaves his seat beside his mother to come stand in front of Cindiana. He points a toy gun at her head and announces briefly and with enough expression so Cindiana begins to cry, great tears rolling out of her eyes and down her face, "I am gon' kill y'all, li'l nigger. Stick 'em up."

"He's only fooling, honey," I tell Cindiana.

"You bet I ain't."

I try vainly to lift the wailing Cindiana onto my lap, but she's as frightened of my white face by now as of everyone else in the room.

"Stick 'em up, nigger."

Bob says, "I think your mother wants you, son." And the little boy's mother, tall, good-looking, elegant, smiles to display her beautiful white teeth and says, in a lofty tone to make me blink, "Why, no, I don't want him, thank you, sir."

Before Bob can make his reply the door to the inner office opens and the doctor steps out. She's a woman, surprisingly, and with her venerable lined face and white hair, as good-looking an elderly woman as I've ever seen.

She asks the people waiting, "D'y'all mind if I see these people first, seeing as how they have to get back to their work." I love that southern accent with its echo of more leisurely ways, of spreading fields and gracious, white-columned mansions. "They work at The Coca-Cola Company."

Perhaps it's my imagination, I think to myself, but there's a subtle change in the atmosphere of the waiting room since the doctor's mentioned The Coca-Cola Company. Where before the mood was one of overwhelming curiosity mixed with hostility, as shown by the mother of the blond boy, it's now a cross between awe—The Coca-Cola Company's a known institution in central Florida—and fear of our project seemingly justified by the fact that we are demanding the same treatment of Cindiana that their kids receive.

It's a relief getting behind the closed doors of the doctor's office.

"Well, what is wrong with the child?"

Bob describes the foot-long worm.

The doctor stares. "You mean you brought her all the way here . . . nigra kid out of that quarter, well, I don't think there are too many there that don't have worms. Dirty, filthy as they are, if they'd ever take a bath . . ."

I say, "What'll they take it in?" and am silenced by Bob's hand pressing my shoulder.

"You can't cure them," she says. "Yeh, I got medicine I'll give you to help this one out now, but it won't be that long before you'd have to bring her back; she'll have the worms all over again."

I ask her why a child like Cindiana can't be cured and she repeats the facts as I've read them: Once treated and cured of the worms, children like Cindiana often contract them again, ingesting the eggs that cling to their hands after they play in soil befouled because of the scarcity of toilets. To hear the doctor tell it, though, you'd have thought the kids themselves were to blame. "And with desegregation in the school, all of that business, well, children like this little gal . . . with her parents being who they are and out of that place . . . she is in a position where she can infect the children out of any of our families in the classroom or on the playground. My little granddaughter . . ."

Bob says, "Well, under the circumstances, doctor, you'll be happy to know there'll soon be new, decent housing with indoor toilets and adequate bathtubs for the company employees."

"Yes, sir. I am glad."

She smiles at us in a way that makes us know she's anything but glad.

ᛰ Chapter 3

We've set ourselves, as of now, two awesome and marvelous tasks: to begin, within our all too manifest limitations, to share, to participate, to partake of the lives of these people we're going to be working with, insofar as we're able and they'll permit us; and to ferret out the people's leaders who will be the ones, if anyone can, to make the project work. Often these indigenous leaders are ignored because they don't hold titles or offices, yet HRI has found in other projects that their ideas and energy and influence are crucial.

Naturally the dozens of Holiness Churches in the area are among Bob's, Stan's, Arnold's, and my earliest ports of call. The largest and most powerful of them is Saint Emanuela and Granny May Lolly's Evening Star Holiness Tabernacle. It is a rickety wooden building, shabby, unpainted, and hardly distinctive except for the shouting, screaming, singing, and music announcing it long before you reach there. And the thing about the sound of the music as we first hear it from the outside is that it's not so different in its essence from what you hear blaring from the jukeboxes of the bars around here.

Inside the walls, though . . .

When I was face to face with Emanuela and Granny May, all dressed up in their "Mother of the Church" white, and the sixty or so other worshippers, truthfully my mood and feeling my first time in that church was like none I'd ever experienced in my life before.

The drums banging. The tambourines racing. The sinners, who'd be saved in front of your eyes, wailing, screaming, and the saved Saints rejoicing, "jubilating with song," as Saint Emanuela puts it.

And the dancing, like the singing: joyous and agonizing at the same time, "crucifying," Emanuela's word again. People wringing wet with their emotions and feelings, so the children have to come with boxes of Kleenex to wipe the sweat and spittle off them.

Cindiana was one of the Kleenex-bearers. "Hi, honey," I said. She answered, "Praise the Lord, praise Jesus," and I couldn't tell from the way she looked at me whether or not she recognized me.

I saw those tired, weary-laden people talking intimately with Jesus: some in tongues, some in words I understood, and others in words I partially did . . . "talking with Jesus, their most beloved friend."

The first experience at Emanuela's church, separate and distinct from all the others I had over my two years in Florida, excited me, a nonbeliever, tremendously. To feel the worshipers being taken over by the spirit is very strange and touching.

The minister, the Reverend Arthur Seaford, whom Emanuela had praised to the skies, was a small man in his late forties with a sensuous face and with a deep, ringing voice and authoritative presence with his parishioners. But he cringed and bowed and scraped to us. "The Coca-Cola Company is so good to bring y'all here. Other Christs is what you are, I can read that in your faces. Yeh, missionaries come to help my poor, benighted people, don't even know theyself how much help they are in need of."

Reverend Seaford takes the text from his sermon from Matthew 4:1-4:

"Then was Jesus led up of the Spirit unto the wilderness to be tempted of the devil. And when he had fasted forty days and forty nights he was afterward mighty hungry. And when the devil came to him, he said, if thou be the Son of God command that these stones be made of bread. But he answered and he said, 'Man shall not live by bread alone but by every word that proceedeth out of the mouth of God.' "

The reverend's presentation so far is very straight, very quiet, and interrupted by only a comparatively few Amens and Hallelujahs. Suddenly, though, there's a shift in both form and mood. It becomes a loud and vigorous quiz, a Biblical examination of the congregation.

"Now, Brothers and Sisters, Christ were *hungry* as we

know from Matthew four after having . . . How long, oh, how *long* had Christ fasted?"

"Forty days and forty nights," the congregation cries out.

"So he was hungry."

"Yes, Jesus! Yes, Lord! Yes, Amen!" the crowd roars and hollers.

"And the devil tried his utmost to tempt Jesus by . . . He say, didn't he, that if you are the Son of God, ha-ha, look who try to tell me *he* be the Son of God, look who's trying to say that. Oh, what are you, a *comedian* or somethin' . . . a comedian? Old devil ask that of Jesus Christ and he says to him, 'Well, let me see you *prove* you are the Son of God by *commanding*' . . . What did he tell Jesus to *command*, Brothers and Sisters?"

"He say to command the stones be made *of bread*."

"So what did *Christ* say when the devil tried to tempt him thataway?"

"He say, 'No, man can't live by bread alone and have to have the *word* of *God*."

"And what do *you* say to what Jesus said?"

"Yes!"

Now the reverend clears his throat and continues the sermon:

"Well, after the devil tempt—try to tempt—Jesus as he done . . . Now, you know because your Bible tells you all of the many temptations old devil lay for Jesus. You know 'cause your Bible tells you how the devil taken Jesus up to the highest mountain and show him all the kingdoms of the world below, all the treasures of the world, saying, 'If thou will fall down and worship me, all these things I will give unto thee.' All these things. And Jesus said . . . What did Jesus say, Brothers and Sisters?"

And it seems that we of the HRI are the only people in that whole church who don't know our Bible sufficiently to answer the reverend's question. The other people, though unable to read the Bible have, nevertheless, succeeded in memorizing it. (Emanuela and other holy mothers would tell me, once we'd come to know one another sufficiently intimately, how shocked and surprised and really sorrowful they were to discover that, though we could *read* the Bible, something they'd give anything to do, we hadn't bothered to commit it "to heart.") The whole church says as one person, "Jesus say, 'Get thee hence, Satan.' "

Now there's even more screaming, hollering, and jumping around the church, and Reverend Seaford suddenly leaves the pulpit and starts walking down the aisle. He stops at our row and goes down on his knees, with his eyes closed. "Jesus fought away the devil. He fought away temptation."

"Yes, Jesus. Yes, Lord."

"You be like Jesus," suddenly comes from Emanuela, sitting a couple of seats away from me.

"Yes, Reverend, you like Jesus 'cause you fight away the devil youself, you do, you do."

Other voices join Emanuela's. "You fight the devil, Reverend, and you won out, thank Jesus, yeh, Lord, oh, tell us how you win."

Reverend Seaford lets his people holler and shout awhile and then, like an actor, comes back to the pulpit as though it is his stage. I say "stage" and "actor" because the reverend's the only person in that rhapsodic, elated congregation who's sufficiently in the world to be cognizant of us visitors and the impression he and his service are making on us. He watches us out of the corner of his eyes as he gives the testimony the congregation has been importuning him for so passionately.

"I'll begin from when I was fourteen and following the crops from Florida to New York State along with my daddy and mama. Now I was sanctified, had been baptized, too, baptized, Brothers and Sisters. Now my daddy and mama were the holiest of the holy."

"Holy. Holy." The church echoes him.

At fifteen, though—he doesn't explain how or why—he'd landed in Harlem. (Why Harlem? I ask myself. Could he be talking about Harlem because it represents a point of connection with us consultants?) Landed in Harlem and found himself for the first time afraid . . . afraid of the evil without, but more important, afraid of the stirrings of evil within himself. "And I say, yeh, Lord, yeh, my friends in this here church, I felt all kind of evil stirring in me, and my heart were inflamed by all of the girls I seen in Harlem. And listen, listen . . ."

"My own body, you know, got to be a whole source of woe, fire, and temptation, now, hear me out, fire and temptation."

From somewhere in back of the church I hear a flinty voice screech, "Ah, poor Reverend, Gawd loved you all of the time and you never even knowed it."

"And the worst of the whole thing, the way the devil tempted me, you know. I sat in the church and thought about the bad women on the outside. I wanted to make them gals. And y'all know what I mean, the evil in my soul, the depravity, the devil in me—when I tell you now, I hate myself even thinking about it today, y'all know what I mean by making them, the bad women never would think of setting foot in a church or praying to God."

He throws out his arms and points his fingers to left and right. "It is written that thou shalt worship the Lord thy God and only Him, and all the time Satan were the one I worshiped. Yeh, it is the truth."

He pauses for a while, breathing deeply, and it seems like Emanuela and a couple of other holy mothers are about to faint.

"Now what I done, Brothers and Sisters, listen, listen, what I done . . ."

"Yeh! Yeh! What did you do?"

"I walk out of the church, out of God's house. And listen, listen . . ."

"Yeh, Lord, we listening."

"Listen to where I walked right on to 125th Street in New York City . . ." Now, for all that he's crying and beating his breast and kneeling on the floor, he can still think to apologize to us he knows to be from New York for what he's going to say next about "them evil, and I mean evil, yeh, I sure does, evil New York whores and pimps. Now, whores and pimps are evil all over, but in New York, they are especially evil, yeh, you bet, if you ain't been there, you know you never can believe how evil those New York pimps, whores, and racketeers can get, and all the same, Brothers and Sisters, all the same . . ."

All the same he was "drawn" to them. "And, well, I just gone along with the evil ones to the dens of iniquity they done, and doing the same wicked things, as they done, the New York pimps and whores. See, the devil say, 'Come' and I never thought to say, 'Get thee hence' like Jesus done. And my good mama and daddy say to me every morning, noon, and night, 'Ain't you ready to give up the devil and come to Christ? Come, son!' "

"Yes, Lord! Yes, Jesus! Yes, Amen!" the crowd roars and hollers even louder than it's done till now. And Emanuela rises from her seat and with tears streaming down her face starts singing:

"Come to Jesus,
"Come to Jesus."

Others join her. So many have tears in their eyes. Yet for all my belligerence to Reverend Seaford, all my seething and simmering over the fact I'm certain he's using me along with everyone else in the church, despite all of this, I feel my own eyes welling. And the holy mother beside me, observing it, throws her arms around me and holds me very close for several minutes.

Reverend Seaford, seeing us, continues his testimony from the aisle beside my row, and if I were uncomfortable before . . .

"Well, I went, like I tell you, yeh, what I done was gone and lay down among the whores, lay down among the swine, the pimps. I was one of them, I made girls fall in love with me and then go out, you know, and sell their bodies for money, for me. I done that. Your own reverend, he knocked the girls, beat the life out of them when they didn't do as I told them.

"Now thank God and praise the Lord, I never killed nobody."

"Praise the Lord." The congregation lows with satisfaction over the fact.

"But almost . . . so deep as the devil was in me, he took my hand and guided it, so almost I killed a man."

A holler goes up from in front of me, and a huge fat woman flops over onto the floor. Emanuela follows suit.

The next one to fall—at my feet—is the holy mother who'd had her arms around me. I lean down and put my hand on her forehead; it's fever hot. Two deacons come to lift her up and walk her around.

"Now I ask you, good people, that if I am a man that was raised to Christ and am still doing all of these things, then you know who have gained possession of my soul?"

The congregation knows who very well indeed.

"The devil, that who have gained possession. See, having

once to ask myself why do I do all of these things, the answer comes easy."

"Yeh, Lord."

"And once that that happened, I say, 'Got to get rid of the old devil. Got to exorcise him, get him out of my life and soul,' you know," he says, almost whispering so all of us in the church, including me, must lean forward to hear his words. "And I went to the little church in New York my mama and daddy gone to, and I got baptized.

"Right there in New York, and there weren't no lakes nor ponds as there is here in Florida. But we found us water all the same, the Lord led us to water, and I got baptized the second time in my life, and my old mama and daddy praying, 'Oh, this time let it take, Lord.' I went to the waters and got baptized and I said, 'Oh, let me be like Jesus, Lord.'"

"Yeh, Lord, you is that, Reverend."

"Be like Jesus and fight away temptation. Fight away temptation!" he shouts, going down on his knees. "Fight away temptation," he says getting up.

And so, on and on, driving all the people to more profound frenzy. Many make their testimonies as the reverend did, but they're hard to understand and, after a while, begin to blend in my mind. And Reverend Seaford suddenly breaks through them . . . I hear him above all the din exhorting testimony from us "honored, oh, *so* honored, bossmen and lady."

Stan's the one of us to rise to the occasion . . . and treat us to a badly needed comic interlude in the process. "Well, now," he says, smiling, "to tell you about myself and my background, I am Jewish and . . ."

"Praise Jesus! Praise the Lord!" The crowd roars and hollers and thanks the gentle Jesus for Stan and Judaism almost as passionately as they'd done the reverend. And it spurs him on to testify at great, and very effective, length. And how is he to know the opportunistic use the Reverend's going to make of his sincerely rendered testimony?

"Sisters and Brothers, we has heard Mr. Stan testify, and it was a beautiful testimony, wasn't it? Now, Mr. Stan, Mr. Bob, and Miss Sara, them coming here, honoring us like they done. It was a great honor, wasn't it?"

"Yeh. Sure were. Thank the Lord."

"And Mr. Stan's beautiful testimony . . . I was so glad and

thankful to the Lord we were all here and able to hear him today."

"Yes, Lord. Yes, Jesus."

"But, now, there was one thing making me feel so bad, Lord, from the time our friends first walked in this here church, so bad. And that is this poor, ugly, old coming-apart church. We ought to have a better place to hear a testimony, a beautiful testimony like Mr. Stan's. We ought to have a fitting church. It . . . I'm talking about . . . yeh . . . a fitting church, Lord. Fitting, yes, Lord."

Now the Reverend's place on the pulpit is taken by a deacon, Lincoln Redfield, a uniquely handsome man in his thirties. His smile, his white teeth in his brown face with the exceptionally bright eyes, is very striking.

"Sisters and Brothers, we all has heard the reverend tell us, we has heard him say as how he feel so bad at not having a fitting church for receiving our honored guests and hearing, oh, yeh, that beautiful testimony of Mr. Stan.

"And we all love and respects our reverend, now am I right about it?"

"Yes."

"Now, I want to show our friends and beloved Rev what we wants our church to be, that we wants a *fitting* church to have them visit in, and that is why I gon' start this here collection with a dollar bill, and I want y'all out there to give your dollars, too. Who gon' be the first?" He flashes the brilliant smile.

"Here my dollar, Brother," one of the young girls, perhaps eighteen or nineteen calls.

"And mine . . . Fifty cents be all I got just now but I'm glad to give it." This from Mary Green, the little mother of the newborn twins Bob and I visited with Granny Lolly. Granny'd told us she "have her health back from the birthing by now . . . have her health back summat and take the babies into the groves with her so she can work some days."

"Fifty cents over here, Brother," Mary says.

In a few minutes, Deacon Redfield raises twenty dollars. I notice, because my eyes are especially riveted in her direction, Cindiana's skinny, sickly mother digging in her pocket.

Chapter 4

We haunted the bars as well as churches in our eagerness to make friends of the people and pinpoint potential project leaders. There are three major bars in the area: Fat Man's, Big Bo's, and Sam Snooker's Do-Drop-Inn. Big Bo's and Fat Man's are tough, chaotic places where we'd been told—by the holy mothers of our acquaintance, who else?—anything could happen and often did. They looked alike in many ways, both housed in two shacks placed together and with paper streamers in every color of the rainbow hanging from the loose plank ceilings.

Both bars might have been as fierce as their reputation. Razor fights and shootings were supposed to be regular occurrences, and the several young girls in heavy make-up and hot pants could well have been the whores the church mothers had described them as being. But the point is that for us both bars were no more nor less than the yes-sir, yes-ma'am world we were unhappily becoming accustomed to here.

Both Fat Man and Big Bo had prior knowledge that some white bossmen and a lady from Coca-Cola would be coming to pay them a visit, and since most of their habitués were company employees, had also forewarned them.

Stan, Bob, Arnold (my husband, on-scene coordinator of the project), and I arrived at Big Bo's at about eight o'clock on a Monday night to be greeted by the proprietor, a large light-skinned man with a handsome expressive face, and nine or ten men and three women customers who rose in unison at our entrance.

They only took their seats again when Bob urged them to, and when we sat down among them and tried to make small talk they merely stared at us with shy interest. Offhand, they seemed very passive, subdued, and fanatically polite. When one of us cracked a bad joke they laughed like hell, when

Bob offered to buy drinks they said no thanks with ingratiating smiles, and when Stan and Arnold talked a little about our project and its people-power aspects they nodded their heads in solemn collective assent, but didn't respond to any of our questions about what they felt the community's needs to be.

After this failure to finger any kind of leadership at Big Bo's, we went to Fat Man's, where both proprietor and customers were, if possible, more frightened out of their wits by us than the Big Bo customers had been. We, therefore, just pulled up our chairs in the middle of the room and told them a little about ourselves, our families, our lives at home, and why we were here. We encouraged them to ask any questions they wanted to, but nobody did, so we concluded with brief, self-conscious talks about the joys of working together and left to many obsequious "Thank y'alls for coming," and a round of vigorous applause as though for film stars. The whole room stood up to pay us obeisance as we walked out.

The third bar we went to, Sam Snooker's Do-Drop-Inn, seemed on its surface to be, with its crumbling ceiling, dirty walls, oilcloth table covers, and rickety chairs, as dreary as Big Bo's and Fat Man's. But Sam Snooker, a tall man in his forties with a powerful wrestler's build and African bush face whose strength and air of intelligence are striking, didn't kowtow in the slightest to us. He told us we'd come at an odd time and doubtless wouldn't want to remain when we learned that there were no ordinary customers at the Do-Drop-Inn that night, only family and friends come to rally round the Snookers in a time of need.

"See, the U.K.'s [United Klans] . . . they could come by here any time now, and, man, ain't no telling what could happen. It be my boy, Larry, and his wife. Hey, Larry, Karen, c'mon over here and meet these folks."

Larry, twenty, solid, earthy, massive like his father and with a deep brown complexion, comes leading pretty, slender, dark-haired Karen by the hand.

Sam's looking hard for any sign of rejection, disapproval, thumbs down from us, and when he's certain in his own mind he doesn't see it, because it's not there, responds to our request (we make it clear we're asking because it's important for us, in our roles, to know, and not just out of curiosity) to explain Larry and Karen's story to us.

It goes back, he says, two years. Larry and a couple of other young black fellows had by then—some six years after integration was first begun in the high school—found a definite place in the virile brotherhood of the school's crack athletes.

It was one of those situations where the white athletes played and worked shoulder to shoulder with the blacks, experiencing a comradeship of equality formulated around winning the game. They had slowly but surely reached the point of believing the color of their skin more or less irrelevant.

And what made all of it especially difficult for the parents and majority of white townspeople to bear was that although they viewed this as a revolutionary happening, it was not (and the young people made it clear it wasn't) occurring in terms of ideology and dialectics but rather plain humanity.

"Then what happen . . . See, every year since I been in this town, and I was born here, you know, the women's club give a dinner to the senior class and their mamas. Well, *white* seniors and mamas, naturally; nobody, white nor colored, ever think of it any other way.

"But the kids, man, them kids, all kids I guess is something else. So like Larry's white teammates get with the ladies and say, 'If you're giving a senior dinner, well, that mean all the seniors then, not just the white ones, it is only right. And if you don't invite the black, well, then, don't expect we're gon' come either.' "

The ladies, Sam tells, suggested a compromise. They would invite the black athletes, in view of their unusualness, but not the other seniors. And certainly not the mothers, lowly, dirty, illiterate orange pickers out of the groves.

The athletes thoughtfully considered the women's proposal and turned it down. They didn't challenge them or try in any way to change their view. They merely told them again, in quiet tones, that unless all the black students—and their mothers—were invited to the dinner, they wouldn't attend either.

And what panicked the women's club and resulted in abandonment of the whole idea of the traditional dinner, according to Sam Snooker (and later reiterated by the few liberal white townspeople we came to know and work among), was the low-pitched reasonableness and utter lack of verbal violence among the white athletes.

And it was in this climate of the white townspeople's quite natural frustration, and even horror, at the specter of their own familiar young athletes suddenly become as new and alien to them as any damnyankee kids that the love affair of Larry and Karen became public knowledge.

The young people had actually known about it for a long time, and a couple of not particularly significant campus incidents had happened because of it. But the situation was transformed into ferocity with the entrance on the scene of adults, mostly members of the U.K.A., United Klans of America.

They, led by Mr. Wilson, Karen's father, a crew chief for another company and a rugged, self-righteous man with the law-and-order mentality of his organization, began "patrolling" the campus with drawn knives and loaded guns.

A majority of the black students were frightened and stayed away from the school. But some, accompanied by adults, came carrying their own knives and pieces. And a few were spoiling for a fight.

In the meantime, Larry and Karen were secretly married, and asked Sam and his new, young wife, Rosebud, to take them in. And although Rosebud was only two years older than Larry, and pregnant besides, she never tried to talk Sam out of what he felt to be his obligation to protect and defend Larry and Karen.

Arnold, Stan, Bob, and I listened intently and quietly, but with great surprise I believe showed on our faces. We thought we knew the community so well and we'd defined it so rigidly in our heads as consisting of prejudiced whites and yes-sir, yes-ma'am blacks. We didn't, in our wildest imaginings, allow for white kids like Larry's teammates nor Karen herself, for that matter. Nor, really, everyone in the bar that night.

"Now, you know, when I ask my wife, Rosebud, what to do about Karen and Larry, she said stand by them."

I'd met Rosebud as well as Ziti and Aaron, Sam's parents, at the Good News Tabernacle, where they've been longtime faithful members and tolerated for themselves despite the fact that Sam is a notorious tavern owner. The old Snookers are both sickly and, Emanuela says, in their seventies, though they look older to me.

Ziti, confined to a wheelchair for almost twenty years, looks like the picture portrait of an elderly Aunt Jemima, and Aaron, a longtime tubercular, is a small, brown skeleton who stares at you with eyes of pain. They are people much like Emanuela, only sicker and older. Their humility, like hers, is inbred deep down by the misery and suffering they'd always felt to be part of black people's fate.

Also, they have recollections of Klan smashings and burnings as they occurred fifty, sixty, years ago in Mississippi. You'd think it would be more than they could bear to start it all over again: the white mobs coming into their territory, now, at this time, when they had reason to believe they were done with it all. You'd think, then, that when it came to the matter of offering Larry, and especially Karen, hospitality, they would have done all they could to influence Sam to refuse them.

Sam laughs the kind of laughter that goes with shaking your head in amazement as he tells us:

"You wouldn't believe my daddy and mama, them two old slave-timey niggers, standing up as big as life, mama grabbing a-holt of the handles of her wheelchair and pulling herself to a standing position so she could look me right in the eye, you know.

"And good old Daddy-O stretched hisself out, too, all two and a half feet of him, and said, 'Larry belong to us, he be our flesh and blood and we cannot throw him away. And, now, Karen, being Larry's, also be ours. And we keep and cherish her, too.' And I told them about we could expect the U.K. to come, just as though they didn't know that for theyselfs. And all they would answer were 'Larry and Karen, belonging to us, well, that is the thing that matters.' So Larry and Karen come to stay with us and so do the U.K. come one day and everybody, relatives and friends, rally round. The U.K. didn't do much at the time, just thrown a burning cross, but the kids got afraid for us older folk, and that were why they gon' North to work.

"Well, then, time gone on and mama say, 'Daddy and I ain't getting no younger and we wants to see Larry and Karen again before we dies. Can't they come home for a visit soon?' And I remind them of the U.K., but it don't make no never mind. So here is Larry and Karen, and, well, we don't know what gon' happen next with the U.K."

Bob and I spent many long hours trying to figure out how Ziti and Aaron came by such strength and principle under the frightening circumstances.

Later—a month or so after Karen and Larry had gone North again and the open hostility was ended—when Bob asked Ziti and Aaron how they had been enabled to take such a stand, they said, or Aaron did, while Ziti nodded approvingly:

"It be the Lord and love of people just going together, you know."

And it was love and the Lord, the best, the only important reasons for all of the good people do, they said that caused so many friends and family to rally round and take turns staying at the Snookers' every night of the week they were under threat. And there were nights, during Larry and Karen's first and second stays there, when eighteen or twenty people, in addition to the ones who lived at the Snookers', were gathered both in the bar and adjoining home.

Tonight's going to be a long one at the Snookers'. We ask Sam's permission to remain there with them. And Sam graciously says yes, of course, he'll be pleased if we do. But, nevertheless, he wants to be honest with us, and so has to say he really can't understand why we'd want to stay. Larry and Karen aren't our problems and the Snookers aren't our people.

We explain to him why we want to stay. I repeat to Sam our strong desire, within our limitations, to share the people's lives here. I tell him that Bob, Stan, Arnold, myself, and all the consultants, wherever we go, want to share what is good or bad in the people's lives instead of standing outside and making comments and judgments, which may or may not then be useful.

His only reaction is a solemn nod. He understands and there's no need for further talk on the subject, and then offers to introduce us to his family and friends. They're tremendously interesting to us, but the two we find most provocative are Johnnie Lou Atherton and Emanuel Elias Smith.

Emanuel Elias, Saint Emanuela's eldest grandson, is twenty-three, only recently back from Vietnam and highly intelligent, power-oriented, and aggressive. I've heard a lot about him from both his grandmother and the white supervisors. All of them consider him to be the dangerous revolutionary of the Coke orange groves. Both blame his radicalism on the damnyankees he fraternized with in the army.

Bob says, "We have been looking forward to meeting you. We've heard a lot about you from your grandmother, Emanuel."

Emanuel returns the greeting with an easy smile but adds, a little menacingly, "Yeh, I heard a lots about you from mama, too, a whole lots. She thinks you're good folk, you know." He hesitates and smiles. "Me and her don't often see eye to eye about who's good dudes and who's bad." He turns to me and says, "Nor about who's good ladies either."

Johnnie Lou Atherton is Sam Snooker's cousin and a quite beautiful woman in her forties. She's tall, slender, and has a strong, intelligent, sometimes arrogant, face.

She, Bob, Stan, Arnold, and I would become very good friends during our years in Florida. And from the minute we met her, we haven't stopped marveling at her, and wondering to ourselves and one another by what miracle she had emerged from her hard life as well-rounded and multidimensional a person as any we've ever met.

And talk about natural-born leaders! We saw Johnnie Lou in action as a leader that night at the Snookers'.

It is midnight or a little after and we've been at the Snookers' for over three hours, talking mostly, with Emanuel and Johnnie Lou.

We suddenly hear the sound of a car stopping, no other sound, but everyone rises up as though there'd been an explosion. A few men grab their loaded guns and kneel, waiting, in front of the window, peeping out at the stopped car.

It is a red pickup truck with two men on the front seat and three in back, unmasked but unrecognizable. They heave out a burning cross, as Sam says they did the first time, and drive away.

Some people look as terrified as I feel and hope I don't appear. But a couple of men, nevertheless, get their guns and shoot them into the air. And Emanuel tells them:

"Damn fools y'all, shooting your guns up in the air instead of at the U.K.ers got you turned into damn cowards. Shooting guns up in the air, hell, who do you think's going to be scared of that?"

Sam says, "Yeh, well, what you have us do, son, go shoot up on the white folks? Well, who you think get hurt worst if we was to do that?"

Emanuel says, "Well, I'm not talking about shooting up anybody but just going to their part of town and doing the same as they done us. Go burn our cross in their part of town is all I'm saying. Like y'all enough Saints here, I want to know what about what your Bible tells you about, you know, an eye for an eye and a tooth for a tooth, that is what I want to know."

The mention of the Saints and the Bible reminds old Pa Snooker. He gets down on his knees and calls on all the other Saints to kneel and pray to God.

A few do and Emanuel's infuriated, "Oh, you nothings, you Toms, you bunch of Uncle Toms, get up off your damn knees."

Now Sam says, "You, Emanuel, calling our people names, well, you and your Communist stuff, sometime I don't mind listening. But tonight you know you be just too much to take and I am here to tell you this be my place, not yours and if the people wants to pray, if that makes them feel good, well they will have freedom to pray so long as they are in my place. And if Mr. Emanuel Elias, Communist, don't like it, why, thank y'all for coming but you know where the door's at, Emanuel Elias."

Emanuel doesn't leave, naturally. Instead, he keeps griping as much to himself as out loud about wishing more than anything in the world that he could "just get some of the people to just stop taking everything the white people do without fighting back. Because, the more hell black people take, the more white people are going to raise. It's a shame what black people take, it really is a shame. I feel sick sometime, I get so mad with my own people."

Johnnie Lou looks at Emanuel with great warmth and compassion. She puts her arms around him and holds him close to her. Oddly, he doesn't fight to free himself.

"Poor young one," Johnnie says, "poor young Emanuel. Admit it, son, your li'l heart is pounding inside of you just like the rest of us. Baby, even though you do be such a big mouth on the outside you are as scared as all of the rest of us on the inside. And ain't nothing wrong with that so long as we stands together, and, you know, don't run away.

"As long as we keep up one another's spirits. Like, oh, who got a joke to tell? You, Emanuel, no, not you, you young ones,. I don't know why, but seem like God left out your funny bones when he made y'all."

Johnnie Lou tells jokes and funny stories about herself for maybe an hour or two and keeps the people laughing until she realizes the effect's begun to pall. "I wonder what I better do now," she says to me. "Yeh, well, I think the next thing to laughing and getting people to get over the tightness in them is to get them all revved up and fighting the way they was at Emanuel before."

She goes across the room to Rosebud and calls her a hypocrite for "telling me how rotten I be just because I happens to like my wine and beer. And all the time you youself be married to a dude give you all the little things you like to have out of all that evil money come from selling whiskey to sinners like me.

"And your old Reverend Seaford be a worse hypocrite than you youself. Preaching at y'all to save the souls of the drinkers and still gladly taken the dust you always giving him, and he know damn well come right out of this here evil bar. It Sam's dirty money, pretty Rosebud, sure be a big help in getting the Reverend his new green Cadillac this year the same as he got last one."

Before Rosebud can answer Johnnie, Ma Snooker speaks up from her wheelchair in furious tone:

"Now, Johnnie Lou, drop the thing about our reverend and his car no matter what the make of it be, and think a minute about you own mama, Flora."

She says, "When Flora been the age of Rosebud here if she would've known the Bible as a young woman . . . I seen her before she done gone from your daddy and you and poor little Bobby, may his soul rest in peace. And I don't like to talk bad about my flesh and blood, but how could she leave her husband and y'all kids for another man?

"So, I told her, 'Remember your Bible, little Sister. The first thing it warn against be adultery, committing to fornication and adultery.' "

Since Ma Snooker's got a great deal to say about Johnnie Lou's mother's "sins," and many of the Saints here are interested in the details, Johnnie Lou's free to use her abundant ingenuity to "rev up" the young people.

"Well, Emanuel Elias, all them folks thinking you be so big and wrong and Communist. Man. And what they think of Larry here, he is just a dumb good-looking ath-a-lete is all. Then push come to shove, and who cause all the trouble and scare the white folks so bad, make them so mad? Well, old ath-a-lete Larry and not big, bad Communist Emanuel Elias."

I'm not at all sure Emanuel Elias'll fall into her trap, but he does, saying:

"Well, maybe you like being in the spot we all are, Johnnie, just because you 'ath-a-lete' nephew was so selfish as to up and marry this white chick.

"Well, me, I am a black man and that means, baby, I want to fight the U.K.'s and white folks for a better reason than Larry and Karen." He gives Larry a long, contemptuous, look. "Now, I would never disrespect my own people enough so I would marry white."

"Emanuel Elias, you are a big mouth but never put your body where the words are at. You only talk about fighting for our rights and showing us to be as good as white people but I proved it," Larry says. "Because a white man don't think nothing of going out there and getting pleasure with a black woman. But he sure don't want to see no black man with a white woman.

"But I don't care what the old white man like, I take my chick no matter what the white folks will do." And on it went between them until we left.

Chapter 5

Putting the program into effect means to us a long-range process, a lengthy beginning involving finding the natural leaders among the people who can understand the language of people-doing-for-themselves and can communicate it; leaders who have enough trust in the principles of self-help and in the company's expressed intentions of enabling change to occur—changes in housing, employment, health, self-determination. And trust in the "culture change" ideas of Bob, Stan, Arnold, myself, and the other HRI consultants.

And so, our first job is the hiring of the community aides who will begin to involve the people on behalf of the program and also serve as links between the company and the consultants and community. Marvelous Johnnie Lou is, of course, one of them.

"You want me? Man, you mean I will be paid for helping my people? Oh, it just be . . ." Suddenly she stopped talking and began to cry. She sat there between Bob and Stan at the beat-up table of the Do-Drop-Inn and cried as though her heart would break.

"Why are you crying, Johnnie?" I finally asked.

And her answer . . . Good God, the passion and compassion there is in this woman, she says:

"The way you are talking about this project . . . the way y'all telling it, well, if it all works out that way, oh, man, my people gon' to fly. And thinking about that makes me so—joyous—it's too much for a heart to hold."

She hesitates, impelled to tell us, and hating to do it, that:

"Another reason I cry . . . Well, y'all give me this high hope, and say you want me to give my peoples the same high hope you giving me. But then, oh, baby, suppose . . . Aw, hell, how could I *know* you and the company ain't gassing us? How could anybody know it for sure?"

It's a question we'll be hearing very often in the next year.

Saint Emanuela's our second aide, and when we offer her the job shows herself true to her nature, which means believing implicity in all our promises and honestly thinking we and The Coca-Cola Company, from Paul Austin on down, are her people's God-given saviors.

The third aide is Deacon Lincoln Redfield, out of Reverend Seaford's church. (I never would have hired him—or Emanuela. But Stan, Arnold, and Bob feel that since the Saints are dominant here it would be a mistake not to have them represented. Besides, they have obvious strengths that could be a great help to the project. Deacon Lincoln Redfield, handsome devil, asks genially at the time he's offered his post:

"I like to know the reason you chosen me. Is it because you think I be a smart dude or that the chicks, you know, just naturally come to where old Daddy-O is at? Yeh, they come even though it can do them no good because I be saved, praise Jesus."

I really am intrigued by our fourth aide and so are all the consultants. He's Jesús Sanchez, a *"señor muy simpático"* if ever there was one. He is not at all handsome in the ordinary sense and looks to be at least sixty, though he's actually in his middle forties. Gray-headed, bent, and with his warm, friendly face prematurely lined by sun and wind. Oh, his eyes are a young person's, though, almost too beautiful for a man, soft, languorous with long, airy, feminine eyelashes that today fill Lincoln with envy ("I mean why Gawd waste them lashes on so homely a cat), and used to fill Jesús with self-doubt when he was a little boy growing up in Guanajuato, Mexico. "My *abuelita*, little grandmother, would boast of me as a boy of *corazón,* soul when, you know, all I wanted to be in those days was *muy machismo."*

Jesús may pick fruit for a living, but his "true, real life" is as a folk and oral poet, a chronicler of the Chicano migrants' life and history from the earliest years in Mexico to today. Arnold and I, during our years in Florida, and Bob and Stan while they were there, spent all the time we could in Jesús' house, basking in the spontaneous sympathy he always showed us and everyone and fascinated by his folk songs and declamations.

My favorites among his songs and poems tell of his

people's exploitation and present hard life. Cries from the heart of Mexican and Chicano migrants about their frustrations, fears, woes, anxieties, hates, angers . . . and dreams for themselves, but especially their children.

> "I am the cry of the poor
> Who work in the fields
> Who water the earth
> With our sweat.
> Our huts and hovels
> Are always full of sorrow
> For we live as animals . . .
>
> "My sons and my daughters
> You will go to school
> And be doctors, teachers, lawyers
> And your children will never know,
> Of the sufferings you do
> My beloved sons and daughters."

Our first meeting with the newly appointed community aides was held on a Saturday night at Emanuela's shack. I'd never been in the quarter at night before and, though I was with Arnold, Bob, and Stan, I was quite simply terrified. Nighttime in an unaccustomed environment is always fearful and, here, with not a bit of illumination of the dirt road passing between the two rows of morbid shacks, it was infinitely more so.

Lincoln, Jesús, and Johnnie Lou are already there when we come.

"Hey, honey, you look scared or something," Johnnie Lou greeted me with a grin.

"Humph, don't you talk like that to Miss Sara in my house," Saint Emanuela whispers. "She ain't scared."

"But, listen, Miss Emanuela, I am scared."

Johnnie Lou stares at me with her large eyes.

"Well, you got a lots of reason to be scared, Sara, you does, really. Like last Saturday night old Sally Standish was coming home from church—from church. Next thing you know this evil dude looking for green on her and not finding it . . . It blow his head, you see, and he knocked poor Sally down and stomped her so bad."

Stan asks for an indication of how often this sort of thing is happening, and the list is both long and traumatic to hear. He then asks for the aides' definition of some of the reasons behind the crimes, and Emanuela's the first to offer her sound, sane view.

"Man, Mr. Stan, these colored men . . . or no, nigra men what these are . . . is mean and . . . A lots of them around here just born killers is what they are."

"Oh, bull," says Johnnie Lou.

"I hates cussing in my house," Emanuela says.

"Then stop talking so goddamn dumb."

"You cussing one more time." Old Emanuela's keeping tabs.

"Gal, if you think this be cussing for me . . . I know some cusswords, Ella, 'd make you turn white if you was to hear them." And now she's had her bit of fun, gets down to serious business with Stan, Bob, Arnold, and me.

"Y'all always saying how the company want to show us we can trust them. Till the time come they can do all of them fancy things they says, get the new houses built, well, sure, that take time. But then, how come they don't right now light up these here roads so you can see who following behind you and not get killed or something?" She shakes her head. "No way they gon' do that, though."

Stan says, "Why do you say no way, Johnnie?"

Johnnie says simply, "Why this company do what no other company in Florida or anyplace do for their workers? Why should Coca-Cola put in lights?"

Stan says, "Because you have a right to lighted roads is why. You hear me, Johnnie, Linc, Ella, Jesús?"

"I hears you," Emanuela says, grinning.

"Me too," Lincoln says.

Johnnie Lou says, "Yeh, Stan, *we* hears you, man. Only question be, do the company hear you?"

Stan says, "Well, I tell you what. I am going to tell Luke Smith about this when I call him tomorrow to report the results of our meeting."

"Tomorrow be Sunday," Johnnie says.

Stan says, "Yeh, I know."

"You mean you gon' call the Prez on a Sunday? How come?"

"Because he asked me to," Stan says. "And the reason he

asked me to is that he cares a lot about the results of our meeting tonight."

Johnnie Lou says, "Hey, Stan, can we be there when you call up the Prez on Sunday?" Her eyes and tone are mocking.

"Sure can," Stan says.

Now the conversation turns to other problems the aides want Stan to present to Luke Smith tomorrow.

"Stan, tell him about the rats in our shacks as big as cats almost," says Johnnie Lou.

Jesús, always striving for reason, cautions Johnnie not to exaggerate; there's no reason for overstatement when the truth itself is so striking. "Tell it like it is, Johnnie, tell him about the babies that been bitten by rats." He adds, "And we can make a suggestion that, you know, if the garbage was to be picked up like regular instead of just being allowed to collect and become a breeding place for the rats . . . And if they got rat poison to get rid of the things in the first place . . ."

"Oh, you keep out, Jesús," suddenly rants Lincoln, his body bent and trembling in anger, his index finger slashing the air for emphasis. "What you know about what's bringing the rats to our colored people's quarter? You talking about garbage and like that when all of the time . . . See, you wouldn't know it, white man, but the main thing bringing the rats is us throwing out what is in our slop jars because we ain't got no toilets in our houses. Well, you got a toilet indoor in your house, white man, right?"

Jesús nods almost in shame.

"You got screens on your doors, white man?"

"Yeh, Linc."

"And you got a bathtub right inside of you house. Hot and cold water, too."

Emanuela is hardly one to sit back silently while we white people are around and the company's being attacked. It's obvious Lincoln's bitterness toward Jesús is, in reality, directed at the company. She says that conditions here at Coca-Cola are infinitely less terrible than in all the agricultural workers' quarters she's known and lived in in her whole long wandering life.

"Well, these places in New York when I was picking apples, well, me and my kids was living in chicken coops all them places." She explains to us consultants. "The bossmen, what they done was to make the coops a little bit bigger and then people, migrant people like us, move in them."

She thinks awhile and says, "Well, now, that ain't right nohow; peoples oughtn't have to live where chickens done, I don't think.

"But when Johnnie and Linc says we got it so bad here with Minute Maid when all of the time . . . Johnnie, Linc, you know them chicken coops and has lived in them, so why you say . . . ?"

She turns to us again. "Them talking about our outhouses here being so bad when all of the time they been in camps like me. Now, they know theyself that most places didn't have no outhouses right convenient like ours, only acrost the road is all we got to go here at Minute Maid. But in these other places, well, they wasn't no outhouses at all. You got to go out and squat in the woods."

She gets caught up in her recollections. "And, too, they wasn't no water spouts right out in your own front yard like there is with this company. Some places, baby, and Lincoln and Johnnie know, just to get you some water, you have to go so far to get it, walk so far in the woods where they is some kind of pool amongst the snakes.

"I think we living right good here and . . ."

That Lincoln and Johnnie Lou hate Emanuela's guts for her acceptance and humility is, under these circumstances, of course, natural. But what we don't expect is for Johnnie Lou to be so overwhelmed by fury she'll spring at Emanuela with all of her force and energy so Bob, Arnold, Stan, and Jesús have to hold her off.

"You white man, take your dirty hands off her. I mean you, Jesús." Lincoln's voice sounds as if a strangler is at his throat, and his body's rigid with anger as he tells Jesús that he, being considered more white than Negroes are, even although he is of Mexican descent, and therefore not believed to be as good as "true whites," has no business even being at this airing of *black* people's housing and other problems.

And here comes Johnnie Lou stunning me again. Explaining more simply and in less uncertain terms than I know I would have done that, though it's true white and Chicano workers are better housed than black ones, there are many other important problems they have in common.

"The colored parents don't have no place for leaving the

kids and babies while they are out working, and neither do the white nor Mexican. Right, Linc man?"

"Yeh," Lincoln must agree despite himself.

"Listen, Linc," Johnnie Lou says, "when the busses breaks down and we got to just sit there till they fixed and lose all of that money, well, the whites suffers just the same as us colored."

Trust Saint Emanuela to say, "Bus-breaking be a act of God."

At this point Stan gets into the act. "Oh, Ella, you're not going to blame God, are you, for the fact these beat old busses break down this often? Are you going to blame Him?"

"Well, no sir, Mr. Stan."

"Well, whose fault would you say it is then, Miss Emanuela?" I ask.

She doesn't answer, and Stan, wary of the blaming game from his experience on other projects, switches from fault-finding to a search for a solution.

"Listen, what do you think the company can do in order to make sure the buses don't break down as often as they have in the past?"

Emanuela ponders a long time. Then, "Y'all knows that better'n me, Mr. Stan."

"Oh, Gawd," Johnnie Lou says, "sure he knows, but he want to know what y'all knows. Fool, don't be so dumb."

"Yeh," Lincoln agrees.

"Maybe git new buses ain't gon' break down," Emanuela says, and we all applaud her so enthusiastically that her face lights up. A smile at first, and then she quickly hides her pride of self in a laugh.

"Git new buses ain't gon' break down," she repeats with real self-assurance.

I don't remember having ever experienced such a surge of pleasure, enthusiasm, and plain hopefulness about what this project's going to be able to accomplish as I did at that moment. And the point is, my feeling's shared by the three aides as well as Stan, Bob, and Arnold.

Johnnie's glowing as she pats Saint Emanuela on the back and says, "Ella, baby, you know some things I never would've thought."

And that bursts the floodgates, it seems, as all the aides are inspired by one another to explain to us consultants the hard circumstances of their working lives. And if we'd thought that these people don't begin to know the details of their neglect, we were very wrong.

They know all too well, and lament the fact that only they, among all the workers employed by the company, have no medical protection aside from workmen's compensation for illnesses and injuries incurred on the job. They're entirely aware of the excellent health insurance program from which all of the company's other workers benefit.

They know, too, from bitter experience that there's no provision for quick medical help if they become hurt while working in the groves. No foreman, no supervisor, or delegated worker knows first aid. And as for outside doctors who would treat their injuries, they know they aren't welcome in any of their offices or community hospitals either. All the aides have personal stories to match Granny May's about the callous turndowns received by the few agricultural workers of their acquaintance who've been intrepid or foolish enough to actively seek help from hospitals and doctors.

"And I'm thinking about all of it," Jesús says in his gentle way. "We couldn't, wouldn't dare ask this company, or could we . . . ? I mean, could the company get a doctor and a nurse, maybe, to be here for some of us that need them so bad, and outsiders don't want anything to do with us?"

"Get a doctor and nurse for us, you mean?" Lincoln takes a drag of his cigarette and laughs ironically. "Why should the company do something like that since we ain't a-nothin' to them but a pair of hands? We ain't people to them."

Johnnie goes on: "And if you ain't people to them, well, you don't expect they gon' worry about you like the other workers, the ones in the plants and all over the company that do be people to them.

"Like, see, when it is raining and we can't go to work. Well, it ain't even our fault. But we will be punished as though the fault is ourn. Like there ain't no pay for us on rainy days.

"Whilst in the plants, well, being indoors rain don't matter to the people in the company plants. But if they was to get sick and have to stay away from work . . . Now this is the worker hisself getting sick, and not the weather raining on you. Still and all, the company says, 'Man in the plant got sick, it ain't his fault, and anyways, his kids got to eat, don't they? So, we gon' pay him for that day if he work or not.'

"Also, why they never stop to think about is this or that grove better or worse for the picking. Like take them groves that is a lots harder to pick than some other ones. One like this grove my sister Lee was on yesterday, the fruit was so skimpy on the trees, anybody could see how skimpy, but she gotten paid the same as people working on the good-growing trees."

She stops talking awhile, and sits thinking, absorbed. "See, the foreman know how skimpy the grove was and said, 'Now these here skimpy groves ought to fetch a better price by any right.' But see, old supervisor don't listen to the foreman neither, just go on, and make up his own mind, don't listen to no foremen nor no pickers."

Bob asks what the aides suggest the company should do about setting picking rates. Should the responsibility of setting it be taken from the supervisors? And Johnnie's answer, not really a surprise to us after this day, is, "Well, the least they could do, knowing we all pickers know better than them what is a good grove for picking, and what ain't, seem like they ought to let the pickers help the supervisors decide."

On Sunday at four o'clock, a time between afternoon and night services at Emanuela and Lincoln's church, Stan, Arnold, Bob, and I pick them up along with Jesús and Johnnie Lou and set off to make our telephone call to Luke Smith. Stan's going to be our spokesman and not only describe what occurred at the aides' meeting but also present Luke a list of suggestions for immediate improvements and changes. They include:

Lighting the roads in and around the quarters, instituting regular supervised garbage pickup, and poisoning the rats. Tearing down the outhouses and building in their stead decent community toilets with proper washing and shower facilities. The aides, of course, would prefer private baths and toilets but are taking into account the company's promise to help the people move out of their shacks and into either their own or rented houses in the near future.

They're also asking the company to bring water into the shacks, install individual sinks, and bring toilet facilities into the groves as well as to supply ice for the workers' water.

Last, but most important, they want the company to make provision for taking care of the babies and children during the hours the parents have to work in the groves.

I still remember my feeling of anger and fear when Stan stepped into the phone booth while Bob held the door open with his foot so everyone could hear the conversation. I had warned them earlier while we were having breakfast, "You ought to realize this whole project will get messed up before it's even properly begun if your man, Luke Smith, doesn't respond exactly as you're counting on him to."

Stan shrugged and shook his head, and Bob said, "I know Luke will handle it fine, I think he's expecting it."

I said, "You know Luke Smith, you say . . . But if he doesn't handle it fine and if he lets these people down—what then? I swear I don't understand how two such logical people as you and Bob can take such a stupid risk with something that is supposed to mean so much to you." I added, "Listen, call Luke yourself before the people get in on it, and tell him the score, let him be prepared."

"That's exactly what they suspect we're going to do," Bob says, "and sensitive as they're going to be to any nuance . . . I think Johnnie Lou and Jesús would see through our act if it were an act."

"Listen, Bob," I said, "if Luke Smith doesn't come through the way you expect, you'll have to find yourself a new participant-observer. This one will be quitting."

"If he doesn't come through," Bob said, "I won't be here to find her anyway."

We could only hear Stan's side of the conversation, but it was clear from what he was saying that Luke Smith was coming through with flying colors.

Later, Stan reported the whole gist of his conversation with him.

"Luke agreed with all our suggestions and says that he appreciated our letting him know how we saw it. There was one point, though, he sort of questioned, that about the new bathroom facilities. Even then, I can't tell you his opinion was different from ours. All he said was that, since the people would be moving into the new housing so soon, maybe that money could be saved. And he didn't really say it could be but only asked me if I thought there was a chance it could be. I told him what you folks had said about how important this was to the people and he said the company would certainly go along with you. You know better than they do what is important to the people at this point, what will make them trust in both Coke and HRI and know we aren't lying about how much this program means to the company."

"So what he gon' do?" Lincoln asks.

Stan says, "He told me to write Bill Kelly a memo listing all our points and saying to go ahead and start working on them immediately if not sooner."

Bill Kelly, formerly vice-president in charge of the Foods Division's personnel department came here from Houston to become vice-president of groves operations. Bob had asked for a "top flight proven administrator who will command respect from all the employees and from the Houston and Atlanta offices as well". Bill Kelly's such a person.

"You guarantee Mr. Kelly gon' do what you say Mr. Smith tell him to do?" Johnnie Lou asks. "You guarantee it, Stanley Silverzweig?"

"Johnnie," Stan says, "I feel safe in saying, yes, I do guarantee it."

"So you trust this here company?"

"Johnnie, yes, especially now, after my conversation with Luke Smith, I can tell you that, yes, I do."

Johnnie Lou studies Stan intently as he talks. She seems to be weighing Stan's every word before saying anything herself.

Finally, she speaks. "Stanley Silverzweig, why y'all here?"

"By 'all' you mean us from HRI, right?" Stan asks.

"Right. And this question, is Coke just paying you a big pile of money, and you do this here Agricultural Labor Project? Is you working for us peoples or is you working to, as you say, make more money off of us for the company?"

Stan explains these two purposes can, will, hopefully, prove, in fact, to be mutually compatible. He says:

"Not just this company and this company less than others, but all the growers in America may think they help themselves by failing to give the people decent working and living conditions, but really they don't. The truth is they're hurting themselves all the time they're hurting the people.

"Okay, take the people here and this company, see, the workers know that no matter how hard they work they can't make enough to take care of their families, keep their kids in good health, give them all they would want to as parents. It can't happen no matter how hard a man tries or knocks himself out.

"So, hell, why try at all, then? Why knock yourself out at all? I know how it'd be for me in the people's place here. I would work just enough to get the food in me and my family's belly and the booze I need if I'm a drinking man.

"And speaking of a drinking man, I know as well as I know my name's Stanley Silverzweig that if I had to live like many people here do, live without hope, I'm talking about hope for my future, hope that at least my kids'll be living a better life than I do, that I'll have the opportunity to give them that life . . . well, if I didn't have that hope, man, I am not strong like some of you people here, maybe I never had the need to develop my strength the way you all have because my living's always come easy.

"So, what I'm telling you now is that if I were an agricultural worker I'd be drowning my sorrows, forgetting there's no hope for me and my kids. I'd drink up a storm. Or do any other thing I'd need to in order to just forget life's as terrible as it is. I know myself well enough to say right here I'd be drunk more often than not if I were one of you."

"Not you, Mr. Stan," Emanuela says.

"Yeh him, Mr. Stan," says Johnnie Lou.

Stan goes on. "Now take me as I have described myself and consider how this can hurt the company. I'm supposed to go to work this morning and I'm too drunk to even stir out of my bed. So I don't show up at the bus and my crew's short a pair of hands. So my foreman's got to find him another pair of hands and might take the whole crew on a detour looking for them before ever getting to the grove."

He stops to take a deep breath, then says, "Or else, say, I get myself up off the bed and come to work drunk. Well, I'm not the only one either staying in bed or coming to work drunk."

"Man, you sure ain't," Johnnie Lou says. "There's more that's drunk than not."

"Let's get off the drunk thing now, and say that, drunk or sober, I've got no reason for sticking around at Minute Maid if I'm treated so badly. I work three days, two, one, and then, bingo, I've had it. I quit. I'm going someplace else for a day or two—always trying, maybe there's something a little better.

"Now you want to know . . . I've been saying the company hurts when you do and you want to know how."

"Oh, yeh, sir," Emanuela says in a tone to indicate she can't bear the company's hurting.

Stan now explains the plant's dependency on a steady flow of fruit and points up the direct relationship to that of harvesters' work patterns and habits. It's certainly to this company's business advantage to be able to count on the harvesters the same as the plant workers to remain with it steadily, report regularly to work, and be willing and able to work a full, energetic day.

"So, if you, as workers, as an important part of the company, which is what it considers all its other employees, get what is coming to you, why, you will then be both willing and able to give the company what is coming to it.

"Now, do you see what I mean when I say HRI's working for the people is also going to benefit the company?"

Johnnie Lou says, no, she doesn't see, in spite of all Stan's said, how we can be interested in helping the workers and the company at the same time. She believes we're here to "get the company off the hook. See, they don't want us telling people how bad things be and so is getting y'all to make promises about how things is going to be so good come soon."

Stan says, logically, that if the company carries through on its commitments to the Agricultural Labor Project, it won't have any need to hire us or anyone else to get it off the hook. The truth itself will do that.

Now Jesús asks what may be for us three the most difficult question of all to answer. He asks, in his gentle way, how much credit our work here is bringing us in the eyes of certain people who may be important to us. He doesn't specify these "certain people," but we know who he means.

There are some people working with Cesar Chavez's United Farmworkers, as one example, who've given up everything to share the life of the migrants they, like us, want to help, but we help the migrant workers while remaining on our well-paying jobs.

It's, truthfully, a hell of a feeling Jesús has aroused, and Bob's the one of us to admit it aloud. But he must add, also truthfully, that we're here out of our strong conviction that if migrancy is ever to be overcome in our time it is companies like Coca-Cola—with all of their assets, wherewithal, and selfish as well as humanistic interest—who are going to have to take the lead in accomplishing it.

Johnnie Lou narrows her eyes a little and says Stan *may* be right. All the same, the general talk around Do-Drop-Inn continues to be critical of us: "The people says y'all's full of hot air and don't care no more about us for all of the fancy talk." . . . "You're gon' collect your big pile of money and be off." . . . "You're working just for the money and once you get it, you'll be gone."

Jesús, nodding, says, "Yeh, some of the people I talk to they said that, really, you don't care about either us *or* the company. Yeh, they really don't even think you give the company a thought, you are just being paid to do your jobs and will go back where you came from when you are done."

Stan says, "I want to ask you, Emanuela. Before I ask anything, though, I want to tell you that Johnnie, Lincoln, and Jesús have helped us more than I can say by explaining to us how the people really feel about us and the project. Now I'm going to ask you to level, too, about what you've been hearing around the church, for one place."

Emanuela doesn't move—doesn't seem to react at all to Stan's question.

"Please tell us, Miss Ella, it's very important to us and the project that you do."

"Some, oh, a whole lots, really, says, y'all be a lie, come in to make the people believe Coke were going to do so much for them and they wasn't going to do nothing for us at all."

Her face is sad as she begs our pardon for having told us, though she wouldn't have if we hadn't forced it out of her.

"Emanuela," Johnnie says very gently to her, "you done right to tell."

"Yeh," Lincoln says.

But their approval doesn't matter, and Emanuela hangs her head because she can't bear to look us in the eye, and there's nothing any of us can say or do, though we all try, to assuage her feeling of guilt and her basic fear of us.

Johnnie Lou says, "Well, now, to me the part that bothers me the most . . . See, to go back to my first feeling, to the time at Sam Snooker's when you first asked me to come and do this job. It was that, you know, if y'all come up here and meet me and believe I can help my people . . . But now, come to find out, they, my own people, feel like I has been bought. They say, 'That Johnnie Lou, see, she'll just do anything to keep from picking fruit.' That what my own people says." Now there are tears in Johnnie Lou's eyes.

"Yeh," Lincoln says.

"So I don't want to work for y'all no more," Johnnie Lou says. "Because my people are not trusting you, they can't trust me either. Anything you do to hurt them, it is as good as if I done it."

"Look, Johnnie," Bob says, "we intend all you and the others have said as a warning. And all we're asking you to do is to take a chance and trust us while keeping your eyes open for any harm we may do. Then, if you want us off the project, you've only got to tell us, and we'll be gone. It's a promise."

Johnnie yells at him now:

"Suppose we does trust you, well, you ain't the real bosses, man. Let your Mr. Luke Smith come and talk to us aides like you done it today. Let's hear from him, you know."

∽§ Chapter 6

Six days after our meeting with the aides, J. Lucian Smith, then president of the Foods Division in which the citrus operation is contained, Donald Keough, and also Joseph Califano, presently Secretary of the Department of Health, Education and Welfare, who was the company's Washington-based attorney at the time, arrive to hold their own meeting with the aides as Johnnie Lou had requested.

Luke Smith is in his early fifties, tall, rather more virile than good-looking, conservatively dressed in sports pants and jacket. Don Keough's shorter, slenderer, with blue eyes and a smile that's open and disarming. He looks comfortable in Emanuela's shack.

"This is the biggest honor to me," Emanuela says.

Don says, "The honor's ours."

Emanuela, overflowing with pleasure, asks, "Could I give y'all something cold to drink, a Coke?"

Everyone says yes, she goes to the icebox to get the Cokes, and I suddenly hear her sigh loudly and exclaim:

"Oh, Lord, how this could happen to me? Oh, Lord, how?"

She stands at the icebox wringing her hands and with a stricken look on her face, and when I join her there and ask her what's wrong she points to the inside of the box still without a word and I have all I can do to keep from exploding with laughter at what I see there—bottles of Pepsi where the Coke ought to be. It's obvious what has happened. Emanuel, probably perturbed by Ella's bootlicking gratitude at the company's big brass coming to her house, had taken this way of expressing his feelings.

"Miss Sara, what I'm gon' do?"

"Serve the Pepsi, Miss Ella."

"I couldn' do *that*."

"Well, explain why you've got to; the people will understand."

"How explain? What I'm gon' say?"

"Do you want me to explain, Miss Ella?"

She nods with tears in her eyes, and I tell her dilemma and our interpretation of it. To everyone's credit they remain serious-faced, no one as much as smiles, and Don graciously tells Emanuela to please relax, it's no great tragedy, and her grandson has quite a sense of humor, doesn't he?

Sense of humor, Emanuela says, sense of mischief, sense of mean-ness, sense of evil's more like it. Then Don begins smiling, giving Johnnie freedom to laugh like hell until, finally, her merriment becomes contagious so the rest of us, including Ella by now, laugh and laugh. She says that if we'll excuse her she'll run out and buy some Coke, and Don jumps to his feet and tells her that, no, indeed she will not. She's an important person at this meeting. He'll go if anyone does because "I won't be missed as much as you, Miss Ella."

The relish and pure pleasure on Emanuela's face at Don's consideration for her, his way of complimenting her and putting her at ease, is really something to observe.

Luke opens the formal meeting by telling the aides he's grateful Bob's arranged this "opportunity" for "us getting to know each other."

"The reason I say it's an opportunity for us, well, let me speak to that point as a businessman first. Don Keough and I, as businessmen, *ought* to know about our employees; who they are, how they feel about the company, their hopes and ambitions. I mean, I'm not even talking at this moment about our human desire to know you as people. I'll speak to that later, but only about the fact it is *good business* to know our employees and *bad business* if we don't."

The aides, even Johnnie Lou, to my bewilderment—I'd have expected she'd be more wary—are drinking in Luke's words with the most obvious acceptance. And now Luke says something to break through my cynicism, too. It's so implacably realistic I can't find room for challenge. It's unwise, he says, for the Coke executives to go on relying as they've done in the past on the interpretations of the workers by the supervisors who "as you do and we—Bill Kelly, Don Keough, all of us—look through our own special glasses. Well, to my mind, it's time you and we saw each other straight for the company's and all of our sakes.

"If we know you as people, as human beings, and if you know us that way, if we can sit down and talk together as we are, then, you know, sitting here with you, you can't ever again be bogeymen to us."

"Nor you neither to us," says Johnnie Lou.

Luke goes on:

"All right, to start telling you something about us as human beings and not bogeymen, I want to tell you first, speaking for all of us in the company, how truly sorry we are because it took us much too long to come here to sit down with you and learn for ourselves what you are up against."

He continues: "Our neglect . . . I hope you'll believe me when I say that we never had bad intentions toward you, but rather . . ."

Don interrupts to explain the meaning of the word intentions.

Luke says, "Ignorance. The one word, as I see it, with which to try to explain our long neglect is ignorance. We just didn't know what was happening here. And I have to admit we took the easy way. Sitting here among you today and feeling good because I know we have finally made a beginning in resolving our mutual problems, I have, nevertheless, to deal with the question I know must be on all your minds. Why didn't we get together as we are today eight years ago when we first took over the groves? And the answer I believe I've made clear by now is that we took the easy way out, didn't ourselves investigate your working—and living—conditions in these groves, but instead relied for our information on people whose whole interest was in keeping us 'happy' and 'self-satisfied.' "

He hesitates a long moment. "I want you to know we're far from being self-satisfied today, and we feel that we as a company have much to undo in our relationship with you and the other agricultural workers. So rather than tell you again how truly sorry all of us are about the past, I'm here to pledge our complete cooperation to you for the future. I'm here to say we'll stand behind you and the people in all of your efforts to change things here."

Now the aides describe to Luke and Don, as they have to us, all the ideas and recommendations that they had come up with. I was afraid they'd be too intimidated to be honest, but they are far from it. Johnnie Lou and Jesús especially talk to the point and in a way that impresses Luke and Don.

When they're done, Luke says they and the company see eye to eye and summarizes in toto, as the consultants and aides together have done piecemeal till now, the hopes and dreams for the long-term program:

> To upgrade working conditions enabling agricultural workers to attain job productivity, job security, and living conditions comparable to industrial employees.
>
> To provide agricultural workers with opportunity to upgrade their skills and educational level so that they have access to higher-paying jobs at the company or elsewhere.
>
> To improve working and living conditions so that the company's citrus grove operations attract top-level workers, with employee turnover kept to a minimum.

He makes it clear also, as Stan did with less credibility, obviously, that the company's actions are motivated by enlightened self-interest and not a desire to become a private social welfare agency.

And the aides—Jesús and Johnnie Lou—express their realization that enlightened self-interest is an important plus for the program.

Johnnie rises from her seat and addresses us all in these terms:

"Well, the way I see it, I'd lots rather take from y'all when we know we got something to give you back for what y'all giving to us. And, too, it ain't only a matter of that, but, you know, if we got something to give you back, then you're glad to go on giving to us, where, if we don't, well, y'all might just get tired of giving and giving for nothing.

"And then one day, man, we think we got it made on this here project, and then y'all come and say, 'Sorry, but you know, we has had it. No more help to the people.'"

Don, sitting beside me, says, "The woman's remarkable," and repeats, more to himself than anyone else, "remarkable."

And Luke says, "What you've just said, Miss Johnnie . . . I want to tell you that, having talked with Bob and the other consultants as much as we have about the program and your strengths and abilities, we came here expecting a lot.

"Well, you people are even—the word I want is stronger, I guess—yes, you're even stronger than we expected you'd be. I have no doubt you can change life in these groves if you're given half a chance. You're going to be given it because it's your right.

"I know from being here today that you can count on yourselves, and I hope you know and believe from even this short acquaintance with us that you also can count on us to do our part."

"Yeh," Johnnie Lou says. "We will count on you and us not just to help the people on this project in the company, but other migrants, too, maybe all over the whole state of Florida, and maybe all over this whole country. I mean, what I'm hoping be we can show them others how to help theyselfs the way we will be helping ourselfs. Maybe, by the time we are done, there won't be no more migrancy at all. It is what I am hoping in my heart anyways."

Joseph Califano says, "Miss Johnnie Lou, I am very interested in your hope that migrancy can be done away with. I am interested for many reasons, including a personal one. You see, I was an aide to President Johnson for a long time; I lived in the White House. And we were very concerned about migrants, very anxious to abolish, get rid of, migrancy in this country just as you want to do. We, too, wanted, more than I can say, to help migrants to a decent life. Yet, with all the power of the government behind us, we couldn't do it. How, then, can you believe you can?"

Johnnie Lou answers simply and confidently. "Well, not to lowrate the government, but y'all isn't *the people, the migrants theyselfs*. Well, *we* be the people, and if we get a boost, we can help ourselfs better than anybody else, even y'all. People can help theyselfs better than other people could do no matter who they are. So that is why I say what I did and hope I be right and the thing turn out the way I think now it gon' do."

"Oh," Califano says, serious-faced, "I want to say you may very well be right. God knows, I hope you are. I wish you the best of luck and do believe what you accomplish, do, for yourselves, may, in the long run prove a lesson to us all."

After Luke, Don and Joseph Califano leave, I quiz the aides on their reactions to them.

"That man, Luke Smith," Jesús says, "I know . . . listening to him I felt uplifted because I know now this Project is going to help the people become . . . He says we're going to have the opportunity I never thought we would . . . And I believe him."

Just then, Emanuel comes in and, lo and behold, all he wants in the whole world, all he's been dreaming of for the last hour or hour and a half is a bottle of nice cold Coca-Cola.

Emanuela answers him back for a change, tells him that "of all the mean and low-down tricks" . . . why did he feel called upon to embarrass and humiliate her at a moment in her life when she "feel good and important, you know, for a change?"

Emanuel says it was no more than a small joke. And Emanuela had better learn to laugh at herself once in a while if she expects to continue surviving in our bitter world.

Emanuela's got no answer, but Jesús does. He tells Emanuel in no uncertain terms that a person has got to feel secure, be sure of who he is and what he's really about, to be able to laugh at himself. Well, Emanuela's got no such inner security, but that Emanuel does is to her great credit, not his. She's responsible, basically, for the fact Emanuel can feel a person of such dignity and worth he can laugh at himself, or so he puts it. The truth is, though, Jesús hasn't ever met Emanuel when he's been humorous at his own expense, but only other people's, mainly Emanuela's.

"And I'm gon' tell you something y'all ain't gon' believe. While you done steal my dignity, Mr. Luke and Mr. Don done help me get it back a little bit," Emanuela adds, to our surprise.

Emanuel, chin up as high as it will go, glares at Emanuela and says, "You, mama, are just a dumb nigger, and your Mr. Don and Mr. Luke, *yuch,* the sound of you calling their names makes me sick.

"Listen, do you think for one little minute . . . You, Johnnie, Lincoln, even you Jesús, do you think you are the only ones they make feel important? See, they talk the same way to the white fat cats as they do to you. So, you ain't nobody special to them, although you may think you are. They only acted the way you say because it is good business, folks, no other reason."

And then Emanuela said something that left Bob, Arnold, Stan, and me sitting there in amazement. She said, "Well, now, Emanuel, if'n you be right that Mr. Luke Smith and Mr. Don Keough go to the trouble talking to me like they done because it be 'good business,' then that mean, don't it, I be important to the whole company, the whole business? And ain't that even better than being important to just them, the two single men?"

Emanuel Elias, as all of us do, stares at Emanuela with disbelief.

"Hey, mama, I sure wish some of my army buddies could hear you now. You are talking about black power, you know it?"

She mulls it over, obviously terrified. Of course she isn't talking about black power the way she dimly gauges its meaning. Emanuel's been preaching black power since he's returned from Vietnam, and she's been scared to death every time he opened his mouth on the subject. The very mention of the word *power* is enough, more than enough, to bring her back to herself and lifelong loving investment in white "good bossman" power like that of the visitors just departed.

"Oh, my God," Emanuel says, "you dumb niggers believing in those liars."

Suddenly I find myself telling Emanuel, "I think if you'd been here earlier, Emanuel, you wouldn't in all logic and by light of your own philosophy have called Smith, Keough, or Califano liars when they told the aides, in so many words, that the supervisors, being middlemen, don't want them to have any kind of personal intimate contact with the workers like your grandmother. See, they know very well the picture of the workers they're going to get from, say, Bill Bennet or Jarvis Liston is gonng to be distorted and misleading."

Emanuel stares at me with his burning eyes. "See, that is the picture they want, though."

"Think into it a little more deeply, Emanuel, and you'll see it's not. It isn't even profitable to think of workers as not having ability because they aren't human."

He lights a cigarette and inhales deeply. "Oh, man, it is profitable as hell. Once you start thinking of your workers as human, it's going to cost you money."

He adds he'd expected a little deeper thinking, somewhat less naïveté from me. He'd begun to develop a kind of respect for me as a "people's writer" of some depth after he'd read a couple of my books last week. And now, unless he questions my genuineness, which he's not at this point quite prepared to do, he's got to condemn me as very gullible, as much a dupe as his poor old grandmother of "smart operators" like Luke, Don, and Joseph Califano.

"They have got you hailing and a-mening them just like she does with telling you how the redneck supervisors are responsible for keeping them apart from the workers.

"Then, see, they'll get with the supervisors. That same Luke Smith and Don Keough's gon' get with the crackers like Liston, Bennet, Old Red, and tell them . . . Well, Godalmighty, don't you know how the white men use the crackers and rednecks and black workers against each other for their own profit?"

He clears his throat meaningfully and gives me a wink. "Wow, I'd sure like to be a fly on the wall when Smith, Keough, and them get with the supervisors themselves. I wonder what they gon' say to *them*, you know, and how far apart it'll be from what they told the aides today."

⋖§ Chapter 7

The training session for managers and supervisors, a four-day affair, is held in a place that's as far away in mood from the ones they frequent on their own as it is possible to get. The Hotel Naples, directly on the Gulf in Naples and entirely ringed by stately palms, is a refined, romantic place, once a rich men's resort, and even today quite upper middle class and with a distinctly *Wasp*ish aura.

We're a motley crew here, consisting not only of the twenty top-level Florida managers and supervisors—including Bill Bennet, Jarvis Liston, and Old Red, who'd made my first day in the groves so memorable—but also our four aides, four company people—Luke, Don, Bill Kelly, and Gerry Abell, who'd come along with Bill to be the manager of the Agricultural Labor Project—and also six of us SRIers. Particularly striking in our group is tall, black Mel Green, obviously attractive to women, in a red, green and yellow daishiki.

Knowing from the beginning how discordant the interaction among such basically diverse people might be, I decided to keep a diary in order to recall precisely, meticulously, what occurred.

Day One

Our first breakfast together. My table included: Bill Kelly, tall, good-looking, the kind of man known as a quiet man, seeming calm and collected in that old-fashioned American way that becomes rarer and rarer today, and Gerry Abell, businessman on the rise at forty or almost, with conservative clothes, bald head, and honest, earnest, nice face. Johnnie

Lou and Emanuela. Jarvis Liston and Old Red. And Mel Green.

Bill introduced Mel to Old Red and Jarvis, and Mel stuck out his hand in greeting. Old Red took it easily, more or less. But Jarvis, who Johnnie Lou swears is a Kleagle, a recruiter in his United Klans' klavern, shook Mel's hand with deep-felt difficulty, under Bill's surveillance, and I wondered how he'd have behaved if Bill weren't around. His face was covered with sweat, and I saw he had the shivers as he took Mel's hand and held it a short moment.

Johnnie Lou, on one side of me, whispered, "What we gon' have for breakfast, y'all know, honey?"

I told her I didn't know, and she said, "Well, if I don't know what knife or fork to use for eating what dish with, I figured it all out even before I come here that what I gon' do be watch you and do just like you do. You eat with a fork and I do too, like that."

Bill Kelly started the conversational ball rolling by commenting on the fine weather, the beauty of the sea, the ripe old age of this grand old lady of resort hotels. But toward the middle of breakfast he was called out for a long-distance telephone call and left us more or less quiet under the force of Jarvis's flagrant, glaring detestation of Mel.

I was the one to break the silence, awkwardly and foolishly, by remarking that the other guests seemed to be watching us with attentive intensity and ears pricked to pick up our every word of wisdom.

This got Mel to shaking his head, and saying to me in a thick southern accent, "Oh, they diggin' us, gal. They jus' sittin' aroun' an' diggin' us."

We all stayed quiet except for Jarvis, who jumped up from his chair and stood behind me. I felt the hot moisture of his breath on my neck, and he sprayed me with spittle as he yelled:

"When Mr. Kelly come back, tell him . . . tell him I ain't hungry. Or, no, tell him I got sick all of a sudden and to please excuse me from breakfast."

Bob and Luke Smith introduced the training session for supervisors together. Bob spoke quietly yet forcefully of his dream that the people here can create a new world for themselves. He told how, through his theory called Normative Systems, "people like you learn to create their own cultures rather than just being the victims of the cultures they happen to have been born in." He talked with intensity, and while his words were probably only partially understood, it was apparent that some people caught his sense of excitement and belief.

Luke explained, in a quietly impassioned fashion, the principles of the Agricultural Labor Project—that it will be effective only if it fully involves the workers themselves in the solutions of their problems; that after years of empty promises it's going to be long-term accomplishments that will count; that there must be some immediate, visible results; that the emphasis would be on self-help, not welfare handouts; that in the long run the program must sustain itself economically; that the complexity of the problems we confront calls for a systematic, sustained approach.

There was something that came through about Luke at this meeting that didn't in his earlier one with just the aides and consultants, a slight hint of controlled aggressiveness. This is a man who knows his word's law, and if it would ever be challenged ...

Late Afternoon

We had finally got around to the pertinent subject of anti-black words and jokes that are an ingrained part of life between the white and black people in the groves, and the company has resolved won't, any longer, be countenanced.

Luke made the point:

"As managers and supervisors, it is your responsibility to make it very clear to all the people in your crews that words like nigger cannot any longer be spoken around here, that those words have got to come out of the vocabularies of anybody who wants to go on working for this company."

Most of the racists we'd already pegged as being compulsive, obsessed, the Jarvis Listons, were so affronted by all Luke said, they didn't trust themselves to dispute the subject. But Old Red, whom the aides, Johnnie Lou included, do respect and like as a person, said, though almost inaudibly, "Well, the way I look at it, sir, nigger, the word nigger, I mean, there isn't anything wrong with it under certain circumstances."

Luke said, "What would those be, sir?"

Old Red smiled patiently and said, "Well, the word nigger . . . Some people, when they use it, it may be an insulting word. I mean, they hate nig— colored people, and the colored people know it.

"But with me, not to blow smoke at myself, but ask any of my people if I am lying when I tell you that whenever they have got a problem, like getting in trouble with the law or their kids go a-foul, and they need my help and advice, well, black, colored, or what, it does not matter to me; they are always welcome to drop by at Mr. Red's house."

"Yes, I know what you mean when you say you keep an open door for your workers, and I think it's a very fine thing to do. But I can't see any connection," Luke said, musing, "between your open door and the word nigger perhaps being insulting when someone else uses it, but not when you do. Can you explain why you say this?"

"Because," Old Red stammered, "so long as my colored folks know my whole feeling about them is as good as it is, then, you know, how could they get insulted if I call one of the bad ones nigger? They call them niggers themselves. 'Come on over here to me, nigger.' 'Yes, sir, Mr. Red.' Well, that is just our way with one another, it is just a name."

Lots of sick northern jokes come to my mind as I listen to Old Red. But, really, now that I know him, a little, I can't make any more such jokes at the expense of people who, like him, are struggling so hard to see themselves and their customs of a lifetime through our alien eyes. I hope, in fact, I can take my cue from them and pitch and plunge into myself as they're doing in an attempt to see myself and my traditions with their eyes.

And as though to accentuate my thought, Lincoln Redfield, of all people, spoke up for Old Red, saying he didn't so much mind the term nigger on his lips because "I know . . . Because I know that, as far as colored people, as far as any people goes, he have got as big a heart as that chair sitting over there. It do not make any difference what their color, he hisself would not hesitate helping any person and really shows a lot of kindness."

Luke asked Johnnie Lou to speak to this point and she

shrugged, grinned, and said she didn't know what got into Lincoln, he sounds more like Emanuela than himself. "The fact be nigger's a dirty word and it don't matter who use it, man."

Luke said, smiling, "Well, Miss Johnnie's said it, gentlemen." He then advanced to the "anti-black or what I call anti-people jokes, nigger jokes, darky jokes, all of these. They, too, will stop as of now."

Bill Bennet, loyal, faithful, utterly devoted to the company, said, "Any order of this company, sir, I aim to do my level best to carry it out."

"I want you to know I appreciate that," Luke said.

Bill Bennet said, "But, see, sir, I am one thing and the white workers on my crews is something else again. Like how can *I* promise you *they* will stop telling jokes they . . ."

Luke said, "As I see it, now, I'm not saying you're in a position to promise anything for anyone but yourself; you're not and neither am I. But there are two steps you can—must—take as soon as this meeting's over and you're back with your men that are bound to make a difference, all the difference. First thing, you tell every man you supervise that 'Around here in this company, we don't tolerate any lowrating of people's dignity through so-called humor, or any other thing.' And, you say, 'Consider this a warning. The next time I hear you tell one of these stories, the very next time you tell a joke reflecting on anyone's dignity, you are fired.' "

Bill asked apprehensively: "And what happens? Suppose he was to tell the joke in spite of you warning him? What do you do about that?"

Luke answered simply, "Why, you do what you've told him you would. You fire him."

"I can understand doing that if it was one man, but you know . . ."

"If it's one man or ten or a whole supervisory force."

There was a burst of laughter to cover up a considerable amount of embarrassment.

After that, though, every one seriously discussed the matter. And some people realized then that Luke's tone as well as his words proved clearly that he meant what he said and didn't intend any argument or deviation.

And many, like Old Red, Mel, and even Jarvis, realized then (as they may not have done during his presentation of the matters of a new, decent wage scale and employee insurance and employee-owned housing and health and child development programs) that the concept of this project had nothing to do with charity but existed rather in the realm of ideological struggle and dignity.

It was something they'd never, in their wildest dreams, envisioned the company supporting. No wonder many, if not all of them, were badly shaken.

And Red, almost as much as an energy release as anything else, said to Luke, "What comes to me, Mr. Smith, is that what you are saying, if you excuse me, well, aren't those things you said what the union, the Farmworkers' Union, they call it, don't they, isn't what you said the same thing they do? I mean Cesar Chavez, if I have got his name right? And won't such a project make it easier for them to get our people in their union?"

Luke answered, naturally and spontaneously, that, yes, Red was doubtless right, the Farmworkers' Union is saying, as he did, that migrant workers are entitled to all the securities and advantages other workers are and have certainly not received till now. As for the Agricultural Labor Project, in its essence, making it simpler for many workers to accept the union, that, too, is a fact.

"But I know from Bob Allen here that Chavez is not the devil he's cracked up to be; he cares with all his heart about the people's welfare, which is not to say, if I'm to tell the truth, that I would be overjoyed to see us have a union in this situation, but I would be fooling you if I told you that we were gonna deny our workers here any rights that we give to any other workers in The Coca-Cola Company. If workers in a plant want to organize, they have the right to have an election and do exactly that, and we have the right to tell them why we don't think it is a good idea. I am committed to the idea that workers here will be no less than workers anywhere else in The Coca-Cola Company. And if that means we are going to have a union here someday, then I say that that's the way it's gonna be. If the workers decide they want a union, then they have a right to it, just like everybody else working for this company."

There was a hush of terrified silence in response to Luke's words signifying a rising panic and culture shock on the part of the managers and supervisors. And in the very midst of all of that, a prime stereotype of the virile black man haunting many if not most of them here today rose from his seat with all his inherent dignity (even Jarvis Liston admitted to me that his Tom and nigger jokes weren't applicable to proud Mel) and told Luke:

"When Bill Kelly asked me to take this job, and right up until today, I didn't know whether I would or could do it. Because as I said to him . . . I don't know whether Bill told you this or not but I told him, 'Well, okay, I'll go down and look over the situation, man, but that don't mean I'm staying, far from it. Because if what this company wants me to be is its resident nigger in Florida to be pulled out, shined off, and shown off every time trouble threatens—See how very much our company cares about poor black people, look at the position we gave ol' Mel Green—if all the company intended to use me for was to improve its own image and get media attention, well,' I said to Bill, 'that company just ain't got enough money to pay me for that.' "

Luke nodded.

Mel said, "Listening to you today, though, Luke, hearing you tell your top people in Florida that if they aren't ready to go with this new way, aren't ready to go with 'people power'—I know these are the top people you said that to, and if they were to quit, walk out now, man, I know you and this whole operation would be in pretty big trouble—I have to tell you I admire your guts and really believe you mean . . .

"See, I wasn't born yesterday. I dig there are damn good reasons behind what you and this company hope to accomplish, what I mean is, it isn't all being done out of the goodness of your hearts. And saying that, you know, well, it's my long-winded way of telling you that hearing you out as I've had the privilege of doing today . . . It is like a lot of people are, like, slick talkers, you know, and I can tell these a mile away because I happen to be one of them myself.

"But what you said came from your heart, and nobody can make me believe it was just another corporate executive making a speech.

"So what I want to say is that, being with you today, Luke . . . Well, you've just made up my mind about whether to take the job or not. I'm proud to be associated with a man like you in such a venture."

Luke shook Mel's hand without speaking, with the silence

between them one of those moments when two people tell each other more without words than could possibly be the case with them. And then he said, sinking many of the supervisors to even further depths, "Mel, your telling me this . . . It's one of the fine moments of my whole life."

I saw Jarvis Liston literally freeze in front of me as he stared from Mel to Luke and back again with that blank expression of people who see their accustomed world blown to pieces and can't fathom the reason why.

Chapter 8

Days Two and Three

The most important, valid, far-reaching elements of the supervisory training as I experienced it were the sharing sessions dealing with "what I know about myself you don't know, and that would help you understand me better if you did."

I had thought at first, and indeed until we were well into the sessions, they couldn't succeed except by some miracle. The supervisors' antagonism toward us from HRI, their view of us as strange, suspicious, dangerous to them . . . Why, I kept asking Bob, should they trot out their inner selves to the likes of us?

And yet . . .

Bob opened the first session. He was, he said, born and brought up in a small town in upper New York State, serene, languid, and with great natural beauty.

"I guess I would've loved my town if I hadn't been poor there. Well, being poor anyplace is a hard proposition, and maybe a small town's a better place to be poor than a big city. I don't know about that. I do know, though, how all the time I was coming up I was made to feel so different from the other kids."

His father was an invalid from the time Bob was very young, and though his mother had worked full time as a nurse, she'd still been unable to keep the family off relief.

"Well, the humiliation of knowing we couldn't keep ourselves . . . And it's strange to remember now there were people who rubbed our condition in—not just to my mother and father but also us kids.

"There was this teacher I had in third grade, Miss Johnson, I'll always remember her name. She'd say to me in the morning, oh, on many a morning, 'Bob I wish you'd go the barber's and have your hair cut once in a while. And I'd surely like to see you in a clean, white shirt like all the other little boys wear.' "

Johnnie Lou sat there, her hands jammed into her pockets, looking at him.

"A teacher doing y'all like that," she said quietly. "Her going to college and all didn't do her too much good, seem like. Well, didn't she know you would've wanted to wear a clean shirt and go to the barber if your folks was able to afford it?"

"Yeh, Johnnie," Bob said. "I think she knew, but, there was a streak of cruelty in her."

Jesús nodded.

He looked at Bob closely, shook his head, and said, "A streak of cruelty in teachers. Yeh. I certainly found that streak when my family and I first came to El Paso from Mexico. I must've been about the same age you were, Bob, when you met Miss Johnson, seven or eight. My teacher's name was Smith."

Jesús said he couldn't tell us about Miss Smith except by comparison to his mother and the other Mexican women out of his childhood. They—his mother and the others—were quiet, polite, meek, and self-effacing, while the teacher was tough, assertive, and, above all, unfriendly to Jesús and all the Spanish-surnamed kids.

"She told us we would be punished if we spoke . . . if we didn't speak English in the school, if she ever heard us speak Spanish even to one another. I remember her words, 'I feel sorry for what will happen to you children if I ever catch you speaking Spanish.' "

And it wasn't the teacher's threats alone that hurt and frightened Jesús, but also the hateful, hurtful words of the kids, mostly Mexican themselves, ironically, who spoke English, and took their cue from Miss Smith. "They'd laugh at me, and sometimes beat me up."

There were either teacher- or self-appointed monitors to assure that, even if Miss Smith wasn't around, the newly arrived Mexican children wouldn't speak Spanish.

Jesús glanced around the room and took a deep breath as though again living through the terrible day of his eighth year when one of the monitors, a third-generation Mexican child, led a group in chasing him out of the playground when he and another child whispered in Spanish during the so-called recreation period.

"Dirty Mex. Dirty Mex." All those big boys after him, so many running feet and such loud cries: "Dirty Mex. Dirty Mex."

Jesús told us how he ran for his life and "might just have escaped" if something hadn't struck him on his shoulder, and a foot hadn't reached out to trip him and force him down to the muddy ground. Then he felt fists pummeling his head and shoulders while boys' feet in heavy shoes kicked his ankles, feet, and thighs. He felt the dirt against his face and heard the words, "Let's feed mud to the dirty Mex." He struggled, retched, tried to spit out the mud but couldn't and so had to swallow it instead.

Later in the classroom his teacher asked what had happened to him. Goggle-eyed with fear, he tried to tell her about the boy who'd tripped him and the one who'd fed him mud.

"Was the teacher mad at those boys?" Old Red asked. "Did she punish them or something like that?"

"Oh, no, all she said was everything that happened was for my good, you know, and someday I'd be grateful to her and the boys.

"After that . . . There was a lot of respect for education in my family and I knew, after my time in Miss Smith's class, that though I would always want education more than—more than anything—I wouldn't want to stay in school anymore. So I learned everything I did with the help of a brilliant older kid who also lived in my barrio."

"Well, why didn't you speak English as Miss Smith, that teacher, wanted you to?" one of the supervisors asks.

Jesús said softly, "I would have been glad to speak English, if I'd only known how. But I didn't. We only spoke Spanish at home and in the barrio where my people lived."

Bill Bennet said, "Well, then, I don't just see anything wrong with her wanting you to talk English. She told you she was doing it for your own good."

"Get kids to beat up on you for your own good. Now you know yourself, Bill, that is a foolish thing to say," Old Red answered him.

Nevertheless, several supervisors did say it. And Bill Bennet said, "Man, think where Jesús would be today if the teacher hadn't *made* him speak American."

"Where would he be?" Old Red looked at Bill soberly. "Well, I'll tell you where he might be . . . not picking oranges in these groves, and that is for sure. Because Jesús has got *brains*, I am here to tell you. And had he have stayed in school like he would have wanted so much, weren't nothing to stop him from being a doctor, lawyer, a credit to his people.

"And that dolgone teacher, she stole his pride away. Making him ashamed and taking his pride in his own language away, in his own people and in his own race. Take that away . . ."

I looked at Bob across the room realizing we had a single thought at the moment. If only Old Red could make the connection between Jesús' experience and the nigger jokes that are told around here.

Well, someday, maybe.

Old Red was the first of the supervisors—he would be—to let down his barriers and open himself to us.

"Listening to Bob talk as he did, well, of course, it was a great surprise to me hearing Bob Allen grew up a poor boy. And, really, I am glad to know that because, well, it means that he can understand something about us who also came up poor.

"Well, I was a poor boy, too, Bob, even though not what you would call relief poor, from as far back as I remember. And just as Bob can sit here and tell us with no shame or embarrassment about his life as a poor kid, well, I can do the same without shame and tell you we were dirt poor, too, nigger poor." He turned to Luke in propitiation. "Saying 'nigger poor' I am sorry, sir. But it is just the way we used to say real poor in Alabama, which is where I come up."

Luke smiled wryly, and said, "Well, it's the way we used to say it in Mississippi, too, but that doesn't make it all right, you know."

Old Red said, "Now, I don't mean we kids ever went hungry, because the truth is we did not. But, you know, Bob, our neighbors in Alabama must surely have been very different from yours up north.

"Because far from making us feel bad like your neighbors did you because you were poor, ours'd try to make it up to the poor people, and especially the kids. Like people had their little gardens and were all of the time calling you in,

'Here, son, do me a favor and pick some of these beans. They are getting overripe, and I would appreciate your mama taking them off my hands, you know.' And my teachers'd bring special treats in for the poor kids: candy, a toy here and there, all of the things your parents would've like to give you but couldn't afford. And, see, they'd save your pride while they'd give it to you, too, by saying, 'Listen, Red, you did so well this month that you deserve a reward for it.' That is some of what I remember about being poor and my neighbors and teachers."

"Red," Bob said, "you're a lucky man to have childhood memories of such good neighbors."

"Well, I guess it is our southern way, if you don't mind my saying so, Bob."

"I don't mind, no," Bob said.

Old Red said, "Bob, Jesús, y'all having talked about what must've been the worst time in your life as kids, I am trying to think about the worst time in my life as a kid."

Once started on his childhood, Old Red couldn't seem to stop, and, listening to him, I hoped he never would. There was, in reality, a large streak of sensitivity and creativity in him as he recalled the animals on his father's farm.

Two horses called Lady and Turnip, brown, sleek, smooth, and "real pretty to look at, you know," in the green bows his little sister Mary took out of her own blonde hair to tie on their manes and forelocks. And three pigs, Red's "particular friends," he called Porkies One, Two, and Three.

"I raised those pigs from babies and never thought, you know, the day might come for slaughtering them. Then it came to be revival time, and Preacher was honoring our family by coming to stay with us."

He laughed with a trace of embarrassment and said, "One of my pigs was gon' to have to be slaughtered to provide Preacher's feast, and my daddy said for me to choose the one. I was too tenderhearted in those days, and couldn't stand for *any* of the three being slaughtered.

"So then my daddy said he would choose the pig for slaughtering if I would not—Porky Number One—and I was gon' to have to help out, I was gon' to have to take a part in killing my pig."

I had to say, "Poor Red."

"Yes," he said, "that was what my mama also said. 'Poor

li'l ol' Red.' And then she told me, 'Well, don't you worry, son, I will handle your daddy. The thing I promise you, sugar, is you ain't gon' be taking part in the slaughter no way.' "

I've met Ma Wilson, Red's mother, a couple of times and she is really quite a lady. A big fat woman of seventy-three or -four, with a full, soft face and musical, lilting voice, she indulges her great-grandbabies today as she must have done Old Red when he was their age with kisses, big hugs, and the southern lovely "sugar-tit" words: honey, sweetie, baby, love.

But, also, you know she's resolute, too, tough enough when her child's well-being is at stake to win the battle, if one must be fought, against Red's father or any other "one-hundred-and-eighty-degree man."

"My mama," Old Red said, "what she did, well, when the day came for the slaughtering and pa came to get me to go with him to kill my pet, my ma stood right up to my father, and said she hoped it would be acceptable to my father that I would stop at the house with her while the other kids go to the slaughtering with pa because, 'Well, we will admit,' she said, 'we will admit the whole thing of our son feeling bad about his pet being slaughtered. And, too, we will admit that the boy, at seven, is tenderhearted. But, as a loving father, can't you give him two years, a year, six months, before him having to become a man? He is only seven years old.'

"Well, my daddy got out his mulberry limb and ready to work on my fanny then, but mama got in front of him and said, 'You can work on his fanny only if you work on mine first.'

"So then I told him . . . I saw he and mama really be gon' to fight it out, and not wanting that to happen, I said, 'All right then, Daddy, I will go along.'

"Your daddy's mulberry or oak limb doesn't mean all that much, so long as you have got a mother who'll make it up to you after he's done with the tanning like mine always did."

I said, "Yeh, I guess Ma Wilson would make it up to you. I admire her a lot, Red."

Jarvis turned to me and said, "Yeh, a lady like her, don't it strike you funny hearing her called redneck?"

"It does," I said.

Then Jarvis turned to Mel. "Does it strike you funny, Mel?"

Mel said, "It strikes me sad rather than funny, Jarvis. I think I know how Old Red, or you yourself, for that matter, must feel when somebody calls his mama a redneck by just remembering how I myself feel when somebody calls my mama a nigger—not mad but sad." He lit a cigarette, inhaled the smoke dreamily, and threw away the match.

"See, any man anyplace gon' call me nigger he can expect to feel my fist in his face because I get bitter, and when I get bitter, man, I get mad. And when I get mad, I fight, you know, that has been my problem all my life. I'll fight easy."

The room's so quiet you can hear a pin drop, everyone watching Mel with all their attention.

"But you call my mother nigger, see, and sure I'll fight you the same as if you call me the name, but also before I fight you I'm going to be crying inside, and maybe won't even be able to hide my tears from you. Then if I know you've seen me crying, man, you gon' to pay for making me show you that little sign of weakness."

Bill Bennet and several other supervisors look at Mel suspiciously. Jarvis Liston is choking.

"What the hell do you mean when you say you gon' to make us pay? You mean you gon' make white men pay?"

"I'm talking about making all men, any men who would call my mother nigger pay for it, no matter what their color."

Old Red looked very thoughtful. "I think I know what Mel means. He says it's not white men only that'd call his mother or other nigra, excuse me, colored, black women, nigger. It can be other black folk that . . . look down their noses at their own people. And it hurts, it does hurt, coming from them."

He turns to Mel. "I know how it must hurt you and yours, Mel, because my people'll do their own the same way, too. Oh, and how bad it can hurt when those folks coming out of the same life you did, and having hit it a little better, making more money or going off to college . . . Well, I have many times heard them say about their own people that, you know, it is typical redneck behavior." He laughed. "So, Mel, I know what you and other colored are going through along that line."

You could almost feel Jarvis Liston and his special cohorts catching their breath at this exchange between the two men. Good God, Old Red Wilson must have lost his mind to be talking on such a level of equality with Mel and revealing himself—and them—to us consultants.

Bob looked directly at them, therefore, when he said, "I guess every father, every parent, wants his child to surpass him. And yet, we all know that if our children, because of all we've put into them, do go beyond us, they're going to look down at our world from where they're at in theirs."

"Yeh," Bill Bennet says.

"Now me myself," Bob says, "see my kids are still young. Judd's twelve and Peter's ten, and they're really kind, by which I mean they wouldn't knowingly hurt anyone's feelings. Yet, where Elaine and I are concerned, they let us know they think they'll be coming into a better world than ours when they're grown up. And they don't mind telling us everything that's wrong with us as well as our world. This is now at their age. I can just imagine then how it'll be when they're seventeen, nineteen, twenty-five.

"What I'm trying to say is I see a connection between our kids more or less looking down on us and our world and black people looking down on other blacks who haven't made it up the ladder as well. I see a connection between our kids and the ones Old Red's talking about as looking down at their people."

The session's really brought home now for those supervisors in the room who have sent their kids to college and seen them take on new values. Bill Bennet's son, Mark, for one, is and has been since entering the University of Miami three years ago one of its most outspoken activists: pacifist, marcher, protester, long-haired, shoulder to shoulder with the blacks. You name your cause, Mark Bennet's a part of it.

Well, if that is Mark's way . . . if he has chosen liberalism as his only guiding light and other activists as his only allies . . . "If that is his way, he's my son, I love him and can't stop because I hate his actions. I can't, nohow, see my own son as my enemy.

"But he, you know, sees me as his enemy, and it hurts so terribly bad. And he sees his mama the same way, too . . . her that, well, from the day that boy was born, he been her life, you might say her whole life. Don't he know we love him no matter what he does? And why can't he love us the same way, too?"

~§ Chapter 9

Feeling quite unexpectedly touched by Bill Bennet's open discussion about his son, I found myself suddenly possessed of this absurd fantasy (or was it so absurd?). I am going to cultivate and come to know intimately—of all people—Jarvis Liston and his family. Once I understand him as the most rabid, fanatical person at the session, feel him on the nitty-gritty level I believe I do Johnnie Lou or even Emanuela, say, I may achieve a new dimension, rapport, with all of the supervisors.

I sat in the hotel bar with Jarvis. I'd invited him to meet me there and asked if I could perhaps buy him a drink.

He stared at me with disbelief. "*You* want to buy *me* a drink?"

"Well, would you buy me one then?"

He asked me what I was drinking and ordered it.

I glanced at Jarvis.

"I guess you're wondering about why I asked you to meet me here?"

"Yes ma'am."

I decided to take the bull by the horns and explained to him that I hadn't had the opportunity to meet many southern whites on an intimate basis and he said he hadn't met many easterners either.

"Arnold and I would like to get together with you and your wife someday soon," I said. "Maybe you would join us for dinner one night when it's convenient."

"My wife likes to stick close to home."

How to get Jarvis to invite me to his house then? I said, "From my short experience, Jarvis, I may be wrong but it seems to me black people are more hospitable than whites around here."

Jarvis fixed his blue eyes on me and they didn't make me feel very popular. "Why do you say such a thing?"

I told him that while we've not been invited to any of the white supervisors' homes, Johnnie Lou, Emanuela, Lincoln, all of them have asked us to visit in their homes.

"And you gon' to eat with them?"

Before I could answer him he said, "Now, me, as a white man, after these days with the nigra aides and Mel Green, I have got to where I could shake hands with them. But as for eating, I don't know if you noticed or not, but I have not ate one single meal in this hotel because if I had've had to, the good Lord knows I never would've kept a bite down."

Something about talking with Jarvis this way brought to my mind a recollection out of my childhood I'd buried deep. I'd spent my early childhood in Wilmington, Delaware, where apartheid was as much the unwritten law as it's ever been here, and there was little, if any, crossing over. As a child, therefore, I'd called dark chicken "nigger meat," and always passed by legs and thighs in favor of breasts, telling my parents, "If you make me eat that nigger meat, I'll just throw it up."

Jarvis's face lit up when I told him. "So you got a idea of what I went through these days." Then, in a suddenly sharp, suspicious voice, "Say, how come you tell this to me but wouldn't tell it in the sharing session then?"

I said that, as I've told him, I'd completely forgotten. It was his experience here that had caused me to relive the one of my childhood.

He gave me one of those searching looks full of things that are better left unsaid and caused me to say:

"If I had've thought of it during the sharing session I would have said it."

"Well, if you had've, maybe I'd've said a couple of things then too, you know, Sara. Maybe I would've got up and tell Mr. Luke Smith when he got done with his speech about 'nigger is a word I want out of your vocabulary,' and some of them like Old Red kowtowing to him, just going along with anything he say . . .

"Well, Mr. Luke Smith, if he had've been outside later where me and the other men were talking about him, he would've heard some things he wouldn't've liked so much. Some of us were really angry men, believe me. And him that is supposed to be so smart and hisself a born and bred southerner. Then talks about vocabulary as though he does not even know that in me and some other supervisors' vocabulary there ain't now or ever will be, no matter what Mr. Smith will say or do, the two words Negro or black.

"So far as I and these other supervisors are concerned, there's only two words for people of that race. The good ones is colored folks and the snakes in the grass are niggers. And if you want to do it, you can just tell Mr. Luke Smith and see if he carry through. I know what he meant when he said, 'I certainly hope you gentlemen can go with this new way . . .' Oh, that man wears the velvet glove but we know what he means by 'I hope you can go with this new way.' It means that, well, if you cannot, then all the years you have put in with this company don't mean anything, and you are done, through, finished.

"So go on, tell him what I told you, and see if he gon' throw this white man out for the niggers' sake."

I said, "Please believe Luke Smith neither wants me to tell him of my discussion with you nor would I do it if he did."

Actually Jarvis is "so sick and just turrible hurt at all that has happened these last days" he doesn't care if I do tell Luke what he's said. He might, in fact, welcome my doing it. Because he's angry at himself for having remained silent in the face of the challenges everyone leveled at "me and my people. I am a hypocrite not to have stood up to them and said, 'What is this you are doing to us white men who have worked for you all our lives almost and given you all our loyalty?'

"What about us loyal white men that is hurting like you say the nigras is? Seem like Mr. Luke Smith don't want to hear nothing about that, seem like nobody want to hear it, you know."

I said, surprised myself at how deeply I meant it, "I want to hear it, Jarvis."

He smiled, very sweetly, and said maybe he's a sucker to fall into a trap I could be laying for him, but he's made up his mind, despite my connection with such nefarious people as Bob and Stan, to trust me until or unless I prove myself "crooked," too.

And then he said in a warm voice:

"You will make me and mama happy by coming to have dinner with us tomorrow night."

I can't help liking Jarvis's wife, Mary. Frizzy-haired and fat, she comes across as a gentle person with a rosy, loving outlook toward life and spontaneous sympathy toward everyone in her vicinity, definitely including me, over whom she clucks from the first moment of our meeting. How sad it is to be away from home and my very own kitchen. And how galled I must be by all those restaurant meals I've got to eat day after day and night after night. She's delighted, therefore, Jarvis had sense enough to invite me here for some home cooking. "Not that I am so good a cook, but anything home be better'n the best restaurant, wouldn't you say, honey, even this simple little dinner we are having tonight."

The simple little dinner turned out to be a very festive affair with such an overfulness of food that I could have thrown a party myself with all she forced me to bring back to the motel and Arnold. I had a great urge to tell her one didn't have to be Jewish to be a Jewish mother—she filled the bill in every way—but contained myself.

There were a good many other people there, too, three married sons with their wives and kids, two young unmarried daughters, Mary's sister and her husband, and Jarvis's brother and his wife.

The men and women eat separately here, the men first, and Mary offers me the opportunity to eat with them but I decline, primarily because I'm not sure Jarvis would find it tolerable. After dinner, though, all of us—men, women and children—gather in the living room where Jarvis is showing off a new gun, a little snub-nosed .38-caliber pistol, "A Smith and Wesson chief's special," as he tells us all with profound pride.

All the men have guns, I notice, and the children, the little boys including Jarvis's grandson, Billy, age six, have toy guns. Jarvis sits caressing his almost dreamily awhile, then asks, "You want to see my other guns, Sara, my whole collection?" He delegates Mary to show them to me, and she takes me on a tour of the house while she's at it.

It's quite an expensive house for these parts, with its television sets topped with American flags in all four bedrooms as well as the recreation room.

Finally we're in the "gun room," a separate room displaying Jarvis's twenty or more guns of all kinds, shapes, and sizes in two large wall cases. Gentle Mary explains the make of each one to me while handling it with . . . self-fulfillment's the only word I can think of, and watching her is one of the oddest experiences of this whole unusual evening.

"Ain't these guns just so beautiful, honey?"

Back in the living room I tell Jarvis both his house and gun collection are impressive, and he says,

"Seem like, you know, you are surprised at me having so good a house."

I'm not at all surprised, actually, because I know for a fact Jarvis is one of the prime moneylenders here and has got to have become wealthy, even very wealthy, over the years. But I say, "Well, I know the company can't be paying you all this much money and . . ."

He narrows his eyes a little, and wrinkles suddenly spread all over his face. Then he smiles a half smile and says, "Yeh, you right about that, the company sure don't break itself with paying us supervisors, yeh, and even so I am a rich man for this part of the country. And people all respect me for the way I done it, made my money the hard and thrifty way. Sara, I see you sitting here and know you want nothing more than to find out how I become sort of rich, but haven't got the nerve to ask, am I right about that?"

"Well, yes," I say.

"See, me being . . . For all you may think I hate niggers, but, see, colored peoples that know their place is something else. I do not hate them and am glad to do my little bit to help them. Well, so far back as before I become a supervisor and I was still a crew chief, well, you know how come I always have a full crew, never no trouble keeping a picker, well, I told them, they knew if they ever needed a little money ahead of time they can sure come to me. Like I was their father or something.

"Their father. My colored people. See, I made sure there weren't any niggers on my crew, only colored people, and your heart really can go out to some of them sometimes. I mean, they need you and count on you to help them with everything, they don't know anything about taking care of their money, and if I hadn't've been around to help them, well, we got no way of telling what would've happened to the poor souls then.

"And I told them what to do with the money. I said, 'Lay off of the drinking, and buy yourself something's gon' last you and your family a long time, good stuff. Well, you can't move out of the company shack and buy you a good house 'cause there ain't none in the colored quarters. But you can buy a good car, right? If you can't buy a good house, well, then, you buy you a pretty good car, let's pay for it. If you get behind in your payments, I'll help you a month or two so you can catch up again.' "

"Well, what did you get in return for your help to them?" I ask as though I didn't know.

He says, as though I'd never asked my question, "As I say, I certainly helped them, I did help them a lot. You can ask anybody if it is not true, that they could come back, and get a payment if they needed it. If he got behind on a payment, he knew where he could come to. And, see, my people appreciated it, and they sort of worshiped me, and always wanted to be on my crew, because, knowing my pocketbook was open to them. Well, I don't like to boast but am only saying what all of the colored people around would tell you if you asked them."

I decided—once more—to take the bull by the horns and say to correct me if I'm wrong but I've heard of pickers who'd borrowed small sums of money from Jarvis and were still in his debt for them ten, twelve, fifteen, years later: Wouldn't he himself say such an operation was . . . usurious?

His bright smile lights up the room as he looks me straight in the eye. It's obvious from his look that my implied and overt accusations of wrongdoing, of guilt, appear so insane to him he doesn't need to answer them except to say,

"Well, see, Sara, sure I get my little interest, but it ain't what you seem to be saying. Ask the colored people what they think and let them be the ones to tell you was I their savior or not.

"Well," he goes on, "one reason I was really wanting to help them to the best of my ability, well, me and Mary wasn't always rich, far from it. When her and me were first married, we wasn't nothing but migrants ourselves. Me and Mary both worked for a dollar and a half a day, each, that's fifteen cents an hour. We worked here, in this place, from the time we was kids, and let me tell you, you worked, too. You didn't go in the fields and sit down, drinking soda or eating sandwiches, something like that. We picked oranges, the seedlings were ten cents a box, a bud was six cents a box, grapefruit was two and a half cents a box, and tangerines were ten or twelve. You could pick from fifty, sixty, seventy, boxes a day if you hustled from early to late.

"If you hustled . . . I know one year Mary didn't have a good dress for church even. I hated seeing her walk in in that old everyday thing, and I figured to buy her a new dress the first week I made fifteen dollars in the fruit. But I only made seven on the grove until the fruit come in. The first week I made fifteen, we'd buy a dress. It took a long time to do it, too."

"Jarvis," I say, "why didn't you borrow the money off of a supervisor or foreman, and buy Mary's dress a lot earlier than you did?"

"No," he says, really without batting an eyelash, "no, me and Mary never has nor ever would buy anything we didn't have the cash for."

"Yet you encourage your pickers . . ."

He interrupts me to say, "Now, then, to go on with our life story, if you want to hear it. Well, my Mary worked just as good as what I did, and then come home and cook, clean the house, take all the care of the kids."

"No," Mary says, "but Jarvis was the one. He worked so good and faithful, the supervisor had got to know it, and made a foreman out of him long before the others had come even earlier than us.

"So we moved into a foreman's house right then. And see, at the time Coca-Cola didn't own these groves and feel everything ought to be done for the niggers and they're as good as white and ought to have as good houses. No, hon'. At the time these groves was Doctor Phillips' groves, and the idea was white people's houses, especial white foremen's, hadn't ought to be like niggers' shacks.

"So this is the way I tell you that me and Jarvis's house the company give us was a nice one. It had a nice kitchen, indoor bathroom, everything.

"And about the money, well so, now we have not got the rent to pay. And Jarvis started off at fifteen dollars a week straight time working as a foreman. And I gon' right on working on the crew for a dollar fifty a day. And we saved our money and we was so happy about everything; we thought we was rich after the long way we come up. Yeh, we thought we was rich then. I think, sometime, we was happier then than now. Because you were closer to your neighbor in those days. And everybody went to church, not just on Sunday as they do today. It was the inspiration to be with good people in God's holy presence.

"All the church people and also all of the ones belonging to our little klavern back then and still do up till today. All has got a whole lots more today than we ever thought we would have."

"Mary," Jarvis says in an angry tone, and she freezes, staring at him awhile.

Jarvis turns toward me and asks, "You know her meaning, Sara, when she talks about a klavern?"

I avoid his eyes and say, "It's a branch of the United Klans of America, isn't it?"

He watches me with an odd, almost mocking look in his eye, and says, "Well, what you think about the Klan, Sara?"

I try to hide my uneasiness but betray it anyway. "I don't know much about the recent Klan, Jarvis."

I don't, of course, tell him about the facts I do know that come to mind—the pictures I'd seen in the newsreels of 1964 of black women in St. Augustine who were beaten and had had their clothes torn off are some I'll always remember. And I won't ever forget, either, the sickening sight of Reverend Charles Conley Lynch roaring out, "I favor violence to preserve the white race," and making reference to "Martin Lucifer Coon."

Jarvis says in a tone defying me to deny the fact, "I guess whatever I tell you gon' be told to Mr. Luke Smith or Keough or Mr. Bill Kelly, the nigger-loving officers of this company."

"I promise you no, Jarvis."

"All right then, I'll tell you." A flicker of a smile, but enough, more than enough for me to catch an expression of the most intense pride. "Well, sure I tell you and tell you glad, yes ma'am, me and Mary both is members of the Klan and were since we were babies, as were all our folks before us. And the whole thing making us feel bad is that we can't just stand up, you know, and be counted like other folks belonging to the Lions or Shriners; proud as we are, we just got to sit back and deny we are what we are, telling lies in the sight of God and man."

His voice is high-pitched, not like his voice at all.

"Well, take all of the sessions we just finished, the sharing, everyone telling all of these so-called deep and proud things about themselves. And me, I ain't allowed to even mention the most important thing in my whole life.

"See, everybody talking about when they were kids, well, you know what I remember best about when I was a kid? Well, in those days there wasn't a law like there is today about you can't wear the robe of the Klan. And my daddy, the way he wore his robe, just watching him put it on was a grand feeling. I never, in all of my life, did feel so close to God as watching my daddy put on his robe, and then going hand in hand with him to a Klan rally."

Mary adds, "About Jarvis's daddy's robe, I remember my daddy's robe, too, and thinking when I seen him put it on that, you know, it's white, as pure as Jesus Christ Hisself."

I ask hesitantly, "If the robe represents Christ's purity, then what is the meaning of the burning crosses?"

Mary looks at me, smiles her quiet, warm smile and says, "Oh, Sara, if you knew us better you would know for yourself that the cross burning ain't only to make people stand in fear."

The smile turns into laughter. "The cross is what Christ died on, right, honey? Now why should it make people stand in fear, then?"

"The ones that do stand in fear," Jarvis intones, "they are the ones ought to stand in fear of Christ, too. I mean they got good reason for standing in fear. And I'm not just talking about niggers now either."

"Well, who are you talking about?"

"White sinners like drunks and harlots, we has got our ways of taking care of them, too."

"Tell her what you done about Billy Reid," Mary says. "He was the worst kind of a drunk, and although working on a job, never took care of his wife nor babies. I mean, there was never enough to eat in that house."

"Yeah," Jarvis nods his head.

"So what Jarvis and the others done is that they got a-holt of Billy and . . . well, you tell her Jarv."

A silence—Mary's contributing to its effect by almost suspending her regular breathing—and then Jarvis looks at me as sternly as he must have done at Billy and says, "We just told him that, you know, unless he started into doing right by his wife and kids . . . that the kids didn't ask to be brung into the world, they were here because he wanted them. And we said, 'Well, we will give you one week to straighten up and do right.' "

"Oh, Sara," Mary says, "and then, after all that they told him, he wouldn't listen but gon' right on with the drinking and neglecting of his family."

"Well, what'd you do then, Jarvis?"

"Beat him up some," he answers succinctly. "Knocked him around till he knew we meant business." He shakes his head, laughs. "Well, so far, the last week, the fellow been doing all right. See, he knows our eyes are on him.

"And Billy's not the only one, no. Right here in this li'l town there's some mean, dirty white men don't think nothing of cheating on their wives, cheating."

And Jarvis, meek apostle of Christ, had, according to Mary, also "taken care of them. The knights has always done what the Klan motto says to do: 'Fight for the Right, Die If We Must, But Always Remember in God We Trust.' "

" 'Be a Man, Join the Klan,' " Jarvis adds with no trace of irony. "See, if you are a man, then you got to look out for the women and children, take care of the snakes in the grass would do them harm. And that is all that we do, all that I have done, and ain't deserving of no credit for it the way that I see it. If you want to have a right to call yourself a soldier of Christ."

So Jarvis, as a Klansman, is not only a racist and nativist but also, importantly, a hard type of Victorian moralist, the hardest you can get. And it is this that Mary, for one, most admires in him.

"And like Jarvis tell you, what makes me feel so bad is because it is really sad the way things are set up at Coca-Cola, say. Jarvis, the way he hisself told you before, with all of the good he is doing in his klavern, well, he can't let them know who he is. Klaliff of his klavern."

"Klaliff is number-two man," Jarvis tells me.

"And now you keep your fingers crossed for us, honey, because Jarvis is running for Exalted Cyclops," Mary says gazing worshipfully into the eyes of her husband. "Exalted Cyclops."

"That is number one," Jarvis explains to me.

"You must have worked for that . . ." I bite my lip and get the word out: "honor. You must have worked for that honor a long time, Jarvis."

"All of my life, ma'am. And that is why it hurt so much to know that if I was to say to them Coca-Cola 'rich men' that I will be elected Exalted Cyclops of my klavern—Exalted Cyclops—they would see me like I am a nothing or worse.

"Well, to me that Mr. Luke Smith and Mr. Don Keough, yeh, and Mr. Kelly too, is every bit as bad as Bobby Kennedy, say, every bit as bad."

I try to keep a straight face at this really sincere cry from Jarvis's heart, and succeed.

He backs up his comparison by telling me:

"See, Bobby Kennedy talks all about the niggers' civil rights, and so do Mr. Smith, Keough and Kelly. Him and them talk the same way about the nigger and his civil rights, that he got, you know, to have all the rights the rest of us do. And the thing is that neither Bobby Kennedy nor Smith, Keough, and Kelly has it in their minds what will happen when you give him his civil rights so called."

He grows silent and stays that way, beating the tip of his foot against the floor.

"What happens, Jarvis?" I finally ask.

He almost barks:

"What happens is he ends up in the white man's bed. You know what I am saying?"

I stay silent awhile.

"Listen," Jarvis says, "a young nigger name Larry Snooker, Johnnie Lou's nephew . . . Does the name mean something to you, Sara?"

I say yes.

"Well, the little gal he run off with, Karen, was a friend of my girl, Jeanie."

Jeanie, seventeen, Jarvis's youngest, is sitting here in the room with us. She's tall and slender with blue eyes and exquisite features, under close-cropped blonde hair. She's just finished playing the piano and singing for us in her high, sweet voice: patriotic songs, church songs, and a sad love song or two. She'd looked at Jarvis much of the time and he'd hardly taken his eyes off her, so anyone could tell he was putty in her hands.

Now he's got his eyes pinned on her again although he's addressing his conversation to me. "To tell you some more about Karen. See, she was always a good, nice little gal come up with my Jeanie from her totting time on, almost. Well, I would've thought I knew Karen like my child, and would have laid bets, would've give you odds she never could become a whore."

There is a silence, a statement he won't make, though it's all right there on the tip of his tongue behind the stern, sullen expression. It's obvious the silence is about Jeanie, whom he can visualize in Karen's place.

"See, you got to know I love my daughter," he says finally, "my baby. But, listen, I find her with a nigger like Karen's daddy done, I'll take this here gun out of my pocket and I'll blow her brains out. You better believe it, too, you know."

In spite of everything, I hadn't suspected that such belligerence, such savage hostility without a saving grace of doubt, soul-searching, self-questioning, was possible even to Jarvis. It seems now he really would, as he tells me, feel justified, his conscience would be clear. "If I was ever drove, you know . . . Well, I talk to Karen's daddy, sometime, and, you don't like to call a good man a coward. But see, I set on his front porch after the girl run off with her nigger, after they had left, and I said, 'Well, man, how could you let that baby go to live among niggers?' And he asked me the quesiton, 'Well, Jarvis, what would you do, being in my place?' And this is just my reply:

" 'What I would do is to blow her brains out. Now I am telling you.' "

Jarvis's face is tight with excitement and I know he's got a lot more to say on the subject when he's interrupted suddenly by a cowbell ringing.

He jumps quickly out of his chair and goes upstairs, saying, to me, "This is my daddy calling. He is a pretty bad invalid. You can come on up and meet him if you want."

Jarvis's daddy is in his eighties, a terribly thin man. Dressed in gay pink pajamas, which seem to mock the ghostly pallor of his face, he stares long and thoughtfully at me when Jarvis introduces us.

Jarvis sits on his father's bed while the old man watches

him lovingly, and holds his hand a minute. I can tell there's a lot between these two, mutual respect, peace, communion, a sharing I haven't often been privileged to see between old parents and their grown children.

"Well, what you think of my best son, ma'am? Ain't he a *man*?" Then, while I'm still gathering my thoughts for a proper answer, Jarvis's father says, "To tell you something about old Jarvis you may not know, and his wife, well, as you see me now is what I have been for nine years, helpless and can't get out of bed. You have to pick me up and carry me to the bathroom or let me use a bed pan, something like that."

He watches me for a while, then says thoughtfully, "The way I see it, a lots of old people like me, some of them pretty well known to me and Jarvis both, you know what happened to them when they get to be like me?"

"What, sir?"

"Their sons take them and put them away, throw them away like garbage. America have changed to where sons and daughters would take their parents like me that was average, that was good, that was a Christian man, and put him in a dolgone nursing home with strangers, with nobody around to give a real care about him."

I'm dying inside as I listen to him. Because my mother will be ready for a nursing home any day now, and although I'm in conflict over it, I know full well that, in the way of my rational world, I'll help place her there when the time comes.

Jarvis's father says, "Who know about even a good, dutiful son like mine in this new, bad America. Maybe him and Mary gon' get tired of doing for me sometime and put me out to pasture. Put me, too, amongst the living-dead old men in a dolgone nursing home."

Jarvis blinks at him:

"Now, daddy, you can't mean . . . Would you think for one li'l moment me and Mary . . . ?"

"Well, son, I dunno." Jarvis's father's smile seems teasing, and his voice bantering, but I'm not certain they are, really. Obviously Jarvis isn't certain either, and I see he's badly shaken.

"Daddy, don't you know . . . ? The day anybody put you in a nursing home, well, I have to be in my grave then."

Jarvis's father remains silent for quite a while, watching his son almost dreamily. "I sure do know it, son."

He closes his eyes and we all tiptoe out.

Here now's another facet of Jarvis Liston I never would have suspected. When he told me what he'd do if he found his daughter, with a black man . . . The hate, anger, and resentment that welled up in me toward him at the time is no more intense, when I come down to it, than what he's feeling toward people "in this country that is supposed to be a good Christian country who would treat their old parents like pieces of garbage, and send them to a nursing home or other turrible place.

"Well, me, as a Klansman, see, if I was ever to think on putting my daddy away, well, the knights would be after me teaching me a lesson about being a good Christian man the same as me and the others done Billy." He nods and asks, "So what do you think of me as a Klansman now?"

I tell him the truth of what I think, tell him I'll never hear any of his messages straight unless and until they are stripped of their racist pathology, which we both know will never happen. As for Jarvis himself, as a person I say that I find him one of the gentle people of prejudice and would only hope he'd want, someday, as I think Old Red's already doing, to rethink his biases and analyze them with an open mind.

"The kind of a man you seem to me to be underneath, I think you could do a fine job with the Agricultural Labor Project if you'd try to open your heart to what it's about."

He interrupts me to say, "See, Sara, I am lucky in that God have blessed me with a good new job . . . so I don't have to go along with all of this about the niggers' civil rights, and nobody giving a little hoot about the white man's civil rights that I myself would die to protect.

"See, I ain't told you yet, but right before you come here tonight, I resigned my job, gave it up after all of these years."

And there's that look on his face of decisive defeat that causes me, by light of what I've come to know about him, to feel not only sorry for him but also somewhat warmly toward him. Which is not to say I can ever embrace him as a spiritual brother or a real friend. But, then, neither can I regard him as I once did, as a total, ruthless conqueror. The truth is that, at this time and in this place, the people are the conquerors, and Jarvis, really one of the "gentle people of prejudice" when you come to know more about him, is the defeated one.

Chapter 10

It's time, past time, perhaps, to solidify all of the workers and their families behind the project . . . to bring them the message the aides have, each in his individual way, begun to absorb. It's time, if our program is, in reality, to follow through on its promise of people power, to organize a broad-based community development corporation with elected officers and a board of trustees whose task it will be to devise and implement the people's programs.

This meeting is our last before the aides begin to visit all of the agricultural workers, either at home or in the groves, to discuss the purposes of the project and ask them to nominate a board of eighteen people including a chairman, vice-chairman, secretary, and treasurer. Any person whose name is suggested is to be considered for elections to be held at a company-wide barbecue on a Saturday not too far distant.

The aides are equipped by now to discuss with the workers the responsibilities of the officers and board members as we've mutually conceived them: liaison people between company, consultants, and the community; administrators of all the programs: child development, health care and family services, scholarships, tutoring, adult education, cultural enrichment, with duties including budgeting, hiring and firing of staff, and the setting of standards for services.

Certain other programs such as wages and benefits, minimum employment age, children in the groves, and lending practices are company-managed activities except that any aspects of them are legitimate subjects for board discussion and recommendation.

"The community development corporation board," Bob says, "would pinpoint to the company the services that people really want to make their first priorities—think are most important—instead of those we consultants, outsiders, might come up with."

Of course, Emanuela has at this point to say that "Aw now, Mr. Bob, I hear you saying that all of the time and I be wanting to tell you before . . . it is crazy to think that we people know anything better'n you."

Johnnie Lou puts her hand to her head, and says, "Oh, you dumb Ella. Remember you telling Emanuel Elias how he taken your dignity away and Mr. Smith and Mr. Keough, them, given it back to you make you feel like you's just as good as anybody else?"

Here she pauses and eyeballs Emanuela. "Well, Miss Ella, where that feeling have gone to by now? Don't you believe the company and consultants?"

Emanuela, never really certain in her mind she's not incurring our disfavor in some way or other (when will she realize she doesn't need to be so afraid of us?), looks at each of us in turn and says, "See, I don't mean, like Johnnie says, us peoples ain't just as good. Well, sure we's just as good the way y'all make us know, it's just that we don't think as good."

"You mean our brains be so much worse than the white folks?" Johnnie Lou asks . . . jokingly, we think.

Solemnly Emanuela admits—again—that, yes, black people's brains *aren't* as good as whites, can't possibly be as good.

There is a moment of hesitation as all of us consultants exchange a look. How discouraging that we aren't further on with Emanuela after all these months she and we have spent together. Stan tells her in a patient tone, "See, Ella, what you're saying about your people not having the brain power the rest of us do just isn't true. These people called psychologists, whose whole job has been to study the subject, know that there are smart and dumb people among . . . Well, I am a Jew, right, so take Jews like me. I know some very smart Jews and then I know some who aren't so smart, and some who are plain dumb. And Don Keough, who's a Catholic, will tell you the same about his people. He's a damn smart fella, but there are plenty among his people who are not. And Bill Kelly and Luke Smith'll tell you the same thing about their people."

So far this whole conversation's predictable. We've had it

a hundred, a thousand times in one form or another since we've come to know the aides. Now, though, Johnnie Lou, of all people, says, "Well, we *ain't* got the brains other people has, and no sense saying we do."

A stunned silence, an overwhelming sense of shock grips everyone, especially Bob and me. We had reason to feel we had probed Johnnie deeply enough to uncover her innermost feelings, and would never have suspected her to be capable of such an expression of we-are-niggers inferiority. We would have to ask ourselves for many months after Johnnie's explosion how we could have missed. How could we have been so shallow in our judgments as to accept her at her own buoyant face value? How could we have failed to realize any person in Johnnie Lou's position who has had it told to her over centuries, "You are subhuman, less than human" . . . ?

Stan, Arnold, Bob, and I have today to blame ourselves for the naïveté enabling us to believe completely in Johnnie Lou's effective act of total psychological equality with whites, and are going to have to penetrate the act, get beneath it if we hope to be of more real help to her than we've evidently been so far.

I personally am not ready yet to try to search deeper into Johnnie. I'd rather comfort her in case, as I suspect, she's upset at having revealed herself to us this way. And so . . . "Johnnie, Johnnie," I say, "you're so wrong about your people being naturally unintelligent; all you need to do to realize it is take a long, hard look at yourself. I don't know many people, regardless of their color, who are what I'd call naturally brainier than you. I say naturally because I'm not talking about the advantages some people have had that may make them seem smarter than others. Sure, they know more facts, speak better English . . .

"Well, take me, for one, and compare me to yourself. I've been to college and have a lot of facts at my fingertips you don't. But"—and I mean it with everything in me when I say—"if push comes to shove, Johnnie, your brain is as good as, if not a hell of a lot better than, mine. You really catch on faster to many things than I do."

Johnnie must have accepted my remark in reality because she said sincerely, "Well, one thing I do know and that is things gon' be different for our young people. If this program gon' work, and, man, it gon' work because the people gon' make it work, our kids are gon' to know everything y'all do because they gon' go to high school and college exactly like you done.

"Now, we know we gon' get the money for sending them, sure, but the other thing be, even with the money they ain't ready to go. They can't never keep up with the other kids there no more'n I can with you, Sara, and Stan, and Bob or Arnold.

"So I am gon' say to the people that we got to get us teachers to get them ready right now. This funding, this budgeting, what that means is, if we want to use our money for paying teachers to get our kids ready for college, it's what we will do."

Jesús asks, "When you talk about 'we,' 'us,' using 'our money,' who you mean by that, Johnnie? Us, the community aides?"

"Not us the community aides," Johnnie says. "Us the people."

"I wish I could go to school myself," Emanuela says suddenly in a tone so low she's surprised when we hear her.

"Nothing to stop you doing it, then," Stan says.

"Well, me," Emanuela says, "I never gon' to school at all, so how could I begin now?"

"What would be a better time than now?" Stan asks.

Emanuela studies Stan awhile, then smiles. "Oh, maybe some other peoples could, Stan, but not me. I be too dumb for all the other people in a school."

Jesús says, "You know what we said at all of our other meetings, Ella. Remember Stan telling us lots of the people'll be like you say you are, ashamed to sit in a class among other people who might laugh at us for not knowing as much as they do."

"I remember, Jesús."

"And remember what we all came up with to do for getting around it?"

Ella says, "Yeh, get a teacher or someone will come right to our own home, learn us there so nobody else know how little school we has had."

"And you yourself said, Ella, you wouldn't mind going to school if that would be the way. Remember?"

"Yeh."

"Well, see," Jesús says, "we can't forget this when we tell

the people about grown-ups also going to school. If we don't tell them that 'your education, you know, gon' be just between you and the teacher,' it may be we'll lose them before anything ever begins."

It's extraordinary to sit here and listen to the aides communicating on this level.

"Now," Jesús says, "let's get to the child development program . . . child development, not child care, as Stan has been putting it to us."

Jesús explains in an understandable yet practically professional manner the difference between child care and child development. He says that in a child care center, children are adequately cared for, kept clean, fed good wholesome food, taught, in a sense, to socialize with one another.

A child development center, however, goes many steps further. Children there learn the alphabet and numbers. They draw, paint, hear stories, engage in psychodrama. By the time they enter kindergarten, or first grade, they can "hold their heads up high," hold their own with the privileged white kids in whose classes they will be because they will have had equal, if not superior, preschool training.

More than that, the child development center, as is every other program of the ALPI, is conceived also as a training ground for new careers for adults. The only person employed from outside the groves will be the director, a person skilled in training others. Everyone else, from the assistant director down, will be drawn from among the people themselves and prepared by both the director and outside schools to carry out their jobs. Before they're done working in our child development center, they'll be capable of working in other centers, no matter how high these centers set their qualifications.

Now Emanuela talks about the contemplated health program, tells it to us exactly as she will to the people to whom she'll be called upon to interpret it.

"Well, I gon' say, 'Dear peoples, first thing in our health program gon' be we will have us a clinic with doctors and nurses and all ain't gon' mind takin' care of us colored and Mexican neither. They ain't gon' mind us no more than if we white folks."

"Oh, Ella," Johnnie Lou says with disgust, "you better not talk about them doctors and nurses we gon' get not minding taking care of us, because that means you still don't understand what we been hearing all these months about the health center will be *our* center, you know. We are the ones gon' help with hiring them doctors, we got to like them, too, you know, not just them liking us.

"And if we don't like them—and we sure ain't goin' to if they got something against us account of our color—then we don't need them here and can tell them so. We can get rid of them and find some will suit us."

Stan adds, "Ella, you forgot to say our clinic will also be staffed by two dentists—hopefully—and their aides."

"Stan," Ella asks, "you really think we gon' be able to find a dentist that he is willing to take care of a colored person's mouth?" Emanuela asks her question with good reason. The truth is that no one of the aides or the majority of other agricultural workers here has ever been in a dentist's office. Bad teeth are often so rotten and loose that they can be pulled out with a string. Those that can't are prayed over by Saints or "touched" by healers.

All the same, Johnnie says to Ella's question, "Listen, our dentists we gon' get for our clinic, they better not have no worry about treating colored or Mexican; they better not if they want to hold on to their jobs and not have us to tell them, 'Man, Mr. Dentist, we has had enough of you, so 'bye, y'all.' "

" 'Bye, y'all,' " Emanuela echoes because she savors the sound of the words, " 'Bye, y'all.' "

Now that we have our dentists put in their places, the conversation turns to the important business of new housing. The aides say, and effectively, they will help the people know that the company intends to dispose of the terrible shacks in which it has been putting up the migrants. They will interpret to the people how living in a company shack—house, whatever—makes "slaves" rather than employees out of the pickers. The company is in a position to control them by putting them out of their homes if they displease it in any way. It couldn't do that with any other workers.

Besides, if agricultural workers' wages are brought into line with those of other company employees, they will not be in need of free shacks like the miserable ones they're occupying now. They will not need handouts to shame them and make them feel less than human.

For these reasons, primarily, the company will make available land it owns on beautiful Lake Clinch for the development of a community of one-family homes. The aides know the company is working with FHA, the Farmers Home Administration, to get government subsidy enabling people to purchase new two- and three-bedroom homes for a down payment of two hundred dollars, which they'll be able to borrow from the credit union, and costing them for mortgage payment, including taxes, fifty-five to ninety dollars a month: a sum they'll have no trouble meeting under the circumstances of the improved earnings for those who will work steadily and therefore want to buy their homes.

"See," Johnnie Lou says, "I know people who ain't living in the company houses, but other shacks that's just as bad or even worse, and, man, they be already paying the same or more money, and them houses don't even belong to them like ours gon' do us. They paying it out to a landlord for rent, and not for something gon' be their own."

The aides talk next about the kinds of houses people may elect to have. There's going to be a housing committee working every step of the way, from inception to completion, with the architects.

Now, though, comes the tough part of the situation: how to arrive at a fair and able board of trustees despite the passionate lines of demarcation in our community. Emanuela, with all her kindliness and honesty, wouldn't see a sinner solicited if her life depended on it. We all try talking to her about the fact this board belongs to all the people, and she assumes a look of deep regard, even of respect, but that's for us personally, not what we're trying to impress on her. "Them sinners gon' kill the board afore it even starts if we ever let them get on it."

And Lincoln backs Emanuela in her quiet certitude and faith, but with an extra dimension. It turns out he himself as a prime Saint, wants to be the board president. He and Emanuela have decided to go out and campaign for his election, as he informs us in no uncertain terms.

"Oh, Lincoln," Bob says, "not only couldn't you be president, man, you couldn't even be on the board as long as you're an aide." He explains to him the natural conflict of interest between board members, who will be the project's administrators, and the aides as its employees.

Bob says, "Say you are our aide and, at the same time,

president of the board or on the board; you're not an officer but a board member who can vote on matters concerning the aides, who are your employees. Now you, as an aide, are being paid at the rate of three dollars an hour, and you think that's unfair. You want four dollars an hour. Now, remember, this is not the company paying your salary, it's the board. So you go to the board, your true bosses, and say, 'Well, I think I deserve more money.' The board has to vote on whether or not to grant your request. You, as a voting member of the board, do you think it's fair that you should be in a position to vote on this question concerning yourself?"

Lincoln flares up. "Well, why in the hell not?"

All of Stan's, Bob's, and the other consultants' rational explanations about why not fall on deaf ears. Once again now we're being brought face to face with the culture gap between us. How could these people, who have never had the opportunity to look out for their own interests let alone be administrators for multileveled groups, be expected to grasp the finer shades of conflict of interest?

Lincoln stares at Bob for a while, then smiles. Bob was to tell me later: "No, you can't say Lincoln was staring at me. He was aiming between the eyes."

Lincoln says, "If I was to be white, Bob, would y'all say then I could be fair?"

"Man, I think you know damn well I'd say the same thing to any white man I'm saying to you."

Lincoln, knowing Bob as he does, must admit the truth and agrees, finally, he'll relinquish the president's job. But he does fire off a rather angry, self-righteous barrage at the fact he'll resign if a sinner becomes president. Emanuela has to tell us, gently as usual, her religious principles will force her to do the same.

It's Johnnie Lou, in a fit of passion, who persuades them how wrong they are. Yeh, she's a tough broad, and everyone knows she hasn't set foot in a church since she was dragged there as a baby. Yet she'd be the first one to nominate Albert Ocea, a stern Saint if there ever was one, for president or any other available office. First of all, he is a strong man, a leader. Johnnie herself had gone to him during a time of personal tragedy there was no particular need to discuss here and now. The man had a heart. And although he'd had more schooling than anyone else around, he wasn't cocky about it.

When Jesús smiled broadly at Johnnie's analysis, thoroughly agreeing with her, the others couldn't openly disagree. If these sinners would accept Saints . . . Nothing here to fit a mood of rebellion, of protest, of brandished fists. And everyone had to agree, in theory anyway, that Bob's insistence the board's and officers' choices are the peoples, not the aides, has, at least in theory, to be accepted.

I went out on occasion with the aides in their solicitations, and was in a further position to observe the tremendous differences among them.

Gentle Emanuela, for instance, has no scruples about saying to her people, all Saints out of Reverend Seaford's church, "See, we got to get our people on this here board, Rev. Seaford's people." With her special skill of a conjurer where other Saints are concerned, she brings before their eyes this potential board meeting of holy mothers all dressed in white and godly outsiders including us consultants as well as Messrs. Kelly, Keough, and Smith, converted to saintliness by now and resolving all the people's problems as they never could themselves in this aura of biblical light and immortality.

"If our board could be made up of all Saints," she says, despite her promise at our last meeting, "that mean our Rev Seaford gon' be the man behind the board even although he do not work for this company. Then we can be sure it be blessed and everything gon' be okay with it."

When I tell her, as I do, she's manipulative, her feelings are hurt, badly hurt. I can't really make her know what I'm talking about, but she promises she'll never do the "evil thing" again, never.

Well . . .

And Lincoln . . . I was out with him once, too, and heard him make such statements to other church elders as this one:

"You pretty li'l daughter, Misty, you don't want her having to go work in the groves like you and your wife, does you?"

"Man, I do anything first."

"Well, I tell you what you do, then. Put my wife Leola's name where it say secretary and yours beside it. That mean our Leola got a chance to be secretary of the board. And you know, the board have got all of these jobs to give away, like aides in the child development center. Oh, man, how you like Misty dressed up in a real nice uniform 'stead of the dungarees for the grove? And working like a lady with the kids to learn them this and that. And going to school herself, maybe become a teacher."

"Oh, man, that be so great," the father says.

"Well, you know the easy way to get it for her, right?"

"Yeh, just put Leola's name down for secretary, and mine down here in this row, right?"

"Right."

"Right, excepting for only one thing wrong, though. See, I sure can't write her name, Linc, can't write Leola's name."

"Here, man," Lincoln says graciously. "I'll write it for you."

"But," the man says, "I can't write my own name neither."

He puts his cross on the nomination sheet, and Lincoln writes both his and Leola's names beside the cross.

"You think this will be good," the man asks, "coming from somebody like me that can't even write?"

"I think it is fine," Lincoln says.

Later, alone with me, Lincoln's somewhat embarrassed. My presence must, after all, remind him of the promise he made Bob and all of us at the last meeting. He says, "Listen, that I done with Misty's daddy weren't so saintly a thing to do, were it, Sara?"

"No," I say, and add, "There's something else wrong, too, about pushing Leola, as I see it. You know how many times all of us have said people have to have certain qualifications for jobs. Leola can't read and write; how's she going to write the minutes, Linc?"

"Oh, well, y'all consultants says everything we got to learn, we gon' learn once the board gets going."

"But, Lincoln," I say, "don't you think it would be better to begin with someone who already can read and write. Then, while Leola's learning..."

"No, I think Leola gon' be fine."

"But, Lincoln, listen..."

"Leola goin' be all right, Sara. Lord, she's gon' be all right because if y'all consultants can't help her to learn quick enough what she got to know, well, there be a better way. Rev Seaford from our church gon' lay hands on her and talk to God, say to please *make* her a good secretary."

I surely can't top that one and don't even try.

Johnnie Lou, though, is a dream to be out with. She goes for her signatures into both the groves and neighborhood bars. She always shows herself true to her generous nature; she's eager to trust people and to prove it to them by giving them tokens of her trust. She refuses to manipulate them into nominating a slate of officers she might herself prefer, but instead outlines the situation to them and insists they make their own board choices.

Jesús operates much the way Johnnie does, altogether unmanipulatively and fairly.

The day of the barbecue dawns cool and fair. And about two hundred and fifty men, women, children, sinners, Saints, and other churchmen, all in their Sunday best, arrive exactly on time. Many supervisors come, too. Some are so hostile we wonder why they came in the first place, while the majority are very polite in a cold, absentminded way. There are a few, however, like Old Red, who are really relishing the situation.

Bill Kelly, impressive, candid, discusses, to a long series of "amens" and "God bless you's," the whole Agricultural Labor Program. He's in the fortunate position of offering samples and examples of the fact the programs are going to begin right now and not at a distant promised time. As Bob has so often reminded us, it's the immediate results that any project needs. They give hope, they help people believe change is possible—and that belief is the real crux . . . These people have been given so many promises in their lives by all the people they worked for . . . next week, next month, next year, "next century," as Jesús once told me.

Further, the company's already begun operating a child care center, preparatory to the planned-out child development center. It's housed in a converted wooden structure and is, as nobody would deny, makeshift. It couldn't have been put together any other way in as short a period because, first, the need was intense and, second, because it was the best, perhaps the only way, to convince the people a true child development center would really happen as soon as it would be possible.

Also, it's already hired a public health nurse, Kaye Clarke, who, before the clinic can become a reality, is making up a staff and soliciting doctors to screen and get treatment for every worker and his family.

And bought new buses that won't break down, as the old ones used to do, and equipped with toilet facilities—to the amusement of some of the supervisors.

Also it's put into effect every promise for temporary relief that Luke Smith made the aides and installed decent toilet and bathroom facilities and children's play areas in the quarters despite the fact the houses will soon be torn down. And put in road lights.

"Honey," Emanuela told Stan once, "we never done told you consultants about it, but for a long time after the road lights come in, we all was watching our electric bills, sure we was gon' be charged for it. Well, I don't need to say we all, because me, I weren't one to think this company would ever, ever cheat us, tell us they would pay for the bill when all of the time they would be charging us, but a lots of the people wasn't like that. Them colored don't trust white nohow, and say, 'Look, the company ain't no better than other white folks. They take all the advantage of you.'

"Then, come to find out, I am right and they be wrong. The company make us little promises and keeps them. It what make us think they gon' keep the big promises, too. I knows they gon' keep them, and now them other no-trusting people got to believe it, too."

Bill Kelly's speech has been applauded and reapplauded. all the food and drinks are finished. And now, finally, finally, here's the hush, hush magic time of the officer and board announcements.

For chairman of the board of the Avon Park–Frostproof–Wachula Community Development Corporation, Mr. Albert Ocea, short, somewhat portly, with a round face, warm brown eyes, full moist lips that collect spittle at the corners of his mouth when he speaks, and a strong voice you listen to.

I don't know much about Mr. Ocea, nobody else seems to either, and yet everybody's got deep-felt respect for him. He lives alone with a small, well-cared for daughter—nobody I know has ever met her mother—in a scrupulously clean shack.

The vice-president, Mack Milton, tall, slender, dark-bearded, is a minister, though not a Saint, and also works as a fruit picker. Like Albert Ocea, he's highly respected and "known for doing good," according to Johnnie Lou. He used to be her foreman and was a crew chief for many years.

"A former crew chief," I say, shocked. "I can't understand why the people would elect such a man to such a job."

Johnnie grins and says, "Listen, Sara, why you think all crew chiefs is just natural bad? Well, the way I see it, there are good and bad in all people. And all people means crew chiefs as well. A man can make it up the ladder and still be decent like the Rev Milton. That man . . . yeh, say, you got in jail and needed money for out and was in his crew, baby, you call him and get whut you need. But that don't mean you gon' pay him all that interest you do them other crew chiefs. In fact, you don't pay him nothing more'n what you owe. Oh, I could tell you stories. . . . He is such a good man."

Mary Reid, eighteen, and one of the few high school seniors here, is elected secretary despite Lincoln's campaign for his wife, Leola. She is as cute and rakish as can be. Laughter comes easily to her. I don't think I ever saw her when she wasn't laughing, and, although being a Saint, she's not allowed to sing or dance in bars or other sinful places—there's plenty of room for dancing and singing her joy in church. But she's a serious girl, too, who intends to be either a teacher or a nurse and work right here in her own community.

The treasurer is Mother Bets, another of the strong women I'm proud to know here. She raised her four sons alone after her husband deserted when the youngest was three months old, but she was never the "hardhearted matriarch" some sociologists would label her and all black women in her position. To say she didn't love her sons or blamed them for their father's actions is, even on its face, ridiculous. She put a lot into her boys and, as is only natural, the more she put into them the more she loved, not hated and despised, them for being their father's sons.

Her boys, grown now, tell me that no matter how tired she would be after coming in from the fields or the groves she always had time and energy to "love us up good," as her eldest son puts it.

The rest of the board consists of seven Saints and five sinners, which may—probably does—presage problems.

⋐ Chapter 11

Actually our staff—company and HRI consultants—is hardly more unanimous in type, personality, and point of view than the board. There are ten of us here at our motel breakfast preparatory to a three-day board meeting to be held beginning today, and you couldn't imagine a more varied group. Agricultural Labor Project Manager Gerry Abell, born and brought up in north Texas, is as ethical as they come and totally devoted to the company. He makes no bones of the fact he's chosen this company for his lifetime career (a conception those of us from HRI can't even imagine) and intends to give everything he's got to it.

Will Gerry be a good manager? I think, yes, he'll be a hell of a good manager. I can't tell yet whether he's as committed as we of HRI consider ourselves to be to the ideas, visions, ideals, of the project. But that he'll be utterly faithful to them is something none of us can doubt. In fact, all of us from HRI who've helped in the conception of the whole project are sometimes inclined to—or actually do—deviate from its principles. But not Gerry. And there have been times, even at this stage, he's called the rest of us to task for doing it.

In extravagant oppositeness to one another as well as to Gerry and our other staff, black as well as white, are Mel Green and young, aggressively militant Jen Lewis. Jen, discovered and presented to the board for hiring, as was Mel, by Bill Kelly, not HRI, was born and brought up in Pittsburgh and worked with, headed up, causes for racial justice since she was very young. She's still only in her early twenties, a small, pudgy, person whose bushy Afro hair style couldn't suit her less. But there is a dignity and self-confidence about her that makes her appear quite a little older. And she, more perhaps than even the other black staff, has, in the few months she has been here, convinced many of the young migrants that black can, indeed, be beautiful. She has also made them know how exploited they have been all of their lives. I admire Jen, and I think she likes me, manages to forget I'm white . . . some of the time. I can't help wondering, though, why the company hired her under the circumstances of the ultramilitancy she's constantly expressing to everyone, including Bill Kelly, not only toward whites but also toward the other black staff members. Mel, for instance, is to her nothing more than a "boojie nigger," a bourgeois black man who, as she puts it, is "in love with the white power structure because he knows he's in a position to gain from it."

She also constantly rains down contempt on Lily Haskins, hired to do attitudinal training, now acting executive director of ALPI, and Dura Mae Everett, housing consultant, who'd had considerable experience in federally supported self-help housing programs. All this despite the fact that able, effective, caring Lily, possessed of a massive, earthy, solid aura of a born fighter is, at fifty or so, a leader for welfare mothers' rights in New Jersey and nationally. And Dura, about as hardheaded, practical, and realistic as they come—on this project or anywhere—is of Florida migrant and sharecropper stock. Still, Jen lumps them and Mel together and defines them all, imperiously and loudly, as sycophantic, reactionary, outdated "boojie niggers"—blind, tradition-bound, "colored friends of the white power structure."

The others here—Arnold, my husband, and on-scene coordinator of the project; Stan; Bob; Kaye; Tom Starnes, recently hired from a Mississippi project; and I—are white.

Arnold, Mel, Lily, and I have been living here at the motel for almost three months, and all the waitresses know us well. Priscilla, tall, blue-eyed, and black-haired, is our waitress today. Her eyes and lips smile as she says, "Good morning, Mr. and Mrs. Harris." And adds almost as an afterthought, "Hi, Mel, hi, Lily." This though Lily's a grandmother.

Jen, persistent in the idea that Mel always encourages white waitresses and other white women to flirt with him, asks us all at the table, "Did you see Priscilla look at Mel with that *special look* [she didn't look at him differently than at her, for instance, or Lily or Dura] and shrug her shoulders when she said, 'Hellooo, Mel,' in that affectionate tone?" (Her tone was the same she'd used to the other blacks, hardly affectionate, and she didn't shrug her shoulders.) Then she turns to Mel, shrugs her shoulders as she maintains Priscilla did, and imitates the voice she says Priscilla used to him, "Hellooo, Mel."

"Well, Mel," she says, "I've got one thing to say in favor of southern belles. They sho' nuff have this way of flirting with black men who flirt with them, and yet keeping them in their place. That shoulder shrug, for instance, is an important piece of business for white chicks like Priscilla leading black dudes like you on, do you know, Mel? It means, 'Man, I might could go for you, and you sure *do* go for me as you're always letting me know. But, if push ever come to shove, and you was to forget your place, nigger, well, I could shrug you off as fast as I shrug my shoulders.'"

Mel never answers the taunts Jen's always throwing at him. But you can tell from his look, they infuriate him. And he usually takes out his anger at one or another of us white staff, most generally Gerry since he's the project head appointed by the company. Today he's assaulting him for some reason none of us, including Gerry, can make any sense of.

Gerry's amazing, though. He remains silent in the face of Mel's overt hostility. He's told me when I've asked him to analyze his feelings toward Mel that he is, quite literally, afraid of them. For this reason, he makes a point of meeting Mel's challenges with silence. Someday, maybe, he'll be strong and disciplined enough to oppose him without exploding—but not yet. He's got a lot of inner exploring to do first.

Mel perceives Gerry's silence, though, not as self-discipline, self-containment, as the rest of us know it to be, but rather as mockery; that's what he's doing, and all he ever does: He's mocking Mel. Mel persists in seeing Gerry as competitive with him, and the rest of us from HRI, and therefore hurtful to the project. He's told us many times when we've pointed up Gerry's efficiency on the project, the vast amount of time beyond his call of duty he devotes to administering it, that Gerry does all he does more out of loyalty to the company and its officers than to the migrants, who ought, by rights, to be his first concern, as they are ours. He would love today to confront Gerry with this so-called fact. But he holds himself back because he knows that if he does he's going to have to cope with some feed-back from Bob, Stan, and Arnold, certainly, and maybe Lily, Dura, and me besides.

"Do you think . . . aside from blowing off steam, which

may have helped you, Mel, though we don't even know about that . . . do you think this kind of unwarranted and un-understandable accusation did any good for Gerry? Or, more important, the Agricultural Labor Project and the people themselves?

Mel, man, cat, dude, people-loving, sensitive one, try using a little of that empathy you claim you've got and the company people, including Gerry, haven't. You want them to put themselves in your shoes. Well, you're the outside consultant, so put yourself in theirs for a change. How do you think it is for them to be forced to adjust to us, strangers in the truest sense. Not alone our ways and words, but everything about us that makes us what we are, all of our deepest values, can't possibly be Gerry's, any more than his can be ours.

But he's got his own values, and they're as significant to him as ours are to us. Just at this time, you may be right about the basic bridges between Gerry and us being Paul Austin, Luke Smith, Don Keough, Bill Kelly. Maybe Gerry does meet the demand to stimulate people involvement, people power, to the best of his ability, and he is doing his level best because they wish him to. But what is wrong with loyalty like that if it makes a person the kind of excellent manager (as even you ought to admit in fairness) Gerry is? Besides, how can you know for a fact that his loyalty to the company is his only motivation? There are certainly plenty of people on the project who wouldn't share your opinion. They feel, and have expressed it over and over, that Gerry cares a lot about them.

And Mel, oddly, gets the message now more effectively than he's done many times during our actual conversations with him. So, he turns his big, warm, easy smile on all of us, definitely including Gerry. (Great God, Mel Green can be charming when he wants to. I've seen him over and over at businessmen's conventions and parties hold the most resistant and obstinate racist and class-oriented people in the palm of his hand, not only offering them the best of what he's got to give but also bringing out the best in them.) Gerry, always fair, has to admit, "Mel's smile, his warmth when he wants one to feel it . . . He can really charm anyone the way he did Luke Smith at the Naples meeting, for instance."

And, Mel, seeming to read Gerry's thought, talks to him at length, and with total honesty, about the Naples meeting.

He repeats to him, meaningfully, what he told Luke. "That guy, Luke, man, what he said came from the heart, as I must have repeated to everyone I've met since the meeting. Nobody could make me believe it was just another corporate executive making a speech. And I know everybody in this room felt the same as me."

Gerry's truly involved with Mel at the moment, very moved by him, and, as is often the case, ready to hold out a hand of friendship if Mel will only meet him a small part of the way. I, therefore, say, "I'd like it, Mel, if you'd tell Gerry about your personal fears of Florida and your experiences in Belle Glade in 1952."

"You mean about me promising the Good Lord and half a dozen responsible people that if I got out of that place alive . . . if I would live to tell the story . . . I'd never again let the Florida sun set on my black ass?"

And now he goes into a new routine. "Oooh, Gerry!" Now he looks at Tom Starnes, too, for the first time since we've sat down, "Oooh, Gerry and Tom, what I said!"

Gerry meets his fake humble look, slowly shaking his head because this is exactly according to his expectation based upon ample previous experience with Mel. No sooner does he manage to win Gerry over to him . . . "See," Gerry explained to me at one such time, "he gets me thinking, and Tom thinking, 'Well, maybe we can work with him, after all.'

"There's nothing I want more and nothing Tom does. We know, from Luke Smith, from Don Keough, they haven't said it in so many words, but we know our futures are going to be influenced. Maybe our future in this company will even depend to a large extent upon the mark we make on the Agricultural Labor Project. And we know that Mel's influence among the workers . . . Well, we need Mel to help us gain acceptability with the workers. It's obvious to us that if we don't gain acceptability with the workers . . . You can say we need Mel Green. And, are, therefore, willing, for this if no other reason, to meet him halfway or further.

"Then when he turns on the 'I-love-everybody-on-this-project-and-please-love-me-back' sincere charm, well, Tom and I want to believe that he's finally stopped holding our being born in Mississippi and Texas against us and is willing to judge us, as we do him, on our present actions and commitment to the project. We've tried, Tom and I both have tried harder than I can tell you, to go out to him in return. As soon as we do, the minute he sees he's got us in his trap again, it's like a cat playing with a mouse, or a spider with a fly."

And, Mel, as though having read my mind, and recollections of my conversations with Gerry, I've certainly repeated to him, says, in literally, his most amiable voice, "Gerry, Tom, Sara's right in me needing to tell you about my experiences here, in Florida, in the year 1952. If I want you to understand me—and I do.

"Well, let me show you the other side of the big, bold, brave Mel Green I try to give people the impression I am. See, to admit to you, as I already have done to some of the other folks at this table . . . I was coward-scared to come to Florida when Bill first asked me. In my little mind I guess I had this mental image of what Florida would be like today based on what it was like when I was here in 'fifty-two. I was in the trucking business then, hauling fruit from Belle Glade to New York or Chicago and Cincinnati.

"And you know how I am about liking to meet new people. And with there not being too much for me to do around Belle Glade, I'd get up early in the morning before my truck would be loaded and go down to this other kind of loading ramp, or loading block as they called it. All the farmers needing, or wanting, daily bean pickers, would pull up there.

"Now, I don't know if any of you were here in the winter of 1952. Because if you had been, you'd sure remember a bad freeze they had all over the state. So at the time I'm telling about, there weren't that many pickers around, the most of them had left for work in other states. And the growers were, like, desperate for people, you would say.

"And the bossmen's stooges were out in full force to get pickers by hook or crook for their farms. And one, a big, scary-looking cat with a long handlebar moustache and a gun strapped on his shoulder rode up to me on his horse. I'll never forget him or his horse.

" 'Boy,' he said, 'I need pickers.'

"I said, 'Well, I'm sorry, sir. But I drive a truck, I don't pick beans.'

"And he pulled out his pistol, stuck it under my nose and said, 'By God, nigger, I want bean pickers.'

"And I said to myself, 'Hell, Mel, I guess you're going to pick beans.' And got on to the truck."

But Mel was luckier, younger, less cowed and beaten than the rest of the men in the truck. And was able, therefore, to escape by jumping into a ditch when the truck slowed down for a curve not too far from town. He lay there for a while in the glare of the sun and tried to cover his head with his hands. He felt dirt in his mouth and nose; he was very sick. After what seemed like a long time, he pulled himself to his feet, swallowing the sour vomit which gushed up in his throat, and staggered out of the ditch and into town.

"Well, see, the reason I even thought I could escape, even dreamed I could, was that I wasn't what you'd call a true migrant. I wasn't born to the life like the other cats in the truck with me. Otherwise, like them, I'd have gone and stayed with that damn man, picked his beans as long as he wanted me to and only left when he told me I could go. And I guess I began to dig that day as I never had before, how damn much my people have always, up till today, been subjected to in this so-called land of the free.

"Now, that cracker sticking his gun in my face may have been the worst of what happened to me in Florida in 'fifty-two, but it wasn't all of what happened, baby, not by a long shot. Okay, the time, as we've said, was 1952, and I hadn't been out of the army too many years. I'd been risking my black self to beat fascism and, you know, keep my country safe for democracy. And though I don't today and certainly didn't twenty years ago consider Florida as black turf, my turf, still it was supposed to be a part of my country I'd been fighting for, right?

"So when I found myself working in Belle Glade and having these dull, dreary long weekends on my hands, I told myself I love to swim, and I thought, 'Hell, all I heard about Miami Beach, the peoples' playground, why shouldn't I go get some fun and sun, too?' And was really shocked to hear . . . well, they didn't allow the likes of me to swim at the sacrosanct beaches of Miami. There was some kind of nigger beach nearby, that was the only place I could go. It made me feel rotten, to put the thing mildly.

"And then there were all these miserable things facing me every day right there in Belle Glade. Thinking back on it all, just getting a damn money order was a hassle for black people, even though there were so many of us there. You walked into the United States Post Office and there was this red line separating white from black money-order window lines. The white people formed right in front of the window. Black people, though, had to sort of lean over from where they were allowed to stand. After all the white folks were taken care of, the black people could lean over and do their business.

"Hell, the first time I walked in sure I knew what the lines were about. How could I not? But I decided I wouldn't pay any attention, just get on the white line, real polite, you know, and wait my turn. First thing, this guard, maybe six foot four and a good three hundred pounds, come up to me. 'By God, nigger, are you blind? Can't you see or what?' "

Jen laughs. "Oh, I did my little things, all right, told him off. With words. But no, I did not burn the building down, bust it up. Well, it was pre-1960, and we weren't into all that in those days, if you'll recall."

Jen grins at him and says precisely, "You weren't into it, Mel. But a whole lots of black *men* were."

This is the strange way the pecking order on this project works, or did during the two years we were there. While Mel rakes Gerry, as good a worker as anyone could be, over the coals, Jen, a heroine of the self-conscious young blacks here (as Bill Kelly certainly knew well she would be before she was hired), does the same with him.

I asked Bill once: "My God, what possessed you to hire Jen? Didn't you know her major desire was to overthrow you?" He said, "I felt at that point that the people needed the sense of dignity Jen could bring, and, naturally, I wasn't afraid she'd be able actually to overthrow us. Anyway, it's the feeling Bob and I came away with when we sat down to analyze the contribution she might make and the chances we were taking."

I hadn't analyzed it, though, and I was always fascinated by Jen's reasons for calling Mel, Lily, and Dura Mae, as she always did, "friends of the white power structure."

"Do you call them 'friends of the white power structure' because they work for Coca-Cola?" I had asked her over a drink one night after a community meeting we'd attended together.

Jen had sat very still with her drink in her hands, looking

at me from under lowered lids. "Their working for Coca-Cola is not the only criterion by which I judge them. Really, I think you would know that yourself, knowing me as you do." She'd given me a dirty look.

I'd met her look and apologized for asking the tactless question under the circumstances of her having confided to me before the meeting that she "feels like a traitor to the black people's cause to be here helping Coca-Cola do anything, achieve anything no matter how legitimate, even right and decently motivated it may seem to be. And what almost drives me up the wall sometimes . . . I need to doubt my own motivations for having ever come to work with Coca-Cola. Well, why am I here? I have to ask myself whether I haven't sold my soul to the company because they pay me a hell of a lot more dinero than I could ever imagine earning any other place."

Then, showing she'd accepted my apology, she answered my question about why she believed Lily. Dura and Mel were friends of the white power structure. Lily and Dura were hard to explain at the moment, but she would the very next time they showed their "boojie faces," which she didn't doubt would be soon.

As for Mel, though, he is easy to explain. Anyone who feels so warmly to Luke Smith, say, as he does, "has got also to feel himself better than the Brothers in the fields and groves. No matter how he covers it up so the people love him like they do, there's still more of a split between him and them, than him and the company officers."

And now it seems the time has come when Dura Mae's and Lily's "boojie faces" are clear as can be. This meeting . . . Up until now, Mel, who's had no particular training in child development, has administered, with aides he's recruited, the makeshift child care center.

Now, however, the longed-for child development center is really in the works. The former single men's dormitory complex of steel buildings, of ample dimensions in a campuslike setting, no longer in use for the formerly required offshore and casual male harvesters, is being converted into a combination medical-dental clinic, living-learning library with the latest reading and tutorial equipment, and, of course, child development center. The latter is intended to house sixty-five infants and children from 6:00 A.M. to 6:00 P.M. and bring into reality all of our wonderful dreams from the day child development had first been mentioned, all of our faith, hope, and desperate craving to create the most perfect center of its kind that has ever been.

Our parents' committees had visited numerous centers, had asked many questions, and read or had read to them every book or magazine article any of us could find on the subject, and they knew what they wanted.

This meeting, therefore, is for the purpose of hiring a trained director, and it's an arduous, tiresome business. Arnold's been working for months, literally, to uncover the most qualified, competent, educator-trainer. He'll be wholly responsible for training the child development aides, after all, and some of them will be directly out of the orange groves. It won't be a simple job. Of course, Arnold and all of us have had an ideal candidate in mind; in view of our respect for this undertaking, how could we not have?

Well, here's all we require from our candidate: He should, of course, be a black or chicano male . . . our kids, like poor, minority kids all over, definitely need close contact with strong black or chicano men as role models. He should also be exceptionally well trained for the education, training, and administration of a topflight child development center. Highly experienced in progressive schools of a kind never before open to any but the cherished offspring of upper- and middle-class families. A generous, outgoing, psychologically healthy person who even if he hasn't solved all of his life's problems, won't need to impose them on the aides and children. Happy, cheerful, relaxed, a person of benevolent presence and courtesy, good manners, extreme civilized behavior. But also possessed of anger and resentment and fury he won't keep leashed in the presence of exploitation and injustice. A man sufficiently sensitive so he'll share the sufferings of the kids and aides he'll be working with. And, though we won't insist on this, sprung not out of the middle or upper class but from among the poor people themselves. That's all we're asking of a child development coordinator.

Arnold begins the discussion by telling our group, unhappily, "Listen, I have to remind you of the job situation where qualified black or Chicano applicants for such a post as ours are concerned. As we really knew from the beginning, though we wouldn't admit it even to one another, there ain't none.

Now, we're listed in agencies all over, advertised in all the professional journals offering . . . Well, our salary's comparatively very high, as you know, and I've portrayed the conditions of life here in central Florida as positively as it was possible to do within, mmm, the minimal bounds of honesty, let's put it like that."

Tom leans forward and looks into Arnold's face. He says, "Life in central Florida is not all that bad, Arnold."

"Hear, hear," Mel says, settling down in his chair and closing his eyes as though to keep from having to look at Tom. "Could I ask what makes a white Ph.D. from Mississippi such an expert on how black people have to live in central Florida? Could I ask you that little question, Dr. Starnes?"

Tom ignores Mel's outburst, as Arnold also does, and says, "First, about Chicano applicants. There weren't any. And only a very few blacks applied. Two young women in particular stood out as lively, concerned people the kids would doubtless take to. But neither of them had work experience in child development. Then there's a middle-aged woman who's had a small amount of experience with a Miami community action program. She wanted to change jobs, but she's not even slightly qualified."

"Well, man, let's hear about the white applications now. I'm sure you found many eminently suitable people among them," Mel says.

"Mel, Mel, quit the crap," Arnold says. "Well, I didn't find many eminently suitable white people, as you so charmingly put it, though I did find one person whose educational and work qualifications are striking."

Mickey Roberts, with a Master's Degree in early childhood education, is presently employed as director of Polk County's preschool programs, and is, therefore, known to all of us, including Mel, who says, "I can't hardly believe it, Arnold. You would hire that southern WASP. You'd impose her on my people? Jeez, I couldn't bear her the minute I met her."

"Whether you can bear her isn't the important thing, though, is it, Mel? The thing that matters is, can the child development committee and the aides bear Mickey Roberts in order to learn all she's got to give them at this critical stage? Damn it, the initial organization of the center can make or break the program. And, Mel, Mickey's known all over Florida as a crackerjack organizer in child development."

Stony and immobile, Mel says, "I don't give a damn what kind of crackerjack she is. If she ain't got love for the people and the kids, we don't need her."

"We need more than love to make this program work, Mel," Arnold says urgently. "Besides, I watched her with the kids. Believe me, she's got plenty of love for them. And they took to her right off as they haven't yet to any of us. As for the adults she'll be working with, they need her knowledge and expertise, not love, as I see it."

Mel says, "I don't care how much she loves the kids. They need to see a black person as a supervisor, an authority."

Lily, sitting across the table from Mel, brings her face close to his. "Now, you listen about black people being hired as supervisors and authorities for no reason except their skin's black. All right, my kids went to this ghetto school headed up by a black man. The principal was black and dumb, man, dumb. If he'd been white, and if my kids' school had been in a white neighborhood, he wouldn't have lasted two weeks.

"And the same's true of some of the black teachers. White parents wouldn't've stood them for nothing. But they were black, see? The dumbest, the lowest, and the board of education foisted them off on us. And we thanked them humbly for doing us such a big favor as to send us 'black authority figures.' A black principal, black teachers . . . Well, what more did us niggers want?

"All right, I'll tell you, Mel, man, what this particular so-called nigger, this proud black woman, wants for her kids. The most outstanding damn principal, the best goddamn teachers the ofay world has got to give. I don't give a hoot if they're green or pink or white as the driven snow with blue, blue eyes and spun-gold hair. I don't want the good people, the experts going to the good, white people's schools while my kids get the poorest ones of the bunch because they're niggers, and are supposed, for that reason, to be able to love my nigger kids.

"Well, now, I'll go Arnold a step better, too. Being black myself, I can do that. Arnold says he don't give a hoot about whether or not Mickey loves the people so long as she does care about the kids. The way I feel about that . . . I'll give you my own kids as an example again. Dig, their principal and teachers don't need to love me or them. But see, they do need to respect all of us enough so they give us a big hunk of all that beautiful knowledge and expertise Mickey Roberts and the rest of them have been picking up all these years in them fancy white schools where you, me, and certainly our agricultural workers never dreamed before we—or our kids—would get past their doors.

"So I agree with Arnold that Mickey Roberts with all that beautiful education and experience will give a hell of a lot more to our workers and kids than any untrained, inexperienced black women with all of the black 'soul' in the world, you know."

Dura Mae nods to all Lily's saying, vigorously, compellingly.

And Jen turns from them to me. Here, finally, is an overt example of what she meant that night in the bar when she couldn't find words for describing Dura Mae's and Lily's "love for the white power structure."

Lily gleans her feeling as well as I do, reads it in her stiff, sullen, frowning face when she looks in her and Dura Mae's direction, and says, "Don't Uncle Tom me—Aunt Jemima me, rather—me or Dura Mae, Sister. Because let me make one thing absolutely clear: Dura Mae and I are as much for the people's rights, definitely including the black people's right to dignity, as either you or Brother Mel. But we all got a different way of assuring they'll get their right. Let's say in front, Sister Jen, that when you come down to the nitty-gritty, all of us on the staff, Coca-Cola as well as HRI consultants, have got the same goals for the success of the project, meaning the people's ability to help themselves, that you yourself do.

"And once they can help themselves, well, then, they may not need a Mickey Roberts. But they sure as hell need her now, and I think it would be a crime to hire an inferior black or Chicano person over her."

Chapter 12

A three day board meeting and training session must begin quite soon, and though Mel and Jen want to answer Lily, with whom the rest of us are in profound agreement, they're interrupted by our three field-work students who arrive, as always, before they're solicited and expected. The students have been assigned by the University of South Florida to work with us for six months, during which they'll receive room, board, and $120 a month for living expenses. Also they've been blunt, brusque skeptics and challengers where the program and the company's motivations are concerned. They see themselves as watchdogs, and again, as in Jen's case, I can't help but respect the company for permitting them to get close to the project in spite of their often and freely expressed opposition—almost enmity.

But, as Bill Kelly generously said, such bright, creative, sensitive young people have a great deal to contribute to the project no matter how they may feel about the company. And he, as well as the rest of us, are genuinely fond of them. All the same, there are many times when one of us must tell them:

"You're saying the company won't keep this promise. Remember all the times you said the same about other promises that were made and certainly kept?"

They never do seem to remember, though, and stand constantly ready to censure those of us of HRI as well as the company people.

Today, the question we're so heatedly debating—the matter of an unqualified black or qualified white child development coordinator—is one they would, naturally, particularly relish. They sit for a while, savoring the situation, and then make it very clear, though no one's asking them, where they stand on the issue.

Nineteen-year-old Mark Gulden, lank and rangy, with stringy muscles, round blue eyes and a large head Afroed to within an inch of its life, backs Jen and Mel as always. Right or wrong . . . Well, being black, they can't be wrong with him. As for all us white staff members, just by virtue of our skin color (he doesn't consider himself white), we're either exploiters or their instruments. This time, however, he addresses himself not just to us white "manipulators" but also to Lily and Dura Mae because we are all in agreement about Mickey. He says we see ourselves, and others also see us, as prime liberals, to use an obnoxious phrase, but aren't we even aware of the fact our chauvinism's peeking out when we insist, with no matter what rationale, upon hiring a white coordinator? We don't belong in our jobs if we don't realize that a white person, no matter how well educated and equipped, cannot possibly be possessed of that beautiful thing—soul. And an administrator without soul for a child development center composed primarily of black and Mexican kids . . . it's beyond Mark even to comprehend our point of view.

Mark's got to face some bickering from his colleagues, though. Anyone knowing these students has to know also they're no more the three musketeers in their way than we or the board members and aides are in ours, and are inclined to disagree with one another quite as often as we do among ourselves.

Marion McPartland, for instance, is eighteen and looks like a stage ingenue, fun-loving and a trifle silly, though she is perhaps the most solemn, thoughtful, earnest student we've got. Her family are white sharecroppers and she hopes to help change the lot of her people. She backs Mark and Mel and Jen "to the ultimate" on the importance of employing black people over white in authority positions whether or not they're as competent. But Bootsie Manners, who is black herself, assents 100 percent with those of us who say qualifications are more important than color when it comes to this job at this particular time.

Now Marion flares up at Bootsie's arrogant assumption that she's got a special sensitivity toward agricultural workers merely because some of their skins and Bootsie's are black. Little Bootsie Manners, being the daughter of Austin Manners, only the wealthiest black funeral director in the county . . . Well, at this point, Marion feels it necessary, although it may be off the subject, to ask who's in a better position to understand poor black migrants' problems or, better, to empathize with them, Marion herself, who's of sharecropper stock, or wealthy, sheltered Bootsie?

"Wealthy, sheltered" Bootsie is about to blow up at these words. She has it on the tip of her tongue, and we're all uncomfortably aware of it, to say to Marion that just because Marion is, or rather is said to be, "carrying on" with Emanuel Elias—it's the gossip among the more hostile townsfolk anyhow—doesn't make her black any more than Bootsie can aspire to being poor under her circumstances.

Stan intervenes, says we'll have to continue the important discussion of a child development coordinator another time. We have now to talk about the substance of the three-day board session.

It will divide into two parts. The first will deal with the main stratagems of negotiating the budget the board has been working on for the past months with the funding agency, presently the company, and presenting it for approval when it's done.

Gerry, of course, will be at the final session to hear the people's proposals and bring them back to the company, while the board members will speak for the people. The second part will be given over to a type of personal sharing, similar to the one we all felt to be so effective during the supervisory sessions and our earlier three with the board.

Stan's hardly done explaining when the board and aides arrive in their small inbred groups. Here are deacons of the church in their shiny black suits; holy mothers in their long dresses, some white, others black. Many wear flowered straw hats and white gloves. And here are the sinners, including Johnnie Lou, in their miniskirts and hot pants. To me the most poignant, maybe because the most genuinely liked aside from Johnnie Lou, is the new treasurer, Mother Bets. Her face so soft and warm, and her loving smile to carry off her tiredness is a tremendous contrast to the huge feet that have swollen to fill the discarded shoes of her huge sons she wore all week at work, and had now put aside to push into the new high heels she sways and flounders in.

But you can't expect tourists coming into the dining room of a tourist motel, who'd never have believed in Mother Bets's existence if you'd ever tried describing her to them, to remain unamused or unbelligerent toward anyone who looks like her. Some are laughing aloud at the sight of her while others look at her with repugnance and bitter animosity. She realizes, of course, but never lets the rest of us know she does. I wish I had her natural poise under the circumstances, but I don't. I stare back at the people who are staring at Mother Bets and I know the look on my face is one that lets those tourists know the umbrage I'm feeling toward them.

Both parts of the conference are, in reality, inspirational to us consultants. Though we had always trusted the people's strength in the abstract, it was a different—and marvelous—matter to experience it in the concrete. Here they were, in the flesh, demonstrating before us their belief in the project and underscoring their inherent fitness for moving it forward—it was beautiful to see.

Even in the formal meeting procedure . . . By now there is hardly any of the chaos we experienced during our earlier meetings and conferences. Stan has presented both board and aides with a set of rules they have absorbed rather rapidly and have doted on ever since. No doubt about it, little Mr. Ocea is the hardest, most sobering and formal chairman you can meet. Nobody is ever recognized out of place or permitted to say a word without acknowledgment. And Mr. Ocea's aided by the whole group in their classic pose of authoritarians erect in their chairs and with their minds on the huge sum of money required for the coming year's program. Medical, child development, housing, scholarship, tutorial, legal aid, voter education, living-learning library, vocational training, cultural enrichment especially aimed at the blacks and Chicanos . . . you name it, the board's listed it.

"This is a serious business we all be here for today," Mother Bets says during the session Gerry's with us and the board makes its presentation to him. "Serious, man." And explains that it's hard even for "educated folk" to figure what the costs of personnel, equipment, etc., are likely to be. And, once having arrived at the figure, being sufficiently secure in it, "right enough," so the funding agency will feel justified in granting your request.

"Who ever think orange pickers like us could do such a big thing as this?" she asks. "Work out this whole big budget?"

But the fact is the people have done it—and effectually, too.

Interestingly, there's only one point on which there is conflict in Gerry's presence, and that's the matter of the living-learning library. The subject is opened by our bubbling young secretary, Mary Reid, who says to us all while looking at Gerry, "As everybody here knows except Gerry, of course, I haven't said much at earlier board meetings about anything we've been talking of here, not housing, not medical care, not child development. I have just been sitting here and writing down what the rest of y'all been saying. Even Lincoln, one time, he said, 'What is the matter with Mary? Is she deaf or dumb or maybe don't care about what goes on here? And her a high school senior?'

"So the one thing I am excited over as a high school student who hopes to go to college is the library we're planning. And I'm saying, Gerry, that when we get it set up, well, I want to know, for sure, it'll have books, magazines, reading matter that has to do with us as blacks and Mexican-Americans, books that I've never even seen in my library in the high school."

Emanuela asks, "Well, what you mean by that, Mary? Baby, you know yourself you got plenty books in your high school." Everybody knows she's talking for Gerry's benefit, and some people are furious with her.

"She means," Jesús answers, "she wants books in our library that will make her and all the black and Mexican-American children and young people proud to be themselves. She wants books and magazines where the great things black and Mexican-American people have done and are doing are brought out and the people shine as they deserve."

Now Mary says, "And, as you know, Ella, because we talked a whole lots about it, though you seem to want Gerry to think we haven't, we also want to have books by authors telling us as black people we have our rights as Americans the same as white people, and if we can't get them by peaceful means, then there are other ways of getting them, you know."

Emanuela looks at Gerry, who's nodding and smiling in obvious approval of Mary's words, and yet feels compelled to say, "Mary, baby, I wouldn't nohow want us to have a library with books like that in it. I git so scared inside when I think of what can happen to y'all if you take the advice in them books y'all talking about now. Baby, I want to see you live you life out and die of old age, you know, and not no bullets or something. But, I know you gon' listen to the books, not me."

Many people, including us consultants and Gerry, try to persuade poor Emanuela times have changed, and black people's self-expressions are not only permitted but even sometimes, though all too rarely, heeded.

Mary, bored by our attempts to reassure Emanuela, heaves her shoulders dramatically, and tells Gerry:

"The board also suggests the budget contain this item, appointing a committee of ten people, including six students who'll probably make greatest use of the library, to visit libraries in other cities—Miami's got a great library for minority users—in order to be in a position to help the staff choose the books, films, recordings, and all of the rest that are going to be of the greatest aid to us, as blacks, Chicanos, and so on. We want to help choose them.

"Another thing we would like the company to consider, Gerry"—Mary's quoting Jen now almost word for word—"is a budget item for the writing of original books a committee of our people will suggest as to subject matter by authors we will choose. We want books about rural black and Chicano kids, migrant black and Chicano kids, and all that they've got to go through in life. And the ways there are that they can help themselves, though their parents never have been able to do it. I want to see those books outlining those ways point by point, written especially for our kids. To us, that is true cultural enrichment."

"Yes, Mary," Gerry says. "I surely do see your point about that."

There is, in fact, only one item in the entire complex budget that Gerry would like to warn us the company may question. And it is one to make us all, including him, look at each other and grin at the originality of it. The board has insisted, and none of us has contradicted them, that the budget for its child development center should amount to $100,000, and Gerry tells them:

"May I say that, in my opinion, the company will turn down this request and ask you to research it further because . . . Now, remember this is my opinion and you needn't act upon it, but I believe the sum you're asking for will not be nearly enough to do the kind of job that needs to be done in child development. I would suggest, therefore, that you do further research on the subject. Thank you very much."

Mother Bets, a shadow falling over her face—she has kept a spontaneity of expression, an abandon and directness in the outward manifestations of her feelings and thoughts that is something like a last trace of childhood on the old, tortured face—says, "Now, do I get your point or am I missing it? Are you really saying you wants to give us more money than we's asking?"

"I'm really saying, Bets, that the company, just like the people, want this to be the best child development center possible. And it seems, at least to me, that you haven't requested enough money to make that happen."

I hear Mark's voice, a little bit startled, saying, "Who would ever think you'd hear the likes of this from Coca-Cola?"

Now it's sharing time, and Bob points up, as he has on earlier occasions, how hard it is for people to communicate honestly with one another and really come to know one another and themselves on a nitty-gritty level. There's not a person in the world—from those of us in this room to the Coke executives who've had their sharing sessions, too—who's not basically afraid to make himself vulnerable (the people know by now what he means by vulnerable) because, really, we live in the kind of world where people find it hard to trust one another.

Stan pursues the concept of trust in his way. He tells us that as extroverted as he may appear now, trust, true trust in human beings including his own family, came very hard, from the time he was a child.

"And yet," he says, in a soft tone, "in these months we've been working and living together I've learned to trust all of you people. So I want to tell you this true story, I'm very ashamed of, about the first time I came down here even before the project began.

"The first person I met was Larry Mack." He turns to look at Larry, a man in his forties with wide eyes and mouth smiling now in a friendly urchin grin. He's one of the Saints of the board.

"Okay, here goes all about Stanley Silverzweig, hypocrite. I was wearing some pretty funny-looking jeans and a shirt when Larry met me. But the truth of the matter is, I really also had a couple of pretty good-looking suits with me that I didn't want him or any of you to know anything about."

Larry's face goes bright with pleasure at Stan's attention to him, and he says, to everyone. "Stan talk about a good suit and all, but, you know, he look like the poorest of the poor, can't afford nothing but rags the first time I seen him. He were wearin' these old blue jeans. How could you dress like that for a first meeting with people?" he suddenly asks Stan.

Stan answers, "Well, see, I didn't know any more about agricultural workers at the time than you did about New Jersey or New York consultants. So the way I had it figured out, I thought agricultural workers . . . I knew what little money you were making, and I figured you'd be dressed in clothes like dungarees, old shirts, like that. And I wanted to try and be on the same footing, and not come around looking like a fancy city slicker."

"A fancy slicker," Larry says, chuckling. "Let me tell you, Stan, you looked like a tramp that day."

Stan says, "Larry, if at our first meeting I didn't look like you figured me, well, I was just as surprised to see you looking like you did. I remember we met on the road as we were pulling into the quarter and you were going out, it was church night, and you and Annie and all of the kids were dressed up to kill. And I stopped the car, I didn't know you were you, Larry, and asked where Annie and you lived. And you got real embarrassed and you said, 'Oh, you're Mr. Silverzweig.' And you said Thursday was church night, and you were sorry about doing this to me on my first night among you, but church has to come before anything. So I could go back to your house and relax and you'd be home as soon as possible.

"And I asked Larry, I said, 'Would it be okay with you, Mr. Mack, if I come along to church with you?'"

Larry tells everyone, quietly, that Stan was the first white man ever to call him mister, adding, humorously, "But that didn't stop me from a-telling him off anyways, you know, about them bad clothes. I said, 'Oh, it would be fine if you want to come to church, but now you ain't thinking of coming dressed like that, is you?' And I said, 'Do you need some clothes?'"

Stan says, "And I said, 'No, not really, I brought a suit along. But can I go into your house to change and wash up?"

Johnnie Lou says, "Oh, Stan, honey, I got a question for you now. I really like to know how a man like you . . . ? I mean I knowed, well, in a way I knowed from the time we first met, you sort of did care about people like us, so now I want to ask you how you felt when you first seen Larry and Annie's shack?"

Stan minces no words in describing his reactions.

"Me, I have a sort of funny way of defending myself from things I can't bear. I just don't believe in it, if you know what I mean. It isn't there for me. It's just like I don't see it as it really is.

"And the truth is, the first place I walked into was not Larry's house, at least that one had Annie's warm touches and there was something homey about it, though I'll never know to this day how she managed that little miracle.

"But the first house I went to was the one next door to Larry's that the family and I had come to live in for a couple of days in order to try to feel out, if it was at all possible, just a little bit of what you've had to experience all your lives.

"And coming into that house, those two little boxes passing as rooms . . . And in spite of trying not to see the truth of the picture, I had, anyway, to think to myself, 'This is America?'

"And that's one thing that came to me, that, my God, I don't know anything about what it means to be poor, and I felt like, what was I doing here? Who was I to believe anything I could do would help people who had had to live this kind of a life? And a part of me wanted to just run away so I wouldn't have to live through any more of this. I mean, I thought to myself, I don't know if I can take what I'm seeing here."

It's quiet for a while after Stan's done talking, everyone sitting in a kind of distraction, when Larry says, "Stan can't stand the whole idea of being in the shack and say to me, he taken his pipe out of the dead center of his mouth where it at, and say to me, 'Oh, Mr. Mack, I got a important question to ask you, but just don't seem to have the words for saying it with.'

"But then he do find the words. 'Listen, man, your wife, she work awful hard to get this shack cleaned up even to what it is now, ain't that right?' 'Yeh, man, sure it is right.' He say, 'Now I gon' ask a question I want you to answer truthful. Your wife working so hard for my coming . . . Well, I brought my sleeping bag I use when I go on camping trips and like that. I got my sleeping bag right here,' he tell me. And I say, 'Oh, yeh?'

"Then Stan say real fast like, 'What I want to ask you, man, do you think Mrs. Mack's feelings be hurt, bad hurt if I was to sleep outside of the shack, on the porch, maybe, in my sleeping bag?'

"And he say something about liking to watch the stars, he don't get a chance to do that much in Jersey where he from, them kinds of lies he tell me, poor Stan.

"He say this and I seen tears in his eyes, and begun feeling real sorry for him so something in me wanted to let him off the hook. But, man, he ain't nothing but a stranger to me at the time, and my wife, she is my own wife. And I say:

" 'See, sir, my wife here she ain't no different from nobody else's wife. Sure, her feelings gon' be hurt if you won't sleep here after she work so hard to make that place right. Well, right as it is possible to get it.'

"So now Stan says, 'Oh, please, I am sorry. I shouldn't even have asked you, man.' And he brought the sleeping bag inside and laid it out on the floor.

"So then I look at his eyes and they so sad, you know, sometimes Stan's eyes get so dolgone sad. And I says, 'Listen, if you want to sleep out under the stars, I mean it won't make all that difference to my wife. So you just do what you do. Sleep under the stars.'

"So Stan say no, he ain't gon' sleep under the stars. And he say, 'I am ashamed to think of something else after your wife done as she did.' And then I see he was crying, got tears in his dolgone eyes."

Next our black staff speak. Their stories are, of course, infinitely more applicable than the white staff's as they tell their tales of the agony they lived through from childhood on. All of them, Mel and Lily especially, are in a position to touch the tragic realities of the inner and outer lives of the board members and aides here in a way that we as whites, no matter how well-meaning and sincere, no matter how determined, could ever hope to do.

They are in that position because they are black and because of the kind of people they are, their inherent dignity.

Now the warm and charming Mel gets up and, with a few words, brings before the people's eyes an apartment located in Harlem as terrible as any of the migrants' shacks, an overworked, overwhelmed mother, a father who'd died when Mel was an infant, and a passel of unhappy, hopeless kids.

Brings before the people's eyes a picture of himself as a young boy and teenager who not only felt unloved and unwanted at home and rejected as a delinquent at school, but also felt certain that there could be nothing lovable or even good about him.

"I may not have come up in the South but I did come up in Harlem . . . and, let me tell you, that can make you feel like a nigger, too."

Mel knows the pain and rage, hidden until quite recently out of profound fear, of being black and poor.

And Lily, with dead-level honesty and passion, tells of life in the mean streets of Elizabeth, New Jersey's black ghetto as child, young woman, mother, and, finally, grandmother.

Clamping it down about all of us, giving the scene, straight and honest, of how it was to be on welfare with your two children because, having no husband to help you, and no skill or education, it's the only way open to you.

Without being too harsh on the administrators and social workers, Lily tells . . . charity is a bitter pill for a proud person to swallow.

Only Lily's pride wasn't all that apparent—or existent—in those days. It had been brought out in her, as in Mel, slowly and in the pain and anguish of heavy probing and soul-searching.

The floodgates opened after Mel and Lily finished speaking, or, more accurately, sharing themselves. And emotion overswept the place, there were tears in the eyes, as the realization hit that these impressive, high-seeming consultants were not only *for* the people but also very much *of* them.

Johnnie Lou, in her game way, takes over when they are done.

"I ain't gon' say nothing right here and now at what Lily

and Mel say, how good they make me feel because knowing they's really my Sister and Brother. But, my friend Stan, I want to tell you this, that if you think that shack next to Annie and Larry be bad . . . Well, maybe you right, and no matter how hard y'all white peoples try you can't know how poor, migrant poor, or, as the white folk down here sometime say, 'nigger poor' can be. Like, well, all us peoples already tell y'all consultants about the chicken coops a whole lots of us agricultural workers lived in whilst migrating. But I never told the story of when I were a kid, me and my brother.

"Well, the first time me and the family start in migrating, I must be around seven and remember me and my family and maybe eight other families living in this here dormitory in Virginia where we was picking peaches, see? Nine families, fifty, sixty peoples live in that dormitory. And the noise, man. And the fights. And all the kids crying. And sleeping on beds of hay, no mattresses.

"And you'd be laying there with the hay sticking right through you. It would stick through you no matter what you would have over you—blankets or anything else. And you know you lay there and get up in the morning with your whole body aching.

"Plus the bed had the biggest damn bugs you ever seen in it. They would come out and crawl all over you.

"And me and my brother, the most of the mornings we was out in the peach groves helping the older ones. But this here one morning, I dunno, I was too sick to get out and so I was in bed all alone. And woke up about five in the morning, everybody was already out, and begun screaming about the damn, rotten bugs. Then, next thing I know, the bossman come and I can still remember him beating me in the face so bad yelling, 'Goddamn li'l nigger troublemaker.' "

I see Johnnie Lou's face loosen up at the seams and melt from strength to horror. The sinew of her face relaxes, her jaw grows slack, and grief spreads along her face.

But being Johnnie Lou and seeing our, particularly the consultants' and students', reactions, she catches hold of herself in a hurry and imitates all our lugubrious expressions in her brash, witty way to make everyone roar with laughter.

"Well, it's all forgot now, you know," she says.

Mother Bets says, "Lawd, Lawd, Johnnie Lou, you must not trust the people here like the consultants say we should when you say it's all forgot. Because you know and all of us do it ain't never gon' be forgot. It gon' be with you to hurt you till the day that you die. Me, I had white bossmen do me that-a-way many times more than oncet. And I ain't never gon' be able to forget. And if you tell the truth, Johnnie, you can't neither."

Johnnie's eyes harden and she shifts her weight from one foot to the other. "Yeh, Bets is right. I can't forget that and a whole lots of other things, worst ones, the white folks done us. Man, for a while there, I hate every white man because I can't go to school, and because I feel like a animal instead of a person."

"Yeh, me, too," says Lincoln.

"Me, too," says everyone else except young Mary, whose experience has, after all, been different from the others . . . and Emanuela.

By now all the students and several consultants have tears in their eyes. And the point is that the aides and board members take it upon themselves to come and comfort us. Mark Gulden, with Johnnie Lou's arms around him, is crying loudest of all. And the moment he gets his equilibrium back, he says, almost unbelievingly. "And to think it's Coca-Cola that's made all of this possible!" So, Mark Gulden, destroyer of systems, even Mark has done a turnaround, a complete one, at this session.

⤜§ Chapter 13

Warm, friendly, dedicated public health nurse Kaye Clarke was the first to be engaged for the worker health program, which would result, finally, in a federally funded health center employing two doctors, two nurses, two dentists, and an administrator with support services provided by clinic aides, dental assistants, technicians and clerical personnel. All except the doctors and nurses are community people who were trained for their jobs by the center staff and through specially arranged courses.

Kaye's job, which began very early in the program, soon after we came to Florida . . . more instantaneous evidence that the company would not renege on its pledges . . . was threefold: to engage a doctor and, along with him, screen all the agricultural workers and their families for sickness and disease: to be a people's advocate, often requiring both tact and toughness, and arrange hospitalization or doctors' appointments for those who would either not know how to go about getting them or likely be rejected if, by some chance, they did; and, finally, to train, from among the groves workers themselves, five outreach people and health aides whose complicated duties I, though generally a wishful thinker, could not envisage them carrying out.

She was also to offer comfort and reassurance, beyond what any outsider could, to those who lived in dread of doctors and hospitals. Or to those who believed, as many of Reverend Seaford's people did, that prayer and the laying on of hands had to be more efficacious than the best medical care. Or to those who believed in incantations of good and bad witches, which doctors and nurses could not hope to counteract. There were also some people, especially among the foremen and their families, who'd had long-term relationships with so-called doctors Kaye soon discovered to be quacks and charlatans of the worst order.

Kaye looked hard for people who had had some schooling and could read and write to be trained as nurses' aides; they had also to be, naturally, both extroverted and respected in the community for presentation to the board. It took a long time to ferret them out, but she and the board finally did.

There is Maudie Lewis, a churchwoman who, although not a Saint, is more or less trusted by many out of Reverend Seaford's and the other, smaller Holiness Churches. A large woman in her fifties with a handsome, expressive face, she laughs a lot and glows like a Christmas bulb when Kaye offers her the opportunity to be interviewed by the board after she herself has spent very significant and revealing time with her.

And Annie Breen, also in her fifties, whose mother and grandmother, now dead, are well remembered as witches with privileged, secret, esoteric, and exclusive knowledge of anything and everything: They were, however, always known as *good witches*. Annie, herself, has, for many years, found both their activities and the legends that have grown up about them in the community, comical. She looks at Kaye a long time after she offers her the opportunity to appear as a candidate before the board, and then asks, but in a good-natured, tolerant way (I've never, in the two years I knew her, heard her sound any way but good-natured and tolerant), "Now, I just want to know, do you want me for this job because of all them stories you heard about my mama and grandma, or does you want me for myself, because you think I am good enough to do the job?"

Kaye says, "I want you for yourself, definitely. And I imagine the board will also want you for yourself."

Annie sits erect in her seat appraising Kaye, looking at me, then giggling and saying, "But the stories gon' round about my mama and grandma having been such good witches while they lived don't hurt neither, does it?"

"No," Kaye says truthfully, "it doesn't."

Then there are the two young women who've managed to get through two years of high school, despite having migrated with their parents since babyhood, and helped them in the groves from the time they were able. Daisy Sikimley is a striking-looking woman in her mid twenties and has three young children who will, of course, be taken care of in the child development center. Jackie Piedmont, though not as attractive as Daisy, has a certain distinction about her, a kind of physical nobility of build and movement, especially outstanding in this place. "You know," she tells us in her quiet way, "Daisy and I . . . well, we been friends since we were kids, and some of our talks, especially since we got to high school and earlier, too . . . there was a teacher in New York State where my family'd always go at apple-picking time who told me, 'When you grow up, Jackie, you ought to be a nurse. I think there is something about you to make sick people more comfortable, something about your way.'

"Well, I didn't even know the meaning of the word nurse at the time. The teacher had to explain it to me. But once she did, it all stuck in my mind. And I told myself, 'You will be a nurse to help sick people when you grow up. No matter what I have to do to become that, it is what I will be.' "

Of course, she didn't breathe a word about the dream to her parents, knowing well that they, in their hopelessness and desperation, would never believe in such a possibility. Also, she'd lived through enough of her parents' daily defeats, indignation, tears, anger, "So, you know, I didn't want to give them another reason for feeling miserable in knowing I had a dream that couldn't ever happen. I knew they'd blame themselves for having no way to help me be what I so much wanted to be, and they had enough troubles, carried enough on their backs."

She laughs a little. "So the one I would talk to about the thing was Daisy. She's three years younger than me, and I couldn't always be sure she understood. But she'd listen, you know, and having someone who'd do that was better than not having anyone at all. We'd always meet back in Florida in the winter no matter where we were the rest of the year."

Daisy's smile is infectious. "Well, just as that teacher in New York got Jackie into thinking about nursing till she couldn't hardly think of anything else, Jackie did me the same way. I decided when I was pretty small that's what I would want to be, too."

Little by little, though, she continues, her dream faded. Agricultural work was tough, her family had sacrificed sufficiently to allow her to finish elementary school and those two years of high school, and couldn't be expected to do any more.

"Well, I had to carry my share of the work . . . how could I not? Especially since my father and mother were getting older and I wanted to take some of the burden off of them. I had to work a lot harder than I'd done before. And at night I'd just fall into bed, you know. There was no time for school, nor any time for dreaming either.

"Well, then I got married, and Bill, being a good worker, and us living with my family and pooling everything, it seemed then like I didn't have to work so hard again. I could go back to school at night, finish high school, go to nursing school.

"But then the babies came, and needed things. Well, three babies are going to be a big expense to an agricultural family. So I had to start working as hard as before all over again. Not only that, but the babies needed care, too. And one thing I had made up my mind about, My children weren't going to be left in the groves all day while the family worked. And, you know, we never even dreamed there'd be a program, with us being able to stay in the one place all year round. And a child development center for the kids.

"I had to leave mine with a granny lady and I didn't really trust her. Besides, she cost money, too. So I worked harder all of the time, and got more tired."

Daisy rises from her chair, stretches, sits down again, and, with eyes on the floor, tells us that she hopes we won't misunderstand what she's going to say, hopes we won't consider her an unnatural mother, but . . . "I got to where I was blaming the kids because my dream of ever being able to become a nurse was all over, there just wasn't any sense to it anymore."

And now, she says, with Kaye's coming . . . "It's a miracle because, really, as I see it, the next thing to being a nurse is to be an aide. And maybe . . ."

Jackie says, "With me, well, sure, it was just about the same with me as Daisy. The older I got, the less possible my dream seemed to be till it just made me miserable, and I said to myself, 'Better give it up. You are what your family always was before you and make up your mind, if you have kids, they'll be the same after you.'"

And at the moment when she finally acknowledged to herself the lifetime dream would never happen, when the truth of her future as well as present was driven like a nail into her soul, she knew the rest of life would be a routine thing to be got through the best she could.

She cries when she tells us this, and, we almost cry along with her. Kaye says, "You won't be as tired at the end of the day as when you work in the groves or doing other picking. You'll be able to do your high school equivalency easily enough at night. And with the scholarships the program is arranging, there's nothing to stop you from going to nursing school. The board will find a way of taking care of the obligations that might prevent you from taking advantage of the scholarships. Take it from me, both of you'll be nurses yet."

The two women are convinced by Kaye and dazzled at the new-old prospect. Their dream is back and shining in their eyes.

The fifth aide, Merilita Sanchez, Jesús' wife and mother of six, cannot read or write English or Spanish, but neither Kaye nor any member of the board doubts her ability to make not just an adequate but a rather excellent aide. She is, along with her husband, one of the warmest, most genuinely friendly people I have ever met, and her face reveals the intelligence, the alertness that surprises and delights everyone who knows her.

The only problem that might have stood in the way of her getting the aide's job would have been Jesús' employment as one. But he has, much to his, the company's, and our regret, been conscience-driven to give up his aide's job some weeks ago. The point is the new salary scale . . . Jesús, as a farmhand at $5.50 an hour, can earn far more than he could as an aide, and for the sake of his children, one of whom is now ready for college, must regretfully give up his aide job. Somebody, probably Mr. Ocea, the president, not Kaye, was the one to suggest that Merilita make application for one of the open health aide opportunities. "That way we will still have a Sanchez as an aide."

"But I can't neither read nor write, so what good could I be?" Merilita asks with her elementary honesty that does not understand guile or pretense. And adds, softening into her magnificently warm smile, "I sure enjoy doing things for people, though."

"That is just it, honey," Johnnie Lou told her "Me, I think you could be the greatest. Right, Kaye?"

Kaye nodded hard to Johnnie Lou's and the board members' pep rally for Merilita. And finally Merilita said, "Well, if y'all think . . . One thing I promise you, board members, Kaye, I do the best I can." She turns to Kaye and says, "You got to promise me that the first time you see I can't do the job, well, you will say, 'Sorry, Merilita, but the job has got to come before anybody's feelings. We can't keep you no more.' "

Kaye says solemnly, "I promise, Merilita."

And there's Johnnie Lou. She's kept very busy by her job as a general organizing aide, spending all her days talking up the program among the people in the groves. But she does have some free nights, and since much of the screening program takes place at night, she volunteers her services to Kaye.

"See, Kaye, like, you know I always wanted to be a nurse myself. It were my dream just like Daisy's and Jackie's. Only I got less reason for thinking it could maybe come true. Well, I ain't even been to high school, and you know how little I been to school at all. But now, see, I like to do whatever I can with you."

Kaye tells her and the board and consultants, too, that she really should spend her nights being tutored to embark on the high school equivalency program.

Johnnie agrees basically, then says, "How about me spending three nights a week and all the weekend at times when there ain't no corporation meetings working at my reading, writing, and everything else I need to and the other two nights helping out y'all? How about that?"

"Well . . ." Kaye says. "Let's try it out, see if you can manage the long hours."

For a month or more Kaye holds daily full-day classes for her aides. Sometimes, too, she has guest lecturers for them, public health teacher-nurses from surrounding colleges, who, far from being unfriendly to us and the project, are moved by it and the aides' total devotion and, therefore, more than anxious to make their own contribution. There aren't many of these, true, but the few there are care very much.

As for the aides, they're thrilled and excited with every aspect of the program. How they work! And they learn far better than we have rhyme, reason, or right to expect they will.

There are, however, problems, of course. Maudie Lewis,

though not as fanatic as Reverend Seaford's people, still has this gnawing feeling that prayer and the laying on of hands may, after all, be more efficacious for many sick people than doctors. She believes in the ALPI program implicitly, she says time and again. But, well, she wants to be perfectly honest, wants Kaye and the others of us to know the pain of operating in two worlds is something she—and her teachers—must reckon with.

As for Annie, well, let's face it, she tells us . . . although she herself is far from believing in her mother's and grandmother's witchcraft, the fact is she saw them with her own eyes affect some miraculous cures.

But doubtless the worst and most universal problem Kaye's got to face is that agricultural workers, who live in such close quarters that any degree of privacy is hard, if not impossible, to come by, learn from babyhood on "to mind our own business, if y'all know what we mean."

A stunned embarrassment grips them at the thought of going into people's homes and engaging them in the personal aspects of the health interview that Kaye's worked out and explained to them must be followed to the letter. How does she expect Maudie, Annie, Merilita, and even such sophisticates as Daisy, Jackie, and Johnnie ever to be able to ask people such questions as those concerning their and their family's food habits and eating patterns? They act as if Kaye is forcing them to break some unwritten law by asking them to pry into areas where neither she nor they have any business.

And when Kaye talks about the critical assessments and objective reports they'll have to make about people's home conditions—the cleanliness or lack of it, for instance—they tell her, some shamefacedly and others in no uncertain terms, they've no desire to expose the private lives of other people.

"Well, to me that is *nosy*, Kaye," Annie tells her. "I think it be very nosy to go into a lady's house to see if it is clean or dirty. It is none of my business, no, not the way I see it. It is plain nosy. I wouldn't like it if some other agricultural worker like me was to come into my house and make a report about is it clean or not."

At times like this Kaye admits to me her job may be a bit more titanic than she'd anticipated when she took it. Her discouragement rarely lasts overly long, though, because the truth is, and nobody knows it better, that, conflicted or not, the aides will doubtless "come through," as both she and they put it.

"I hate every minute of asking these questions you making me, Kaye," Annie says after she's made her accusations, "but, sure I be . . . am willing to try since you say it is for the good of the ALPI and my own people." Kaye, once she's got her aides in her corner, manages to engage a dedicated, devoted young doctor who's bound to be of help in inspiring them even further toward the program. Dr. Epstein is new to the area and as interested in the success of the program as are any of us.

A majority of people Kaye, Dr. Epstein, and the aides contact for screening understand its purpose and also know they can get medical help and hospitalization (a situation formerly undreamed of by migrants and agricultural workers) through their new coverage by the company's insurance plan.

But some—out of the groups we've discussed earlier and others we didn't know existed, although doubtless we should have—couldn't understand the program and wanted nothing to do with it in the first place. They'd become habituated to their ills, learned stoically to live with them . . . *preferred* living with them over examination by Kaye's medical crew and, certainly, by doctors and nurses they don't know and therefore mistrust a lot more than they do Kaye and Dr. Epstein.

I'll always remember, for instance, a three-generation white family named Graves who, in order to get away from "the damn niggers," squatted, isolated, in makeshift shacks they'd put up themselves in the woods and far away from the people's regular quarters. A couple of pigs rooted behind the shacks and a pack of huge, foaming hunting dogs emerged from under and around the shacks to challenge our exit from the well-equipped Winnebago, which served, at the time, as Kaye and Dr. Epstein's traveling medical office. We merely sat in the Winnebago as the pack closed around it jumping and snapping.

Then we saw a fear-inspiring, heavy, far-bigger-than-life man, probably in his forties, barefoot and wearing nothing but a pair of much torn underpants, emerge from one of the shacks. In a voluminous voice, powerful and incredibly loud, he bellowed over the dogs' barking: "Whatcha want here? Whut y'all doing here?"

Still in the Winnebago, Kaye explains the purpose of our program, and says, "Please, would you call off your dogs so we can come out and talk to you?"

He appraises us all closely, scrutinizing every feature on all our faces, and stops, finally, at Daisy, who's the aide of that day.

He doesn't call the dogs off, and stays silent while Kaye continues with her explanations. He studies Daisy intently as Kaye talks. His stare at her is penetrating, and a slight smile plays on his lips. He does not seem to be listening to a word Kaye's saying.

Finally he speaks. "Well, I will let you talk to Gramps, see whut he say."

"About what?" Kaye asks.

"About calling off the dogs and letting y'all out of that car."

"Gramps, Gramps," he calls. And a man in his seventies, or perhaps older, comes out of the largest shack. He's got a strong, wrinkled, beautiful face with warm, powerful eyes that set us at ease . . . for a minute. But he's followed out by about a dozen or so men, women, and children, some seeming as antagonistic toward us as the heavy we'd first met.

Besides, Gramps's mien and manner of talking to us is obviously not calculated to set us at ease. "Whut the hell y'all want here?" he asks. "Who in the world has sent for you?"

Kaye repeats our purpose to him as the dogs continue barking around the Winnebago and everyone stares at us as though we are from Mars.

"Well, whut you bring that nigger gal around for?"

Kaye explains Daisy's function.

"Ain't no nigger gal coming out around my and my family's place."

Kaye exchanges a look with Daisy, who says, "It seem to me this is no time for fighting the white-black battle. Let's take advantage of what he's willing to give at this moment. It may not last too long after all. You all go on out, Kaye, and help whoever you can."

It turns out, after Kaye has decided to take Gramps Graves at his word where Daisy's concerned, her skin color is hardly his one anxiety. When he sees us, and Kaye as our spokesperson, actually coming out, he says loudly, "Oh, damn, can't you see I don't want *none* of yous on my land?"

I say to Kaye, "I don't see there's much to do here, do you? And time's going fast. And so many people need this team."

"Yeh," Kaye says, "I know what you mean. I guess we'd better get going to where we'll likely be more welcome."

At just this moment Dr. Epstein, who's been exceptionally silent throughout, looks out at one of the teenagers surrounding us, a tall lanky, long-fingered boy, and whispers, "No matter what, we can't leave this place until I've had a look at that kid with the long fingers . . . until I've heard his heart sound. I'll bet my bottom dollar just from seeing him from here he's got a serious heart disease."

Kaye begins talking to Gramps again, pleading with him to at least let the boy be examined. Then Dr. Epstein joins in, and after a whole hour or more of their talk, Gramps Graves, still glowering, says, "Well, the rest of y'all can come out, but not the nigger."

The snarling pack of dogs has not, however, left us yet, and Gramps delegates somebody to bring him a big stick. Then, wading through the dogs with stick a-flying, he clears a path for us. "Remember, though, the nigger stays in the car."

Daisy's dignity, under the circumstance, is remarkable. She smiles at us and kind of bunches up in her seat, makes herself as inconspicuous as possible.

Dr. Epstein's extraordinary, too. Instead of immediately examining the boy who's caught his attention he makes a game of the whole business, showing his medical instruments and especially the stethoscope to Gramps, who's intrigued. "This is used for examining people's hearts," he says and stays silent till Gramps himself asks him to examine his heart. He says, when he's done, "My, but you got a strong heart, sir. Here, listen to the sound of it yourself."

Gramps does. "Yup. My heart sure sound strong to me, too."

"Now, would you like us to listen to your whole family's hearts?"

"Okay," Gramps says, and directs Dr. Epstein in the formalities the examinations must take. First off, he is to listen to the heart of the frightening heavy who first greeted us.

"His heart's almost as strong as yours, sir," Dr. Epstein says. "Here, listen for yourself."

Gramps does.

Finally, Dr. Epstein—and Gramps Graves—examines everyone's heart and comes to the boy who'd caught Epstein's interest in the first place.

"Sir," Dr. Epstein asks, "may we talk privately with you for a minute?"

Gramps says yes, and Dr. Epstein asks, as though consulting a highly respected colleague, "Mr. Graves, did you hear any difference between the heartbeat of that last grandson and the other members of the family?"

"No," Gramps says, with a certain perceptible degree of finality.

"Then would you listen again for me, please?"

"Why I need to do that?"

"Because I myself heard a difference," Epstein says, "and it's important enough so I wonder if you would hear it, too."

"I told y'all in the first place I didn't hear no difference."

He agrees to listen to the boy's heart again, however, and says afterward, "Yeh, could be there be a small difference between him and all our other hearts."

"If you listen again," Epstein says, "you may find it's a lot different."

Gramps does and says, finally, "Yup, it is a lots different."

Dr. Epstein takes the better part of two hours to convince the old man that he should let us take the boy to a cardiologist. By winning Gramps's cooperation so far, he also persuades him to enter the Winnebago and allow the rest of the family to come for the complete examination, Daisy's presence notwithstanding.

It's been a triumph all right, although it's taken most of our day. Well, mine was certainly not wasted. I'd never conceived of such a patient, *personal* practice of medicine.

I remember, with lucid distinctiveness, another time I went with Kaye, Dr. Epstein, and Annie, the day's aide at that time, to the home of a family named Billings, so dirty, so smelly that I felt sick inside and could hardly keep from throwing up. The man, Thomas, lying on a floor mattress in a drunken stupor when we got there, was tall and pitifully skinny.

The woman, Arethera, was also skinny, unanimated, dull-eyed, and seemingly retarded. She held a baby in her arms, a replica of herself. From the baby's general appearance I would have judged him to be less than a year old, but Arethera told us he was "going on to three."

Arethera, upon examination, was revealed to have a cardiac condition, and when Kaye took her to the cardiologist he informed us another pregnancy might kill her.

I sit with Annie while she takes the family's medical history from Arethera. It's my second time in the shack and I've grown more or less accustomed to the dirt and smell. At least I don't feel every moment as though my stomach's turning over. At first Arethera seems hopeless when it comes to answering any of the questions Annie puts to her. She smiles once in a great while to give us some faith she's not completely oblivious to us and our purpose. And that's that.

We leave after an hour or so and tell her we'll come back tomorrow. This second day seems to prove my hypothesis founded on the first day with Arethera. A huge, almost unbridgeable communication gap exists not only between Arethera and me, which may be natural enough under the circumstances, but also between Annie and her.

"Do you ever give your baby milk?" Annie asks.

Arethera whispers, "He ain't a true husbin'. We's common law, be all." Then, turning to me. "He beat me last weekend and the one before. He git drunk every weekend and beat me up bad." Then she says something neither Annie nor I can understand and lapses into a long silence.

Suddenly she laughs wildly. "I were once a purty gal, real, real purty. I had some flesh on these sticking-out, homely bones, and I really once were a purty gal." There is an unexpected touch of animation in Arethera's face as she talks about her former appearance, and Annie and I note it and decide she may not be beyond the medical program's help after all.

After a long silence Arethera asks, "You know how come we all be so terrible skinny here?"

Annie says, "Please tell us, Arethera."

Arethera says, "See, that man Thomas, all he allow me for to buy food for the family is five dollar a week. A week! Well, who could get decent food on that kind of money? And, sometime, I go out picking myself, not in the Coke groves, 'cause they has got all the pickers they need, but in one or other grove. And make a li'l penny. Well, Thomas takes whatever I am able to make away from me. It still be five dollar a week for feeding us all. No matter if I work or don't."

Now that we are, finally, communicating with Arethera, Annie suggests she may want to enroll her baby in the child development center. She starts explaining the difference to Arethera between child care and child development, but soon realizes she's not reaching her with any of this message, and so begins talking instead about the good nutritional breakfast, lunch, and snacks her baby will receive at the center. "The baby will come nice and fat there and won't be too long till he get to look his age, you know."

Arethera asks incredulously, "They gon' take care my baby in that center and feed him like I can't do myself?"

Annie answers positively.

"Man, that is so fine," says Arethera. But adds, after all, "Naah, I can't let him go to no center." She slumps into her seat after she says this, hides her face in her hands and doesn't say another word.

Finally when Annie and I get up to go and tell her goodbye, Arethera says, encouragingly, "I like y'all coming and maybe I let my baby go to that place after all. Where they gon' give him good food." Then stands up suddenly and grabs Annie's hands and mine in her own skeletal one, saying, "See, he be the only company I got since I ain't purty no more. That is the reason I want to keep him home."

Annie reports our findings at a meeting Kaye holds with her aides, and it gives Kaye an opportunity to launch yet again her attack on the aides' concept of "nosiness," to explain for the tenth, the hundredth time the difference between neighborly "nosiness" and professional concern. It makes an impression this time, and Jackie says, "You know, Kaye, the thing that strikes me most . . . well, I happen to know Arethera and Thomas, they don't live too far from us. And I was thinking, just hearing about her telling Sara and Annie how she used to be pretty, well, I'm thinking if we could get her to the beauty parlor once in a while, get her a few decent clothes, she might start taking some pride in herself, keeping her and the baby clean, and maybe even sending him to the child development center. Also, if she gets back the pride she must once have had in her appearance, if we can find a way to give it to her, it may even spill over into the way she will keep her house. She might clean it up some." She stops talking, then asks Kaye, "Well, as a part of the health program, is it our business to do something like this, get her to the beauty parlor and so on?"

"What do you think, Daisy?" Kaye asks.

"I think, yeah," Daisy says.

Everyone agrees there are other priorities, though. Arethera must be given more money for buying food and also be taught the rudiments of decent nutrition. And there's no question in any of our minds but that the enlistment of Arethera's baby in the child development center is the most immediately pressing aspect of the aides' work with her "once she got some pride, self-pride. Then she gon' take it in her baby, too."

It's a revelation, one of the year's wonders, to realize how far and fast these aides have come, not only in realizing they've reason to be proud of themselves, but also, as important, that they can take pride in their new skill at imparting self-confidence to people such as Arethera.

Maudie says, "Talking about us helping Arethera, the business of giving her belief in herself through getting her looking good, I got something to say about it, but am afraid somebody's feelings in this room be hurt if I do."

Annie says, "Remember what Lily Haskins and all the consultants always tell us. The project is most important and we can tell each other anything so long as it be for the good of people and not just because we want to be mean to one another."

"Well, this I has to say concern you, Annie," Maudie says. "And I think it is for the people's good; well, Arethera's anyhow."

"Speak it out then, baby."

"Okay, if Arethera suppose to get self-pride by her getting a couple nice clothes and going to the beauty parlor, well, seem to me then, neither me nor you, Annie, can be the ones to help her that-a-way as much as say, Jackie or Daisy could do."

"No." Annie shrinks back in mock horror. "Girl, Maudie, is you trying to tell me . . . ?" She laughs loudly and says, "Listen, honey, if you hadn't've said it first, I would've said the same thing myself. I mean, it follow, don't it? Daisy and Jackie being so smart about clothes and staying pretty..."

So Daisy takes Arethera's case over from Annie and goes almost immediately to confer with Arethera's mother-in-law, a warm, smart, courageous lady who turns out not only to disapprove of but also to be enraged by her son's treatment of Arethera and, especially, the baby. When Daisy describes the child development center to her, she agrees the baby must be enrolled there, the sooner, the better. She says, "How much it cost a week? Five dollar? Well, me and the little one's grampa be glad to pay that much." She also volunteers to contribute money for some new clothes and a monthly visit to the beauty shop for Arethera.

Before Daisy and I went with Arethera on her shopping trip, we brought several Sears, Roebuck catalogues for her to peruse. She flipped through them looking at all the pictures of dresses, pants suits, and especially hot pants.

"I be too skinny to wear some pants like them, hunh?" she asks. "Baby, my legs look like pipestems, don't they?"

"Oh, you can gain weight easy," Daisy says sagaciously, "so long as you listen to Kaye, stay on her diet."

"Yeh, well, how I do that?"

Daisy discusses with Arethera the diet Kaye wants her and the baby on and gives her extra money the board's allocated to "put you on your feet till you become strong enough to go to work yourself." Then firmly, forcefully, she says, "I'd like to shop for the right kind of food for you and the baby. I'd like to go with you to shop, if that'll be okay."

Arethera nods her head affirmatively. "I guess it be."

That day Daisy worked with Arethera to clean her house up, too.

The beauty shop and new clothes and Daisy's presence seemed to work for Arethera. Not only did she and the baby gain weight and health, but she's been enabled to go to work and earn money for her and the child's support. She's even begun keeping her house clean. It's become almost a pleasure to visit with her. Besides, Daisy's brought her to community and open board meetings. These also helped open new vistas and possibilities to Arethera.

A couple of months after Daisy'd had all her successes with Arethera, however, she came to work in a near panic. Arethera's husband, full of bombast and fustian, had gone to

Daisy's home and threatened her and her husband "for putting all these here crazy ideas in my wife's head."

He was sweating badly, Daisy said, and his eyes were wide and frozen by contrast to the constantly moving lips. "And he had a gun in his hand, not only that, he was aiming it at my head. So my husband put his foot down. Much as I hate giving up on Arethera now, well, my husband's not giving me any choice. So . . ."

Johnnie Lou, who's also present, asks Kaye and Daisy if it would be all right for her to take over with Arethera where Daisy's left off.

"It'd be a shame if, after the poor gal have come as far as you, Daisy, have help bring her . . . I just can't see giving up on her now. And, see, *my husband* don't know nothing about her husband nor no gun."

Daisy and Kaye, of course, shout hosanna to this suggestion of Johnnie's. And Arethera loves the idea of working with Johnnie, the prime liberated lady in these parts.

"Who need that damn man anymore that all he do is beat me and my baby?" Arethera's come to ask of Johnnie, and Johnnie of us, over and over again.

But Arethera's drama, directed for so many months—and so well by Daisy and Johnnie—has, after all, a sad ending. Arethera not only leaves her husband but also her home and the project. And without a word to Kaye, Daisy, Johnnie, or any of us.

Daisy and Johnnie Lou go through a period of intense emotional sorrow over what they consider to be their own failure as well as the fate they predict for Arethera and especially the baby, who'd begun doing so well in the child development center.

Johnnie's voice as she discusses Arethera's going is plaintive, profoundly sad. Her "report," as she terms it, is almost a cry, a lament from one who has herself recently realized hope in her life.

"Well, see all of the time I been with Arethera, and seen all the changes in her and especial her having this new hope life can be good after all the bad she has been through, I wonder where her hope for her and the baby was at on the day she run off and left this place."

Fortunately for the mood of Daisy and Johnnie and the

other health aides, the program, from its inception, has had many more triumphs than failures.

There is, for instance, the case of a Chicano woman—Mrs. Perez, in her early fifties or possibly younger, grossly overweight and a diabetic—who was in the midst of a stroke when Kaye, Dr. Epstein, Merilita, and I arrived at her home. She was lying in bed after having managed, somehow, to accomplish all her home tasks. The house was clean, neat, and filled with warm, good Chicano food and coffee smells.

Kaye takes Mrs. Perez's blood pressure and hardly needs to describe it, as she does, as being "way out of bounds." And Dr. Epstein, feeling her all over, says, "She has no reflexes on her right side, and there's no question but that we've got to get her to the hospital immediately."

Mrs. Perez understands little English but she intuits what Kaye and Dr. Epstein are saying, and with tears running down her face, tells Merilita in Spanish, and with all of the will and spirit possible under the circumstances of her stroke, that she won't leave her house no matter what Kaye and Dr. Epstein order. Her husband and children, even though they are grown, need her at home.

But why do they need her? Merilita asks. And she answers there's no one else to cook for and serve them. All the children are men, after all.

"I'll come and cook for them and serve them while you're getting better," Merilita says in her gentle way.

Mrs. Perez hesitates, then says, "You have your own family to care for, how can you also care for mine?"

She flashes Merilita a look of frustration as though wanting to tell her and all of us to keep our noses out of her life.

"Merilita," Kaye says, "you've got to tell Mrs. Perez . . . I know this will be hard for you but you've got to tell her she'll die if she doesn't get the medical care she needs. And then her husband and sons will have to do without her forever, instead of the couple of days it will be if she lets us take her to the hospital now."

Merilita stares, horror-stricken, at Kaye. "I'm sorry, but I can't tell her that."

Kaye pats her on the shoulder.

"Come, on, Merilita, it's the only way. I know how it makes you feel, but you have to do it."

There's a moment of hesitation, then Merilita, kneeling by

the bed and keeping a loving hand on Mrs. Perez's face, tells her.

Mrs. Perez keeps looking oddly at Merilita all the time she's talking, as though she's the one to blame for her condition. She doesn't answer for quite a while, but when she does it's at some length.

Merilita tells us: "She says she will go to the hospital then, but wonders how she, a Chicano, could get in. And more than that, who will pay the bill? I told her about the company medical insurance and she said okay, we can go then."

Mrs. Perez is back cleaning and cooking for her husband and sons—she's somewhat devastated to find out they were able to get on without her—in less than a week. And Kaye's got her on a diet Merilita's supervising.

She tells us cautiously: "I can't promise, but I do think Mrs. Perez will keep to her diet."

Then there's a fifteen-year-old boy, Lawrence Jones, an invalid all his life, who stares at Kaye, Dr. Epstein, Maudie, the day's aide, and me with the kind of blank look that shows he doesn't expect anything from you and has nothing to offer in the way of trust, sympathy, or rancor. The whole face has a look of brooding, tense sullenness. All the same, Maudie is able to find out, pull out in her interview with him and his mother that he has a long history of nosebleeds. Dr. Epstein refers him to an ear, nose, and throat specialist. He's hospitalized and operated on for removal of a nonmalignant nose tumor.

I saw him soon afterward and couldn't believe the change in him. He teased and bantered lightly with me, all the sullenness was gone from his face and manner as he told me he's "healthy as a horse now and on the high school football team."

Then there is James Ralston, a foreman, a strong-looking, very tall man who came through the company medical program, although he had his own doctor. "See, my voice has been changing on me and I have told my doctor that two times. But he said there wasn't nothing wrong, for me to just forget about the thing. But . . ." He lowers his eyes and tightens his lips into a thin line. He's ashamed to admit he's plagued by the symptoms, and finds himself worrying despite the doctor's order not to.

Dr. Epstein doesn't enlighten James Ralston on the matter.

What would be the use? But he does tell Kaye and me with bitterness and commendable salt on his tongue that James's doctor is one of the most immoral, incompetent quacks around and preys primarily on the black people who, like James, can afford to pay his fee.

He refers James to the same ear, nose, and throat man who saw young Lawrence. As with Lawrence, surgery's the answer; there's a tumor on James Ralton's vocal chord that happily is not malignant but might well have turned so in a couple of years.

Now, more than ever, the need for a clinic, a health center, is apparent. Dr. Epstein, Kaye, and Arnold (who will need, eventually, to secure funds for the clinic and organize it and, therefore, often goes around with the medical team) have seen that the company workers (as well as other migrants and the permanently stationed rural poor) are suffering from a host of ills, serious ones, like high blood pressure and heart conditions that, untreated, can result in death any moment. Also, there are many people who have been operated on and never sought out or received postoperative care.

As far as dental care, 99 pecent of the people Kaye, Arnold, and Dr. Epstein saw had never gone to a dentist, and their teeth, even the children's, were rotted. Arnold always came back to our motel room, after going along on medical rounds, frenzied and overwrought at what he had seen. And I recall him saying once:

"You won't believe this, but I have seen exactly one person, one person, whose teeth weren't absolutely rotted. It is a small baby who is just beginning to get teeth."

Most of the doctors and dentists, out of their own biases or sensitivity to those of their patients they know to be prejudiced, had no relish for treating poor people, especially black or Chicano migrants, and made the fact amply clear. Of course, there were a few principled doctors and dentists who would have been happy to take care of people who needed their services so desperately. But even these could hardly be expected to seek out sick people, as a poor people's clinic with outreach, an important service, would do.

And the people could not have known who the empathetic doctors were. Even if they had known, they were too beaten and hopeless, too filled with the true stories Granny May Lolly and others like her had told them of the attitudes of doctors and dentists toward the likes of them to believe there might be any caring ones. As they saw it, to be sick, and remain untreated, was their unchangeable fate.

As for public facilities for poor people, these were so lacking that the whole business seemed to me, when Arnold or Kaye would describe them, to be stories out of *Catch-22*. In one county, for example, Arnold, Kaye and two aides spent a whole hot summer's day trying to find the county clinic office where children who'd be going to school the following fall could, hopefully, be immunized. They walked through the entire town, all looking for a clinic sign. There wasn't one. Arnold stopped several people on the street and asked if they could tell him where the county clinic was. They looked at him in amazement. Most didn't know there *was* a county clinic. The ones who did know had no idea of its address.

Out of desperation, Arnold said to Kaye, "Let's ask the druggist. He should know if anyone does."

But the druggist didn't know either.

They then went to the United States Department of Agriculture and asked the agent there if he knew the address of the county health clinic.

He smiled. "What's the matter? Can't you find it?"

Arnold had a hard time holding on to his temper. "Look, sir, we've explored the town from beginning to end [actually, the entire town was three blocks long and one wide] and we've asked numerous people for direction. We've also asked your druggist, who couldn't help us either."

"Listen," the agent said, "I'm sorry to have been facetious with you. But I'm cynical, because . . . Well, when you get there you'll see for yourself. Now, what you do, is walk down the street you're on. You'll see a Western Auto store and a dress shop. The county clinic's located between them. It's got a glass door. Go in that door and walk up a flight of stairs. That'll be it."

"Well, we saw that place you're talking about," Arnold said. "We saw the auto store, the dress shop, and the glass-doored building. But there was not *one* sign to indicate that this was the county clinic. How in the hell can people be expected . . . ? I mean, you don't really think the people who have to use the clinic would have the aggressiveness we had to steel ourselves to in order to find it? I don't think that, in my whole life, I've heard anything so stupid, so *insane*."

The agent smiled again. "I told you we here were cynical. Well, now you realize a part of the reason why."

When Arnold, Kaye, and the aides finally made it to the clinic at a little before five, they found no patients, naturally, and the chief nurse and her assistant getting ready to leave. They discussed the problem of the children needing immunization, and when they concluded, Arnold said, "By the way, we had a terribly hard time finding your office. It took us the whole day. Very few people, including the town druggist, knew where it was either."

The two nurses exchanged glances, and neither one said anything in answer to Arnold's statement.

"Tell me," Arnold asked, "why is it you don't have a sign on your door?"

Silence.

"*Why* don't you have a sign on your door?"

In a gentle, almost saccharine tone, the chief nurse, young, stout, dark, and very self-assured under the circumstances, said, "It's a matter of practicality."

"Hunh? What do you mean, a matter of practicality?"

"Well, you see," the nurse, still calm, still contained, explained, "if we did have a sign, did announce ourselves, many people would come for services we just are not equipped to give."

Arnold responded to this by saying, "I don't understand what you're doing here then. If you can't serve the people who need you . . ."

The nurse said, "As I see it, the ones who really need us will find us." And added, as though it were a justification, "Three years ago we did have a sign, but it was removed when our building was painted."

"And you never bothered to put up another one?"

"No, sir," she said, still contained, still calm and self-righteous.

(When Arnold told me this story he said his stomach crawled throughout the entire interview; it felt ulcerous and dangerously acidic.)

On the other hand, the other county health centers Kaye and I visited, except for Polk County, didn't seem of much more help to the people, even though they did have signs on their doors. They were concerned primarily with public health having to do with examining water supply and garbage collection and such. Also immunization for babies, and disease prevention. Some did provide insulin for diabetics, and drugs for tuberculars and people with VD. But if a person had a heart condition, say, or a kidney ailment, or any illness of such a type, he would be expected to go to a county hospital. Honey Jean's experience at a county hospital being, unfortunately, far from atypical, and well-known to migrants and rural poor alike, absolutely discouraged them from seeking help there.

After Arnold and Kaye's survey of health needs in the area had been completed, Arnold, accompanied by Johnnie Lou, visited with people out of the Migrant Health Service in Washington and, with indignation, clarified the whole desperate situation to them. Immediately grasping the need for a clinic such as Arnold visualized, they referred him and Johnnie to their regional office in Atlanta. There they met Dr. Howard Yaeger, Dr. Tom Pheasant, and administrator Ed Rogge.

"Man, we were sure lucky to get to know them three fellows," Johnnie Lou says. "From minute one that Arnold begun explaining what was with us, they, all three of them, seen the true picture of how us people have all these here needs if we are to stay healthy. The whole talk, from the beginning, was like heart to heart. The first thing they say after Arnold were done talking, and they have asked a whole lots of questions and me and Arnold answered them . . . The first thing they say were, 'Look, Johnnie, Arnie, how soon you think we can get on out there to your place, see what give, and, above all, talk to the people?' I mean, they wasn't nothing like you maybe expect of men in their position with all of that money to help you out with. Nothing standoffish about them. Really, they can't hardly wait to get they hands into the thing of helping us get the clinic that, by now, just from what Arnie and me tells them, they got the same feel for us needing it as we do ourselves."

The first to come to visit after Arnold and Johnnie's contact in Atlanta was Dr. Howard Yaeger. He was young, enthusiastic, extroverted, and entirely in the people's corner. It was he who arranged to bring some of our staff to a meeting between the people and their county health officer and his chief nurse, in an almost completely Chicano and Mexican area.

"I happen to be fairly well acquainted with both the health officer and the nurse, and they are . . . well, callous is a mild word for them. They've absolutely no compassion for the people they're here to serve. And, God, even if they did have, I don't believe they'd know how, these people's needs being what they are." He hesitates. "I just thought I'd warn you so you wouldn't be too shocked at what I'll guarantee you're going to experience there."

Arnold smiles at Howard cynically. He says, describing his conversation with the nurses, "Damn, Howard, I think I turned shockproof after that."

"You want to bet, Arnie?"

When we arrive at the school where the meeting is to be held, perhaps half an hour late because we'd had to attend another meeting, we see fifty or sixty migrants and rural poor, dressed in what must surely have been their Sunday best, standing quietly in the parking lot.

"Howard," I say, "I thought this meeting was to have begun half an hour ago."

"Yeh, well, you can see the school doors are still locked tight. The school authorities aren't any more concerned with poor people than the medical authorities are."

Arnold nods. "You know, Howard, I recently conducted a survey of several agencies in addition to the medical ones, and God knows you're right. I visited school superintendents, child care people, and so on. What I found made me very angry. Take the child care aspects. I was given glowing reports of day-care services for migrants. Come to find out, though, this supposedly fine program, federally funded, incidentally, was taking care of the kids from eight A.M. to three in the afternoon. Such a farce in view of the parents' working hours."

"Sure, sure," Howard says.

Arnold says, "And the inadequate amount of money available for all services for agricultural workers, not just the ones without permanence, even the ones with. You can't believe how damn low welfare payments are around here. And if that's not enough, there are all kinds of barriers placed in the way of people in the most extreme need from getting on to the rolls."

Another half hour has gone by while we've talked, and the

school doors are still shut tight. I'm growing terribly restive and angry; so is everyone in our group. You can easily see our feelings on our faces. But the people are resigned; there's not a trace of dissatisfaction on any of their faces, and some are smiling good-humoredly.

I approach a small man whose eyes remind me of Jesús', and say, "Can you tell me, sir, how long ago was this meeting planned?"

"Maybe six, seven weeks ago, ma'am."

"You arranged for a room then, right?"

"Yes'm."

"Well, how come nobody's here to let you in?"

He shrugs his shoulders. "They is often late to let us in."

"Doesn't it make you mad?"

Gently, he says, "That wouldn't do no good, because if they was to think that, you know, we will be mad, then next time we need a room chances are they would turn us away. See what I mean?" He smiles at me again.

"How did you come to arrange this meeting?" I ask.

"Oh, we didn't do it ourselfs. I mean, how could we? Because I think they would turn us away if we try." He points to a priest, wholesome, red-faced, very German-looking (we learn later he speaks only German), and three elderly Spanish nuns we discover speak no English. "Well, they are the ones says we need better medical help than we getting, and has got to tell the doctor and nurse about it."

At last a janitor comes to open up the building, and, somewhat later, another man comes with the key to the library where the meeting's to take place.

And now here is the county doctor, tall, lanky, and obviously disinterested in the whole idea of this meeting. His head nurse is a small, skinny, sour-faced woman who seems to share the doctor's attitude toward the people; she neither looks at nor speaks to anybody.

The doctor opens the meeting. He has been told the people are not satisfied with the medical care they're receiving. All right, then, he's here to hear the specifics.

For a while after this introduction, nobody speaks. Obviously everyone's too frightened.

"Well," the doctor says.

"Well," his nurse echoes.

The nuns, in Spanish, urge the people to express themselves. Surely, they say, the people can't, mustn't, believe they'll be punished in any way for telling the truth. The doctor and nurse have taken the trouble, despite their busy schedules, to come to hear for themselves. They are here, after all, to secure improvements, make changes. But this isn't possible without the people's cooperation.

A small, wizened man rises to his feet. He wants to tell the story of his wife. She'd had a heart attack at home, and he'd been terrified, not known what to do. He'd called his minister, and the minister had called an ambulance to bring her to the hospital. It didn't come. The minister and the man who was speaking had called again, and again, many times. "Well, the ambulance never done come, and my wife, getting no help, well, she upped and died." He sits down with tears in his eyes and a sob he tries hard to control, but can't.

An older lady tells her story. Her only son had been hit by a car on the highway, and she, too, had called an ambulance, numerous times. The ambulance never came, and the boy died on the road.

A pretty young girl (how long can she remain looking like that, I wonder to myself) gets up after the woman sits down and says, "See, I were having a baby, and my husbin' taken me to county. When we come there, the nurse asks does we have our own doctor, and we has to tell her, 'No, we don't got a doctor.' So she say (shades of Granny May Lolly and Honey Jean), 'You can't come in this hospital then.' And then she turn to my husband, and said, 'Let her have her baby in the field or the woods where most migrant womens have their babies. I mean, your wife ain't no better than the rest, is she?' " Her husband sits, shamefaced, beside her. What must he be feeling, I wonder, about his manhood?

There are many more such horrifying true stories told in soft, frightened voices without a hint of bitterness in them.

And, now, at the nuns' urging, the people discuss, still in tempered, subdued tones, the county health center itself. They say they don't know, and seem to have no way of finding out, the center's hours. The nurse says, "We do, you know, advertise our hours in the newspapers."

A timid voice from somewhere in the back of the room pleads, "But most of us can't read English. We don't read papers in English."

"Well, we also advertise in the Spanish paper."

There are two Spanish newpapers in this community, and so someone with less temerity than the others asks, "Please, ma'am, which Spanish paper do you advertise in?" It turns out to be the one nobody reads; everyone reads the other . . . everyone who can read, that is.

The meeting, from its beginning, seemed a necessary but masochistic ritual. Everyone of us knew, and told one another, that nothing, *nothing* would be done about anything we'd heard here tonight.

Howard Yaeger was, however, convinced, due to the meeting and Arnold's survey, that a medical and dental clinic of the kind Arnold had discussed with him was an immediate necessity for the community. Unfortunately, however, he left HEW soon after our first meeting with him. Arnold then worked with his similarly dedicated colleagues, Dr. Tom Pheasant and Ed Rogge. They made it clear they would consider funding a medical and dental clinic, but that there were a lot of details to work out. A proposal would have to be written, a visit to the proposed site would have to be made, responsible agents would have to be appointed, "in kind" contributions from the community would be required—but it could be done if we would put in the time and the effort.

It was worked out. It took nearly three months, but it was developed according to the regulations and the law. A three-year program was worked out aiming at less and less dependency on government assistance. The first year's budget was $169,000. The company would donate, rent-free, a fully remodeled, carpeted, air-conditioned facility eminently suited for a clinic and make available further funds through the project itself. Also, the State Department of Health and Rehabilitation, through its Migrant Health Funds, would provide $28,000; the National Health Service Corps, $14,000; and the Regional Medical Program, $9,360.

Arnold, Tom, and Howard looked toward a staff of eighteen for both the medical and dental clinics, and hoped they'd be able to obtain a doctor, dentist, and perhaps also a nurse from the National Health Service Corps. However, the law states that the provision of NHSC personnel must have approval by the local professional association and by the local governing body.

Arnold, realizing from the beginning that the association's

attitudes could be expected to be far from favorable, began to talk with some influential and empathetic doctors he hoped might help him obtain medical association approval. They promised they would try, but were not hopeful they'd succeed.

It was an empathetic doctor who, on June 7, 1972, placed the matter on the medical association's agenda. Tom Pheasant came to Florida for the occasion, even though neither he nor Arnold had a chance to speak, the presentation being made by the president of the association.

The doctors' decision was that they had no objection to bringing in NHSC personnel if all the doctors on the board felt as they did. Since everyone was not present, though, a committee was appointed to canvass the absentees by telephone.

A couple of days later, Arnold received a letter specifying the doctors' approval. He felt triumphant, thrilled. He then secured county council approval, unanimous except for the chairman, who had been absent but who had set the stage for approval. But then, all of a sudden, all hell seemed to break loose at the medical association. Doctors began calling the committee chairman and others favorable to us, angry at the decision of the board. They subsequently withdrew their approval, giving as a reason that it had never been proven that more medical help was needed in the area.

But Arnold did not take the blow lying down. Instead he organized among well-known establishment people a citizens' committee for medical services. Their attesting that there *was* need for more service had its effect.

He also persuaded the state medical association to reason with the county group, which by now had a new argument. Our doctor would have to be licensed to practice in Florida. It didn't matter, or so they said, that he had passed his federal boards. The state association was able to work out an agreement with the county that specified a doctor would be able to come and work without a Florida license until the new boards were given in June or July.

An agreement was also worked out whereby our doctor would be hired and paid for out of state funds. In that way we got our doctor and the medical association saved face.

Now Arnold began working on approval for a NHSC dentist. He sent out material describing the program to all the members of the dental society and asked that he and Tom Pheasant be permitted to appear at their monthly meeting. The program began with a presentation of slides on peridontics that went on for an hour and a half. Finally—finally—Tom and Arnold's subject was reached. Tom talked about the National Health Service Corps' dentistry program, pointing up that making poor people conscious of the need for tooth care sometimes resulted in those people's seeking out private dental care, and could be a boon to practising dentists. Arnold talked about the project and emphasized the fact that 99 percent of migrants had been found to have multicaries. Certainly, dental care was a number-one need for them.

Again, as at the medical meeting, there was hostility masked as concern. Since the dentist would not have passed the Florida boards, the migrants would be denied expert dental care. Some said—though they had to know everyone in the room realized they were lying—they gave free treatment, and that to bring in an outside dentist would be an infringement of their economic rights.

Then there was the dentist, raucous, and having to be put down by the chairman from the beginning, who challenged Arnold's statement that the county commissioners had approved the idea of an NHSC dentist as well as a doctor. He said Arnold was lying and he knew it because he'd had lunch with the commission chairman "and he told me the commission had *not* voted the way Harris said."

Fortunately, Arnold had brought with him the council's certified letter attesting to approval. He handed it to the hostile dentist and asked him to read it aloud. He did, embarrassedly, and had, like it or not, to admit the letter was authentic.

But the disapproval continued. "Standards of service," etc., etc. People repeated themselves time and again. It became eleven o'clock, eleven thirty.

"Finally," Arnold says, "both Tom and I got sick of the whole thing, and I said to myself, 'Hell, I'm going to go for broke, since it sure looks like we've got nothing to lose, and a lot to gain.' So, where I'd formerly been gentle in my tone, I became quite aggressive. I told them that the story of human relations in America had never been described better than by the Frenchman de Tocqueville. I said, "Remember his saying, 'America is a strange and unusual country. When Americans realize their community has a problem that must be dealt with, a few, the ones who are able, get together, form a committee, and do what needs to be done.' I'm sure you all know, I don't need to tell you, this is how the United Way, and all other agencies of its kind in American life, have assured the well-being of its people.

" 'Now I am challenging you, the dental association of this county: Do the generous, the American thing. Affirm *your* Americanism, don't deny poor people dental care. Approve this service.' "

Arnold's waving of the American flag was more successful than he had any feeling it would be. The dentists held an immediate vote and our clinic got its NHSC dentist.

Chapter 14

The new child development center, in a complex also containing the medical and dental clinic and living-learning library, is easily one of the most physically exciting centers I've ever been in. Created to meet the needs of children from six months to five years who will be there from 6:00 A.M. to 6:00 P.M. it has, first, a warm, gay infant room with its carpeted area for floor play and a sufficient number of crawlers, beginning walkers, crib mobiles, jumpers, baby and adult rocking chairs, baby bunk beds ... and you name it.

The truly provocative rooms, though, are those especially designed to challenge the older children's creative instincts and prepare them for public school, which is attended by many kids out of privileged homes. It has got its own two rooms in a housekeeping corner, imparting a realistic setting for dramatic play and permitting a good number of children to become involved at the same time. And a library unit displaying books on top and having, on bottom, a storage area for puppets and other such playstuff. And a woodworking area with tools where the children can reach them without calling for adult help. There is, besides, a block corner, a painting area where four children can paint at the same time so interaction as well as creativity will be encouraged, crafts tables, and, last but not least, a music and reading area.

Despite all the inventiveness and good intentions, however, this center had a far more frenzied, explosive beginning than the medical program either had or could have had. Part of the problem was, predictably, the makeup of the clashing staff. Though no more varied than the beginning medical program staff, with its righteous Saints, sinners, poets of profanity all, witch people, voodoo people and two self-named radicals, there was one essential difference. Medical program staff worked mostly alone and on their own with individual

Birth of a Vision 165

guidance from Kaye and only occasional group meetings, while in the child development center the whole bunch was thrown together and expected to meld into a harmonious whole.

Naturally there were many fights of epic proportion among the clashing aides. As for their communication with one another, however, the Saints told the sinners in no uncertain terms how they were driven to frenzy daily by their sight and sound, their loud voices, bad manners, and inappropriate clothes—hot pants and miniskirts. The Saints didn't mind the fact the sinners' clothes and general behavior would be sending them straight to hell. They had, after all, relegated *them* there long ago. What did infuriate them, though, was their firm belief the sinners would, in the end, sway the babies and children so they'd be damned, too.

And the sinners would get more and more enraged at the condescension of the Saints, who also outnumbered them. And though the Development Corporation Board, not company staff and consultants, had hired them, they persisted in blaming us because there were more Saints than sinners, and talked often, especially when we were within earshot, about how Mel, Bob, Stan, Arnold, I, all of us, had deliberately granted the "power" to our "pets," the Saints.

One time I heard an argument between a sinner and two Saints. The sinner was an overpowering very black girl of nineteen named Janie, and the Saints were Annie and Lizzie, small, thin girls with small, thin voices.

"I gon' scrinch you you go on talking like that about the way I look when all the time the two of you be old ugly faces yourself. Scrinch you just like you are animals to be cooked."

I stood around waiting to intervene when poor Annie and Lizzie would require me to. But, as it turned out, they didn't need my mediation. Why would they when God and Reverend Seaford were on their side?

I try to talk, to joke both sides out of their towering rage and tearing passion, but know, in front, how ineffectual I'm bound to be even though I could always talk and joke with them on other occasions. I'm right, I am ineffectual, and all I've succeeded in doing by my interference is to make both sides mad at me. All three girls eye me for the first time with unconcealed hostility and I hear Janie say when she thinks

I'm out of earshot, "She be white, so what the hell she know about what us Negro folk go through?"

"Yeh," say Annie and Lizzie. And for a short moment I have the satisfaction of believing their anger at me is a unifying thing for them. But before I can even properly congratulate myself I see Janie making a sudden lunge at Annie and Lizzie kicking Janie in the back.

And if the Saints and sinners aren't affliction enough, there are also our two radicals, Jen-idolators naturally, to be reckoned with. First of all, Jen, in her self-loathing at having become part of the project, had carefully trained them to detest both company and consultants. Furthermore, she and we had, at more or less the same time, arrived at the same conclusion. Her time on the project, for the people's sake, primarily, and her own, incidentally, ought to be concluded. Nevertheless, her followers were convulsed with raw, demonstrative sorrow from the day her going was first contemplated.

"Jen's gon' to go away from us. Jen's gon' to go away."

"Yeh, they sending her away, the company and consultants sending her away."

And when Emanuel Elias and the students, with their special brand of high-pitched, all-out aggressive hostility they believed only to be worthy of the "project's watchdogs," came to the center and were joined by the two radical aides, they managed to create a great whirlpool of sound and confusion out of all proportion to their number. So, even if, as could happen on occasion, the Saints and sinners were relaxed . . .

The trouble with hostility is that it bounces back and forth like a Ping-Pong ball. It's contagious, throws everyone off balance, snowballs, grows beyond all reason without any link. "Bad vibes," as the young put it, are catching, so that both Saints and sinners who had neither a stake in or realization of what *this* fight was about were bound to join it anyway, either on our side, so-called, or Jen's and the radicals'.

Though we'd beg and plead, "The children, the *babies* need you," they listened as little to us at such times as to their opposition among the other aides.

Then Mickey Roberts, over whom Mel and Jen had fought the others of us so hard, came to direct the program, and the company and the consultants, except for Mel, standing alone now that Jen had gone, felt the wind of grace on our brow.

And yet, speaking for myself, I found that, like Mel, I didn't take to Mickey as a person. We weren't friendly and often disagreed. But instead of talking through my disagreements with her as I did with the rest of the staff and must admit she tried to do with me, I avoided confrontation, which might have been valuable to both of us, and, instead, talked behind her back, particularly to the black staff. I said, though I realize now I put her in a position where she really had no other choice, she was patronizing, had no sense of humor. And didn't come to realize until recently that, being sensitive to my feelings and even, sometimes, overt actions toward her, she had little reason for showing her true self, including her sense of humor, to me. And, like it or not, I had to recognize also, she might well be, doubtless was, a natural teacher, one of those rare human beings who give and respond utterly to children, and seem able to draw them with magnetic effortlessness. She has a way with them, of talking, gesturing and bouncing along, hypnotism by words and movement that holds the three- to five-year-olds spellbound. "Now I'll show you how to dance, how to dance."

We shoved the chairs to the corners of the room, leaving the center entirely bare. Mickey danced gracefully around. "One, two, three, kick. One, two, three, kick. Now who's going to dance with me?"

Five-year-old shy Sharon, who'd not said a word to the rest of us, even including Mel, who used all of his charms to reach her, raises her hand and I can't believe it's she joining Mickey on the floor.

"Now, Sharon, let's sing together while we're dancing. One, two, three, kick."

"One, two, three, kick." That's Sharon's voice . . . I'd sometimes suspected she didn't have one.

"Great. That's right. This is great. You really have a lovely voice, Sharon. And you're a wonderful dancer. Any other wonderful dancers around? Sure, you're all wonderful dancers. Everybody in this room is a wonderful dancer and singer. You'll see. One, two, three, kick . . ."

Mickey worked her dancing and singing spells until every able child in the room was in the center of the floor. And those who weren't able never took their eyes off her and the children who were dancing.

The older kids continued dancing and singing even after

Mickey had left them and gone into the infants' room with its six infants from six months to two years. She picks the babies out of their cribs one by one, rocks them on her lap, and sings to them, tells them stories and just plain communicates with them.

The three infant aides, Mary Ann, a pretty Saint of twenty-two whose mother is an important member of the board, a vice-chairman of the child development committee; eighteen-year-old Jane Felice, also a board member's daughter; and sinner Lily Belle, in tight sweater and hot pants, to reveal her striking figure, stare at Mickey as though she's insane.

"Why talk to little babies like these ones here?" Mary Ann asks in stern disapproval.

Mickey explains that babies learn to talk by being talked to. She adds, "You yourselves are going to have to talk to them from now on, talk to them, sing to them, tell them stories."

"*I* ain't talking to no *babies*," Mary Ann mutters under her breath but loud enough for Mickey and me to overhear her.

"Yeh." This from Jane Felice.

"Oh, Gawd," Lily Belle laments out loud, "I never knowed when I took this job . . ."

Mickey tries again . . . and again. "The way babies learn to talk . . ." She leaves the room after a while and I'm alone with Lily Belle, Jane Felice, and Mary Ann. They all look tragically first at me and then one another, and begin speaking together in some untranslatable, to me anyway, potpourri of grunts and monosyllables. Finally, though, Lily Belle, talking so I understand her, assures me she's "not going to speak to no babies won't even know what in the hell I am talking about. You got to be crazy."

Next, Mary Ann and Jane Felice say they want to know what I think of Mickey's insane notion. I explain it doesn't seem the least bit insane to me, that the aides themselves will doubtless realize after they begin carrying out the program how valid Mickey's strong feeling is in reality. I tell them that in four, five years, say, when the babies are ready for school and talking infinitely better than the ones who've never been talked to, they'll have reason to be proud of themselves and the job they will have done.

"No," the three of them answer in unison. "No, no, *no*."

I'm about to say more when Lily Belle interrupts me to ask, "Listen, Sara, do we have to do everything Mickey say do around here?"

"Well," I hedge, "it seems to me that Mickey, with all of her experience..."

Mary Ann, her eyes flashing expressively, interrupts me to say to Lily Belle that though she, Lily Belle, may have to take orders from Mickey, neither she nor Jane Felice are in her position.

"Well, why that is?" Lily Belle asks, back again on the wrong side of the fence.

With a quite disgusting smugness Mary Ann says, "Well, Jane Felice and my mama, being on the board and the child development committee, you know youself, Lily Belle, they are Mickey's bosses. And my mama, especially her being one of the bigshots, listen, gal, all I got to do is to tell my mama how Mickey is giving me a hard time. And you bet your life she gon' get rid of her for me."

So this is what our ideology about "people power" has ended up being. Mary Ann—and her mother—are not the only ones in whom we consultants may well have gone beyond practical reality in our and the company's desire to instill self-respect and a sense of their own dignity. We've influenced the board and all its committee members to believe (as Bob, Stan, Mel, and I are certain in our minds we should have done and must continue doing) they're ready to lead this project *now*. Although, naturally, they'll become more sophisticated and meaningful forerunners when they're educated and better trained for the responsibilities as well as the vanities of leadership.

Arnold, Lily, Kaye, Mickey, and Dura believe, on the other hand, that education and training must precede the assignment of being leaders and, incidentally, arbiters of our and other staff's accomplishments with hiring and firing powers. They say we all know in our hearts we're giving the board false impressions of their ability, lying about it...

And our lies can be exceedingly hurtful to the people we so much want to help. Naturally, Arnold, Dura, Mickey, Kaye, and Lily would diagnose Mary Ann's hoity-toity declaration to Lily Belle not as personally arrogant but rather a natural response to *our provocation*. It is we consultants who have incited the people like Mary Ann to express the kind of unrealistic, frightening sentiment she's displayed here at the child development center. They constantly warn us we're being too precipitous, too high-pitched in our all-out campaign for dignity and selfhood among the people.

And when I repeat Mary Ann's statement to them, who can say, they all challenge, that the girl is speaking out of insolence or any other such reason inherent in herself? All she and so many others are doing is *obeying us*. Answering in the only way they can, given the circumstances we've created, Bob's, Stan's, Mel's and my summonses to them to just come on ahead and be leaders. They are, when you come down to it, no more or less than triumphs of our subliminal persuasion.

My head tells me . . . But my heart says that despite all the conscience-pricking examples like Mary Ann, our way—Bob's Stan's Mel's, mine—will be proven right in the long run. I hope with everything in me, as I know all our opponents on the staff also do, that the way we're doing, giving recognition to the natural leaders *now* and not at some long-off date when they're trained and educated, is the proper, the only procedure under the circumstances.

God, how I hope it'll work better in the future than it seems to be doing now. I hope but don't know whether it will or not. I just don't know and neither do the rest of us, including the company people. But the company's willingness, eagerness, even, to go along ought to be encouraging to the consultant staff. Bill Kelly, Gerry Abell, Luke Smith, Paul Austin, Don Keough, promised an atmosphere of noninterference and, despite heftier and heftier financial outlays, are carrying through on it without stint. Well, I think to myself, if they're not perturbed by this kind of experimentation, why should we be? And yet . . .

Being with Mickey, seeing the problems she's facing with her aides, I feel an urge to talk (unburden myself?) to her about the matter, although I've never done such a thing before. I tell her I think, wonder, rather, whether we aren't barking up the wrong tree when we urge such heavy responsibilities as hiring and firing of staff upon the board at this particular time. She says what she has so many times before, that, yes, of course we are. In her case, for instance, we have created a situation where she, as a trained person, can't function as she should, created the kind of situation where the aides, feeling they'll be protected by the board, can, as so many do, refuse to accept her guidance, but rather go their own way. The ultimate losers, of course, are the children. "I so wish you could see, agree that..."

And, in spite of having opened the subject with her, I say, "I can't agree with anything that might impinge on the board's power; you know it."

"Yes, I suppose I do know," Mickey says, a little sadly. And the barrier door that has been between us two, as between Mel and her ever since she's come on to the project, closes yet one more time. And I must admit to myself, if no one else, it is I, like Mel, and not Mickey, who's to blame for the fact there is such a door.

My own life experience and training have, when you come down to it, prepped me well for coming to know and identify with the psyches of migrant blacks and white southerners like Old Red and even Jarvis and Mary, but did not begin to prepare me for dealing with educated, able southern whites like Mickey. In my simplistic assessment, and despite her devotion to carrying out her overwhelmingly difficult job, I saw her as able, yes, but as prejudiced against blacks like Jarvis merely because she had lived in the South a long time.

I was closed to her because my own emotional needs demanded I be, and I'm really ashamed as I sit here now and think back on the whole situation wherein I blamed Mickey for everything that was wrong with our relationship. And if I ever thought to censure myself for any part of it, it was not because, as was the case, in reality, I had closed myself to her out of prejudice but rather that I hadn't "handled" her as "her kind of people" had, of necessity, to be handled and treated by "my kind," with oily, hypocritical diplomacy.

The assistant coordinator of the child development center first discovered and presented for board approval by Arnold, not Mickey, is twenty-eight-year-old Millicent Green, completely charming-looking with her small, almost fragile features and shiny hair. I had to like Millicent very much from the day I met her for her unusual quality of naturalness, her reassuring simplicity that made everyone except the bellicose sinners of the center feel good. It came at you from her eyes, as if directly from some source of love and loyalty in her. You met her eyes one time and had, ever after, to say to yourself, "You can rely on this lady even if, as is the fact, she's not only a superactive member of Reverend Seaford's church but also a firm believer in ghosts and witchcraft."

"You know, Sara, one time before I find Reverend Seaford, yeh, for a long time really," she told me early in our acquaintance, "I was possessed of evil spirits, to drink, smoke, and do all them other wicked things. I gon' with strange men, too. At the time, you know, I thought I was just a bad person, and never even thought I was possessed.

"Well, I was arrested for drunk and disorderly, on many a time. I knew the inside of the jails of every place I lived. Then, too, my three babies got three daddies and none of them be around today. When I asked the men to marry me account of I was carrying their babies, well, they laughed at me and called me names.

"Then come a time I could not eat nor drink nothing, not even water, because I was rooted by a lady that my mama had a fight with.

"See, my mama and this lady were in jail together, and it was there they had the fight. So my mama say to the lady, 'Just you wait till I git out of this place, I gon' have you cursed till you will wish you was dead.' And the lady laughed at her and said, 'Who gon' have who cursed? I am getting out of jail before you can, and I gon' curse you where it really and truly hurt you at, in your kids.' "

Millicent smiles her beautifully effusive smile. "Well, the way you see me today, a godly woman and healthy, that lady cursed me not just to do all of them evil things but, too, to become sick with snakes in my belly. And they crawled around inside of me, and bit me till nobody could stand me around because I was always screaming and crying.

"But none of us knew what was wrong till my mama come out of jail and told us how I was rooted by the lady there." She lowers her voice and says, "Well, then, she helped me out of all I were suffering by going to this good witch and paying her thirty dollars to get the spell off of me and put it on that lady instead. So that is the way it was. First the snakes left my body and taken their place in hers, this lady's that rooted me in the first place. We hear tell how she begun suffering awful bad from snakes after I didn't have any more trouble with them.

"Then the other miracle to take all of the evil and people's curses out of my heart and soul were done by Reverend Seaford. He laid his hands on, and said how I gon' be a good woman from then on. And I ain't sinned anymore since. He done the same for my mama and she ain't sinned either. Never gon' to jail again and knows she never will."

Although Millicent's only been to third grade in school, she's a genuinely bright person underneath the superstition and had, against the overwhelming odds of her earlier life, taught herself "to read, write and count some."

If there was anything about Mickey during her early months at the center that should have changed my negative attitude toward her it was her and Millicent's relationship, their mutual liking and respect, their outgoingness and warmth in each other's presence.

"I sure do *love* Mickey," Millicent told me. "The way she try to help us all out and don't care how much time it takes her. I mean, with her learning me . . . She said, 'Millicent, you and me, honey, is going to work together to make you a real good assistant coordinator, the best.'" She grins her bell-ringer grin. "See, the way it work, when I am with Mickey, I believes I can be good and maybe best."

And Mickey, in her pragmatism, gave Millicent, besides verbal encouragement, the kind of new self-image bound to come under the circumstances of all the new techniques for functioning she acquired pretty early on.

Menu planning and smart food purchasing for the children's lunch and two snacks. Staff training and programming. The "art," as Mickey put it, of bringing out parental involvement and education to the children's needs at home.

Mickey also managed to train Millicent in record time in what none of us had visualized her ever being able to accomplish. To keep the budget and tremendously complicated records the Department of Health, Education and Welfare requires before it will reimburse for the lunch program.

"You must be a natural-born arithmetic genius," I told Millicent once in a burst of admiration. And she responded, "Oh, Mickey is the one, and without her . . . Well, I dunno if I ever get along in the center if Mickey was to leave. And, you know, I pray night and day she never gon' leave here, never."

And now Mickey's own training of Millicent's accomplished or almost, she also manages to arrange for her to take courses in child development with an instructor at the community college, Rita Lowe, who's a fine choice for teaching Millicent. She's been around some during Mickey's and Millicent's training sessions. And, already, before she sets foot in the classroom, Millicent and Rita, with Mickey's overt and subtle aid and inducement, have formed a mutual admiration society.

Despite my negativism I have, of necessity, to recount to Mel all I've observed of Millicent's fabulous accomplishment and Mickey's literal consecration to help it all happen. And Mel, making less attempt than even I had done to understand or appreciate Mickey for this, says I'm coming through loud and clear at the moment as the exact opposite of the person he'd conceived me to be since we'd begun working together: an unflinching opponent of attempts by white chauvinists like Mickey to impose their own middle-class white values and mores on the black people and aides.

"Goddamn, Sara, if you don't sound like a chauvinist yourself."

I open my mouth to ask if he's kidding me, but can tell from the pugnacious look on his face, that he's not. I want to tell him then, all of a sudden and despite my own illogical rancor toward Mickey, that if he, as an intelligent black man who cares about his people, can't recognize Mickey's strong points, or, as important, refuses to utilize them, I want to say that if Mel, as a representative black leader, gets caught in *that* trap, then the outstanding feature of America's racial problem is its absurdity—on the black side as well as the white.

Instead of honestly expressing my feelings, though . . . "Yeh, Mel," I say as I almost always do to him even while thinking how it is that while I'll challenge white staff or consultants or company people on any and every issue, I'll never (at least I never have yet) defy Mel or other blacks even though I may feel them to be very wrong indeed. It's a question of moral courage, I admit to myself, not for the first time. White guilt, resting on my shoulders as it's done for a long time, incapacitates me for being as useful on this project as I could otherwise be. Popular with black workers and staff? Oh, yes, yes, indeed. But valid in the contributions I make to them through the project? Well . . . anyone who has the overpowering need I seem to for black love and sanction at whatever cost . . .

Mickey, of course, doesn't have any such need. She's here to do a job to the best of her ability. Period. Exclamation point. And I have, therefore, seen her succeed where others of us, staff and consultants, have failed.

Kaye came, soon after Mickey had begun her work in the center, to instruct the aides about examining the children for signs of colds and other contagious illnesses and getting the sick ones to the medical clinic first and, then, home if that seemed indicated. The Saints, following Millicent's leadership, carefully took her instructions in. But the sinners simply stared with their inscrutable expressions that collectively told Kaye (as they'd once done Mickey) they were in the hands of a madwoman who set impossible tasks they couldn't hope to carry out.

"Man," Ancie Lewis, a sinner leader, blurted out, "what y'all think we are anyway, nurses or nurses' aides? Well, we can't tell no sick kids from well ones. Kaye, we can't do it."

"Can't do it," her claque echoed.

Kaye didn't, as Mickey would have and eventually did, challenge them for their uncooperativeness. (There's a little of me in her. She also needs black love and sanction even if not to the same degree I do.) But instead said in her nice way that she herself was to blame for the aides' not comprehending, seeming to comprehend, what she was driving at.

"Let me try again, ladies, to make myself clear."

She did try again—and again—in such a simple way the aides could not possibly have been as puzzled and perturbed as they let on they were. And when Millicent had the good head to challenge them on the whole matter, they didn't respond to her but rather turned to me and said, "How we can do something we don't understand, Sara, how, hunh?" And I . . . like Kaye, I pretended to take them at their face and told them yet again what Kaye had said all those many times. Naturally enough, they didn't "understand" me a whit better than they had her. They understood Mickey, however, before she'd even opened her mouth, and as though by magic. They glowered and glared at her but carried through on their duty with no more argument.

On the days Mickey wasn't at the center, in the morning,

however, they gave poor Millicent the same hard time they'd done Kaye and me.

"We ain't no nurses or nurses' aides, Millie, damnit, and we don't know how . . ."

"But Kaye showed you . . ."

"Man, she herself knew we couldn't understand her, and Sara done the same. So what you running *you* cotton-picking mouth for?"

I sat by, and in the name of noninterference never said a word to help Millicent even after she'd demanded the sinners do their jobs and they asked who in the hell she thought she was to dare to demand anything from them.

"Listen," she answered with tears in her voice and eyes, "I am assistant coordinator, assistant coordinator. And you gon' do what I say do when Mickey ain't around, or else . . ."

Her unexpected strength froze the sinners for a moment but no longer before they, led by Ancie, began mocking her. "I am assistant coordinator, assistant coordinator." And Ancie added, "Well, you ain't nobody all by youself, Millicent, you know. *Nobody*. It just because you the pet of that white woman . . ."

"Yeh," the radical Betty Sue, who looks enough like Ancie to be her sister, said in a loud voice. "You the white lady's pet like you are her dog. That is as much as she care about a nigger pet."

"Nigger pet, nigger pet," the sinners continued tormenting Millicent until there seemed nothing for her to do but telephone Mickey and beg her to get to the center as soon as possible.

She came with her confident long stride and voice and dispersed the sinner aides, despite their malevolent looks, to examine the kids. Then she turned to me and said, "Those aides tormenting Millicent as they do and creating the problems they do in this center, well, I've just about had it and Millicent has, too. If I had my way, if I were allowed to be an administrator in the true sense, I'd soon change things around here. But, since, as you consultants never stop telling me, this center's the board's responsibility, Millicent and I'll appear and explain all our difficulties at the next meeting. If the board comes through, if they can undertake their responsibility in action as well as name . . ."

If they can undertake their responsibility in action as well as name, if they can meet this trial by fire . . .

The board meets on Saturday night, and, due to the fact of the holiday, I'm grateful to see almost everyone's there. Mr. Ocea calls on Mickey to take the floor and she explains, first, her own problems with the sinner aides and then Millicent's. She tells how powerless Millicent feels to cope with their attacks on her basic worth and dignity and explains how they've bullied her.

Midway in her recitation, Chairman Ocea, calm as always, sighs loudly and says he doesn't understand why Mickey needs to talk for Millicent. Surely someone who functions in so important a post is capable of discussing her own problems.

Millicent then stands up and, addressing the board in a calm, constrained, rational tone, perceptively analyzes the situation by saying, "I don't like to give orders to nobody, but know it is my job when Mickey ain't around. I mean, the babies and kids is most important. They are the one reason all of us is in the center in the first place. Well, our jobs and us learning new things, new skills," she says quoting Mickey, "well it's a good thing and I am so glad for us all. But the kids is still *the most important,* see to it that they gon' get a lots better chance in life than any of us ever have. And if, you know, the only way for the babies and kids to get what is coming to them and only don't because some of these aides hates *me* so much, well, then I think I don't belong in the center and I am here to tell y'all on this board that then I like to give up my job if y'all don't mind."

Almost all the board members, sinners as well as Saints, are very moved by Millicent's devotion to the program, and are certain in their minds she won't be the one to go.

Now Ancie, at Mr. Ocea's request, presents her and the other sinner aides' view in her usual adamant fashion. Millicent is both an incompetent and (despite her church affiliation) unregenerated liar who'd never have been appointed to her job in the first place if the Saints hadn't levied such pressures on her behalf.

Of course the Saints react strenuously to that accusation, and practically all of them want to answer Ancie. But, interestingly, Johnnie Lou does, too, and she's the one Mr. Ocea recognizes first.

"I am ashamed of y'all, Ancie, and you other ones doing Millicent the way you done. Now, as you know, this education committee and the other people on this board . . . Well, as a community aide myself, *I* got to answer to them. And so do you and you whole crowd, Ancie Lewis. Now, is what you want us to believe . . . that it be Millicent's fault you and the rest don't worry about the babies and children or if they are sick or well?"

Ancie, who's always loved and admired Johnnie for her humor, spirit and independence, lowers her eyes and tightens her lips into thin lines.

"Well, Ancie?"

"We ain't no nurses or nurses' aides."

"But Kaye shown you what to do and Mickey keep on showing you, too. I know that. Well, just tell me if you think I be wrong, Ancie."

Silence reigns among Ancie and her followers.

Mr. Ocea says, "Ancie, ain't you gon' to answer Johnnie's question?"

"Yes, sir."

"Well, then?"

A voice, not Ancie's but another sinner's, roars out, "Well, we don't want no Reverend Seaford Saint giving us orders, don't want Millicent and all the Saints thinking they better than everybody else."

"Just you leave Reverend Seaford and his Saints out and talk about yourselves and the way y'all treat those kids," Johnnie Lou says.

Another sinner, a board member named Jeanine, about Johnnie's age, says in her very controlled, almost arrogant tone, "Saint or sinner, like Johnnie Lou first say, the ones matter most be the babies and kids. And, you know, well, if you don't know, this whole board be here to tell you . . . we don't care *who* we got to fire if they won't do right by the babies and the kids. Do y'all hear me, Ancie?"

"Yes'm," Ancie answers.

And now, in a marvelous merger of opposites and a meeting I'd never suspected could happen here of those two extraordinarily different worlds of Saint and sinner, Mother

Bets says, "Johnnie, Jeanine, y'all be right in saying nobody in that child development center that don't put the kids ahead of everything can stay there; we will fire them sure as shooting. And you was talking to the sinners.

"But all the same, me being a Saint myself, I can say here and now the Saints ain't always behaved right to the sinners, far from it. And I believe Ancie and them when they tell about how the Saints in the center act like they be so much better than the sinners. Well, I act that-a-way myself sometime and I want to tell you now, since we been meeting together on this here board, I am ashamed of myself for sometime acting like I be a better person than, say, Johnnie Lou.

"Well, I sure know by now I *ain't* better than her and it be what I want the Saints working in the child development center to know. You ain't no better than the sinners working there, and everytime you act like you think you are and make the sinners mad . . .

"Well, just remember you be hurting the babies and kids just the same way, so, the way I look at it, you Saints is as much to blame for all of the trouble in that child development center as the sinners.

"And, see, as a member of this here board, well, I am here to tell you, we would fire Saints as good as sinners if you don't think of youselfs last and the babies and children first. If *you* can't do that much for the kids, well, the way I see it, y'all Saints then, you don't belong in our center. No, little Sisters, you just don't."

All of us except Lily, who has been working hard and long behind the scenes for almost two years now to create this kind of tolerance among board members, are amazed at what's transpired tonight. And we really gasp in disbelief when Emanuela, of all people, rises to her feet and lets fly at the center Saints in much the same way Mother Bets has done.

The whole meeting leaves a good taste and proves a pungent stimulus to staff, consultants, and, more important, all of the center aides. Saints and sinners alike request the board through its education committee to take a more active role in the center than it's done formerly. "I think it be good if us in the center could meet with y'all on the committee one time a week. Then we could tell you our troubles and you could help us out about them," Millicent says eagerly.

Mr. Ocea then asks the other aides how they feel about Millicent's suggestion, do they go along with. All of them nod their heads yes.

Chapter 15

So after all the chaos and wrong beginnings the board can and doubtless soon will function on its own. We of HRI have helped the people on their way, no question about it, and so we're both proud and happy. But some of us, especially I, are also heavy-hearted. Because it's obvious by now the program can well go on *without us*. And the company people, from Bill Kelly down, are well-equipped and emotionally tuned to give the people the help, less all the time, they're going to need from outsiders.

Actually there are two other community development corporations with boards and special committees like the one I'm writing about that the company has helped build and with which we consultants have worked closely. And, almost, some of their working members are at the same stages of competency and independence as are my friends, my favorite people here: Johnnie Lou, Jesús and Merilita, Mother Bets, Mr. Ocea. Others, of course, didn't start out with their potential but were rather as victimized by society as Emanuela. Still, they, like Emanuela herself, have also made almost unbelievable progress.

Emanuela. Who would ever have dreamed during the early time of our acquaintance with her that she'd feel secure enough in herself so she'd be able to blast out and instruct the young Saints out of the child development center on the meaning of cooperation, adjustment, and, above all, commitment to others, the center's babies and kids in this case. And who would have imagined she'd ever come so far as to confront, not meekly either, the white power structure. Lily tells us with an expression of extraordinary pride on her face, the firsthand story of that confrontation.

"See, the aides, Mother Bets, and I were going to see the county health director about the need for more services to our people. And, listen, Bob, Stan, Arnie, Sara, you would've been so proud of Ella if you could have seen her with this snippy little receptionist. She didn't like us and made it . . . oh, she made it quite clear she didn't see us as anything but a bunch of 'pushy niggers,' and she wasn't having anything to do with us. And neither would the doctor, if she was to have her way with us."

Johnnie Lou shakes with silent laughter, her arms crossed over her chest all the time Lily's talking. "Man, old Ella were the greatest."

"Well, I wouldn't be nothing if it hadn't've been for y'all on the health committee and Lily showing us." Ella grins with more genuine joy than I've ever seen her do. "See, for a couple of weeks before we gon' to see the doctor, Lily were training us to act it out how we will be when we got there. What we gon' to say to all the people and how we gon' look while we was saying it."

I may be imagining things, but the tranquil "good colored folks" voice with its touch of sadness . . . Emanuela's voice seems stronger, a lot more her own this morning. "Yeh, and one of the first things Lily tell us was, 'Y'all know some ain't gon' like the sight of us in that office. Now I ain't talking about the doctor herself, she is our friend, but all the people we are like to meet before we even gets to her.' Then Lily say, 'Okay, Bets, say the person y'all meet before coming to get to the doctor herself is a little gal receptionist. Now how you think she gon' act to us when we tell her we wants to see the doctor?'

"And Bets say, 'Oh, I think she gon' to act very bad.' Then Lily say, 'Well, how *you* gon' act?' And Bets say, 'Well, I gon' stay cool, but all the same I gon' make it my business to get us all in the doctor's office if she want to let us or not.'

"Well, next thing Lily tell us do be to act out this here thing. She say, 'Now I gon' be the receptionist and you gon' be y'all selves, the committee our board delegate to talk things around here through with the doctor. Now we got to be very polite, can't say nothing ugly to the gal no matter how ugly she may be herself. Because a person has got dignity and know right be on his side, they don't need to be ugly or not polite. All they need do is be strong and stick to their thing.'

"So, next, Lily be the receptionist the way she say, and

Johnnie Lou was us, one of us. And Lily tell her, she said, 'What y'all people wants here? This is the private office to the doctor, you know.' Then Johnnie said, 'Oh, yes'm, we know this her private office and we be here to see her. We has got a appointment with the doctor.'

"Next Lily has say that if the receptionist talk like that, well, no matter what she say and how she try to find out what was us and the doctor's business we wasn't to tell her. But neither was we gon' lose our cool and say, 'It ain't none of your business.' Instead we was to talk this way, 'Our business be with the doctor herself, ma'am, and we got this appointment with her, you see.'

"And Lily say no matter how many times she ask the question, well, we answer it the same way all the times. So Johnnie Lou done that . . . 'Our business be with the doctor herself, ma'am.' Then Bets taken Johnnie Lou's place and say the same thing whilst playing along with Lily as the little white gal receptionist. Next come Mr. Ocea saying the same thing. 'Our business be with the doctor herself, ma'am.'

"And now my turn come and I do all right, you know, so long as all it be is play acting. But then . . . oh, dear Lord, what happen then, oh, man, I was so scared. See, the day come when we gon' to the doctor for real, no acting then. And come to get upstairs where at the doctor is, well, there be a li'l gold-hair gal, and turn out to be the receptionist just like Lily say. Then Bets, being our committee chairman, say to me, 'You gon' do all of the talking for us, hear, Emanuela?'"

She looks as frantic and fear-ravaged as she must surely have been at the doctor's office as she tells us, "Now I never expect I be the one to do the talking, never. But Bets was the chairman and she say do it." She lowers her voice to relate the rest of the story:

"Well, then the little gal talk just exactly like Lily tell she will do, saying, 'Well, y'all, what your business with the doctor?' And I be so scared of her being white, so scared to talk to a white gal. But then I seen my own people, Mr. Ocea, Johnnie, Bets, Lily, everybody look at me with they eyes, and saying, 'Go on and do it, do it right the way you done when you acted it. Don't go letting us down now, hear?'

"And I look at the white gal staring and I get so scared of what happen if I talk up. But then I look at my people, them looking at me saying, *'Do it, do it right!'* And, see, I get even more scared of doing my own people wrong than the little white gal. And so I walked right on up to her and said, 'Our business be with the doctor herself, ma'am.' I say it again and again every time she ask her question."

"Oh, man," Johnnie Lou says, "I was so *proud* of Ella. All of us was. I mean the way she did her thing . . ."

Like some purifying ritual Emanuela says, smiling happily, "Well, see, then, after a long time, the doctor herself come out and shake all of our hands. Then she says, 'Oh, I be so glad to see you people because we got such a whole lots to talk about.'

"And that li'l white gal just sit there with a look on her face like she can't believe the whole thing. And me standing there, well I can't believe the whole thing neither. But it done happen, *it done*."

"And you, Ella, was the one to make it happen," says Johnnie Lou.

Yes, I have to tell myself, even Emanuela will be . . . is right now, though she'll deny it . . . able to cope with our leaving. Her peers and colleagues can do as good a job as, if not better than, we in being catalysts toward helping her know she's as much a person herself as she's always figured the "good, kind white people" to be. Johnnie Lou, Mother Bets, Mr. Ocea, they'll be the ones in the long run who'll make it possible for Emanuela to quit accepting the myth of white supremacy in all things.

. . . Some six months ago Ella moved out of the company shack and into her own home on beautiful Lake Clinch, which she was now able to finance. Her house, like many others here, has a living room with dining alcove, a modern bath and kitchen, which is both her and Beulah's (Emanuela's mother, who lives with her) pride and joy, and four bedrooms, sufficient to accommodate the whole family and also give privacy to those, like Emanuel, who need it.

Bob, Stan, Arnold, and I were with Ella on the day she moved into her house, which she furnished with new pieces she loved and could afford through company-encouraged cooperative buying and loans made without interest through the employees' credit union.

"You know," she said, "this day be the happiest one in my

whole life. Whoever thunk when . . . oh, I be so happy, people, so happy." And she collapsed into tears.

After she recovered herself she asked us, "Please, y'all, it be a big honor this first night in *my house* if y'all stay and have supper. See, the way I gon' make it today, everybody, the whole family gon' sit down together and eat. Well, living in the shack, even when we all get plenty money . . . why, Beulah herself, making thirty, thirty-five dollar a day since the project begun. And then there was my money, too, the good money I get for being a aide. And, sometime, Emanuel, with all of the money he be making, sometime he put money in the pot, too. So, there is times when we got two hundred dollar or more in one week. And, you know, there was times before this project begun when me and my whole family wouldn't see that much money in a year."

She looks at us all in turn and says, "But, see, before, living in the shack and all, even money don't make no different. Me and Beulah and my grands never did eat together. Never. Then Lily shown me this here picture of people in a family just sitting together and eating the way we only done at church suppers, and I decide, well, we gon' do that, too. Me and my kids and my grands gon' do that. And, tonight, Lily gon' come, and Mel and y'all, Stan, Bob, Arnie, Sara, will you break bread with us tonight?"

"Ella, dear, nothing could keep us away," Bob answered for us all.

"Well, what I gon' make you really likes?"

"Whatever you and the family'll eat," Bob says, "we'll love it, too."

She gives out a deep sigh and shakes her head sadly. "White folks food . . . See there were a time when I known how to make it. But now . . ."

I say, "Ella, believe me, Bob means it when he says all of us would love the kind of food you'd cook for the family."

"You mean," she asks, "soul food, like Emanuel say?"

"It's what we mean, Ella," Stan told her.

Her bright smile can light up the room as she agrees soul food's what we'll have then. All the same I'm surprised when dinner time comes and she does actually serve us the food she'd promised.

So is Emanuel surprised and says mockingly to Stan, Bob, Arnold and me. "See, if y'all white folks don't like our poor nigger food, well then, you don't have to eat it, you know. Just make believe, take a bite here and there, and then it'll all be over and you can be sitting in your nice white folks' restaurant."

"Now come on, Emanuel," Stan says, "that's not funny and it's cheap."

"Yeh," Lily says.

"Yeh," Emanuela says.

"Hey, Bob," Emanuel says, in a quick change of mood, "did you ever think in your wildest dreams, mama'd be able to talk back to me this way? Hey, did you ever think the day would come when she would serve black folks' food to the likes of you white consultants?"

"I never did, Emanuel," Bob answers. "Not in my wildest dreams."

Later, I say to Lily, "Listen, were you surprised at Ella serving us white folk soul food?"

"Oh, Sara, I wasn't a bit surprised, no." Before I can ask her how come she's not surprised, she reminds me of the fact Emanuela's been getting private tutoring for the past four or five months from a black elementary-school teacher. "And, you know, she's not only teaching her the three R's but also the beauty in blackness. I sat in on one of her classes once. It was wonderful. And when the two of them were done, Miss Buford said to me, 'Honey, the thing about Emanuela is she absorbs like a dry sponge.'"

I sit there, my mouth gaping in astonishment at all I'm hearing from Lily. I'm really thrown this time with wondering how I could have been so wrong in the way I'd judged Ella to be.

And Lily told me how, kindly but honestly. As a white, she says, I have great empathy for blacks, *as a white* . . . "But, see, honey, teaching a black woman like Ella that, you know, just because you're black, it don't mean you got to all the time get back. I'm sorry but really only another black person can really, *really* succeed with something like that."

And now Lily tells us Ella's also spending almost all of her free time at the living-learning library, which I feel, after long investigation, may be one of the best-equipped places of its kind in the country for minority users. As for Sam Morrison, the library director, he's dedicated, young, and above all imbued with the ideal of helping blacks like Emanuela learn to respect and love their heritage. I know how much he's done for other workers, but have, nevertheless, to be surprised at his success with Emanuela.

No question about it, black staff people like Sam Morrison are marvelously equipped to carry the ball far beyond where we first threw it. He's able, beyond any doubt, to give Emanuela, and the many others here who are like her, pride in her blackness and herself on an emotional level we whites could never have hoped to achieve, although, God knows, we tried with every good intention in us.

October 20, 1972. All of us consultants, with the exception of Lily, I'm happy to say, are going home. As it happens, Arnold and I have a joyous assignment awaiting us. A trip around the world to write a book and participate in making a documentary film featuring our interviews with women in Africa, the Far East, and the Middle East on their changing position. It's my childhood fantasy come to reality fruition.

All the same, I'm very sad, as all of us are, over leaving the groves. Stan, Bob, Arnold, and I talk about what we meant to the people and they to us, concentrating, as has to be in the end, on our loss of them rather than theirs, such as it will be, of us. We tell each other, in our distinct fashions, how much beauty we felt in our time with the people here and how badly it hurts to leave them. And when Bob says to me, "Listen, Sara, if you and Arnie were to be called back here, would you give up your new project to come?" I answer with no hesitation, "You bet I would."

PART II

Two Women

To realize how far the workers of the company have come in accepting themselves as people and, sometimes, as in Johnnie Lou's and a number of other cases, as people with responsibilities to the more disadvantaged community at large, *leaders*, in fact, instead of just "pairs of hands," one must know something of their lives and backgrounds.

For this reason we are reporting here Emanuela's and Johnnie Lou's life histories, as they themselves know them and told them to us during the middle part of our time in Florida. Although both are, as we said, symbols, the earlier lives of the several people who make up each one have been written in their words, not ours. And we are sure that if they told us their stories today, the mood of the telling, certainly in Emanuela's case, would be different. She has now, finally, we are happy to say, come to a realization of the way she was always exploited by *whites*, as well as certain blacks, and would never tolerate such exploitation today.

As for Johnnie Lou, she was, we think, fated to be a leader of her people. Her personality and early background (contact with her father, brother, and Sam Snooker, who "would not take nothing off nobody") prepared her. However, as she herself always said, the project channeled her energies, lessened her resentments ("I might have ended up in jail instead of ALPI"), and made her know, for a fact, how capable she is. Above all, it gave her the opportunity to do what the love and warmth in her had always driven her toward . . . helping people less fortunate, and certainly less able, to a better life.

๑§ Saint Emanuela

"When I growing up," she tells, "my mama died when I was a little bitty old girl. Well, my Aunt Bets and Uncle George say I was about nine months old when she died. And my daddy died a year later. So I really don't know nothing about them, don't know nothing about no mother nor father.

"Aunt Bets and Uncle George was the ones that raised me. We lived in Virginia on Mr. Robert's place. Lots of colored did. They was renting from him like my Uncle George. He were the nicest white man, Mr. Robert, sometime giving us colored children pennies and candy, or something like that. I just love him to pieces, but my Uncle George called him bad names and say he should be fair about not taking no three quarters of all the crops we raise 'stead of giving pennies and candy to the kids. He never like hearing me or my brother, Tommy, say, 'We loves Mr. Robert." Sometimes he beat us up bad if we was to forget and say it when he was around. He were a mean man, Uncle George.

"Well, Mr. Robert also have this girl me and Tommy love, Miss Lydia Rose. And she said she was my friend. And she would tell me, 'When you know I be at home, you come to the house and I will have you a loaf of bread and a slice of meat cooked.' And I would stand around her house and watch for her to come out on her porch. And then, across the road I would go a-jumping right into that back door. And she would have my bread set in there waiting, along with my meat, and tell me, 'Here your food. Come on and eat!' I say, 'Yes'm.' I would get it and she would tell me to go out and sit down if it was in the summertime. Go outdoors and sit under the tree and eat. Oh, I just love Miss Lydia Rose to pieces like I done her daddy. Uncle George didn't nohow like my loving her neither and sometime beat me over that. Me and Tommy, too.

"Aunt Bets were a nice lady, though, my mama's sister. She were real purty, too, and always say my mama been the same or maybe even purtier than her." A moment of smiling silence. Then the lie comes. "They was Indians, you know, mama and Auntie Bets, with a whole lots of white blood in them, no African in them or that whole part of my family. Auntie Bets herself, see, she have long, shiny, good hair, and she talked soft and kind. And she work for old African Uncle George. She work, she work like a little slave, the way me and Tommy done, too. My uncle giving the orders, and us there have to do everything he say, do, the most of the work around the place. And while we was working, my aunt would offer to us about her grandmother and granddaddy, my great-grandpa and -grandma. They was Indian also with good shiny hair. And she told us about how they say they come over in this country, in American country. She told how they were bought. They was put on stools and sold."

All of a sudden she remembers the source of her story, a thin, young man in daishiki and Afro hair, who bore a vague resemblance to Malcolm X. He had conducted black culture and history courses for the board in its early stages and told, in practically the same words Ella'd used for describing the plight of her so-called Indian and white grandparents, about the "African slaves who were brought here from Africa, and, you know, put on stools and sold."

Humiliated because she knows we must recollect all she does, she talks fast and furious as a cover-up. "Well, the Africans wasn't the only ones sold on the stools. The Indians like my great-granddaddy and -grandma was bought over here the same way. But that African Uncle George . . .

"See, because my Uncle George . . . there was this thing he done, I can't never excuse him for." Ella becomes a different person, her body turned rigid with anger, voice hoarse with fury, not her ordinary bootlicking voice at all. "Well, he near kill Tommy, and make a cripple out of him for life when he were twelve year old, or something like that. One day, while ma and him was doing the hoeing, his right foot begun hurting bad. He tell me and my uncle, 'Uncle George, I got a pain in my foot and can't hardly move it.' And George say, 'Aw shoo, there ain't nothing wrong with you, boy. You go on and work right on.'

"I felt real bad when I seen him. And, everyday, the pain

got worse, and his little foot come on commencing to get worse. So they carry him to a ol' granny lady. And this lady look at the child and she told us that his foot were all out of place. He need doctor's care, but his poor little foot have been bad so long . . . we have waited so long to bring him until the child had took too much of a sickness and was gon' to be a cripple for life. And in all that time, my uncle only taken him to the granny lady. He never once taken him to the doctor. And after I known what were gon' to be with him, poor Tommy, my uncle, him, I want to kill him, to choke the breath out of him. He cripple my only brother by never taking him to a doctor. He cripple Tommy like he used his two hands to do it to him."

Ella knows. Instinct or some other kind of intelligence causes her to realize we have it on the tip of our tongues to ask her when, before the agricultural program began, doctors were ever available to families like hers, and what migrant or sharecropping families, if any, she'd known in those days or knows today in other places than this who had been able to take their children to doctors instead of granny ladies. And she doesn't want to breathe a word about that. It might mean admitting her uncle was not the only one to blame for Tommy's condition, that the "kindly" Mr. Robert also had a share in it, and that goes against her grain.

A hesitation, and then the love for Tommy and fury, hate, anger, and resentment at her uncle meld together in a state of physical fatigue which seems, always, to take care of Ella's inner boilings. She shuffles her feet underneath her chair, gives us her nice, warm friendly smile, and, in a friendly, benevolent voice evocative of her beloved Reverend Seaford, explains how Tommy's condition was, after all, a vital part of God's own beautiful scheme.

"He got Jesus after he turned cripple, you see, and give Him to a whole lots of us that might have stayed heathen if it hadn't have been for him. God done . . . God made my brother His instrument. And one day he called me and say, 'Sister, come here.' And I gone there and he said, 'I got Jesus. I got religion all in my soul, and I rather have Him than even a good foot. And I want you to get Jesus, too, because then you be feeling so good all of the time.' And he told our friends the same as he done me. Knowing he gon' to be a cripple all his life, and still being some happy because he had

Jesus in his soul." Emanuela tells how she stood for a long time over the floor pallet that served Tommy as a bed, looking at her brother and thinking to herself, "If I could have Jesus like Tommy does."

She would never have to cry at night again or "pay too much mind to my hunger that come on me all the time when I weren't with my white folks and getting fed by them. If I have Jesus like Tommy."

She looked for Him first in her aunt's Holiness Church, the "most joyful and rocking" one around. She recalls it well, a plain frame building on a brick base with windows painted different shades of blue and turquoise and violet and pink. And with a choir of gifted young girls she would have liked to have been part of but never believed she could, who sang "Rock of Ages" and "Sweet Jesus" and "Stand by Me."

Emanuela talks especially and at length about the revival season for soliciting unbaptized teenagers and younger girls of her own age when women shouted and jumped and screamed, and deacons ran around grabbing fainting people.

And the tall, handsome, virile minister walked time and again past the rows where the young girls sat in their gaily colored dresses, waving his arms and asking, "Who's ready to come to Christ tonight? Who's going to come? Come to Jesus. Come right now."

And many of the bad, or "good-time," girls, the ones Ella knew for a fact to be having rough-and-tumble sexual affairs, for instance, volunteered to be baptized and washed clean of their sins. And the deacons and old women looked at them with tears running out of their eyes and sang, "He will save you. He will save you."

And Emanuela, yearning to join the ones in the front row at the mourners' bench, and keeping her mind tuned on Tommy, begging him to help her stand up and speak up when the reverend said, "If you are a sinner, repent tonight," but feeling herself, somehow, incapable of doing it. It was like she was tied hand and foot so she couldn't move up off her bench, and like there was a muzzle on her mouth keeping her from saying, "Jesus save me, I repent."

"And then all of a sudden I could say it. Jesus done come to me. He come to me just the same way He done Tommy. I was eleven years old when I first feel my religion. It was on a Wednesday and I never will forget it. I weren't inside no church but just outside of our one. It was six o'clock and I set me down underneath a old oak tree, sit down there and prayed and prayed for God to come to me like He done to Tommy and let me to stand up in church and say, 'I am a sinner and want to be baptized.'

"And I tell Jesus . . . I didn't know nothing about my mother at that time, not what she looked like or nothing . . . and I tell God that if I have Him in my soul, please to show me my mother. And she come before me dressed in white. And she walked up. I heard someone say real soft, 'Ella, Emanuela, honey, this is your mother.' And I turn around and look. And there was somebody standing there. And she looked and smile at me, and said, 'This is your mother. And I'm gon' to see to it you get Jesus in your soul now, so you gon' join me in heaven when your time come, just like Tommy gon' do when it get round to his time, you know.'

"And I remember just how good I felt. I got back to the church, and all of the people had begun coming out the door, the service was finished. And I started hollering, 'How glad, how glad I am I got Jesus.' And everybody were so happy for me being purified, and wanting to be baptized."

Baptism at Emanuela's childhood church, as at Reverend Seaford's and all of the other Holiness Churches here, was the biggest occurrence of the year. Most families saved all year to buy new dresses and shoes and socks and underclothes for their baptismal candidates, all white, to symbolize the fact they were entering the church pure. But Emanuela's uncle refused to buy her a new outfit. Never before, in all the frustrations she'd known, even including Tommy's crippling, had she felt such savage and vain anger against anyone as against him.

"I keep on wishing God to strike him dead on his feet. I say, 'I love you, God. You know it. But he don't because he is hurting one of your little ones. Look-a here what he do and strike him dead on his feet.' And then I begun sobbing and crying. I guess I were crying most all of the time before the baptism. I used to sit there in the house thinking of cutting myself in the heart and disappearing forever. But I knowed I never would get to heaven if I didn't get baptized. And then I think to myself, 'Better pray for a miracle, O ye of little faith.'

"And the miracle taken place. My white family I was

working for, baby-sitting and washing diapers and sweeping the floors and sometimes doing the windows, I started off with them at fifty cent a week. And I would clean up the stove maybe ten or eleven times for a sack of flour to bring home. And, sometime, they would give me meat for cleaning the stove. I was carrying a lot of food, not just my money, my fifty cent. But they would give me a bag of sweet potatoes, as much as I could tote, sometime. And when our cows was low on milk, she give me milk, and she give me butter, my white lady.

"And one day she seen me sobbing my little heart out and asked me what were wrong. And when I told her, I never will forget it, she told me, 'Don't you worry none, I will buy you them baptismal clothes and they will be as fine as anybody's there.'

"And she bought them. Them was the first fancy clothes I had. White shoes and dress and slip and even panties. They was beautiful."

"I baptize you in the name of the Father, in the name of the Son, and in the name of the Holy Ghost. Amen," the Reverend said as he ducked Emanuela swiftly under the water. And the Sisters' and Brothers' voices rang out loud and clear, "Take me to the waters, take me to the waters, to be baptized!" Emanuela came up coughing and sputtering, her hair dripping with mud. And her white dress dark brown. "I look down at that dress and think, 'It might be ruint. And then again it might not. But it be all for the sake of the Lord that Miss Sylvia give it to me and what matter if it be ruint?

"But the li'l white shoes, I still got them in memory of Jesus and Miss Sylvia. And, see, it was a white lady done that for me. All of the good I ever have done for me or mine were done by the white folks. And that were from the time I was little till, well, right now.

"And even my Pearlie Mae, the white folks done her the best ever and the blacks was just as jealous as could be, you know."

Pearlie Mae is Emanuela's forty-year-old daughter and the mother of Emanuel Elias. She's a pretty woman with a café-au-lait complexion and strangely perfect teeth in this world of multicaries. And as Emanuela tells us proudly, she had a white lover. Or, rather, there was a white man who took Pearlie Mae to bed with him when he felt like it and then paid her off in his own way. The whole mood of Emanuela's recounting of her daughter's relationship, such as it was, is one of feverish euphoria, romanticism, and pitiful pride that revealed from the first day I talked to her what the project would be up against in its attempt to inculcate a sense of black pride in those like her.

Mr. Charlie (that, ironically enough, really was the man's name and Emanuela has no awareness of its contemporary significance) was, according to her, an admirable person. "Well, first on first he were godly, and used to tell all of his colored folks that, you know, whatever you have or ain't got, your soul, if it is clean and shining, be the best part of everything.

"And he hisself was the living example of all his preaching. His poor wife, Miss Eloise, had cancer and he were as good to her as the day is long. He have Pearlie there just taking care of her, just that and naught else. He pay three dollars a week for that. And he pay me five for cooking for Miss Eloise and the rest of the family. The cooking and cleaning weren't that much, though. Miss Eloise were the most of it and sometime need me and Pearlie both to baby her up right.

"I done more crying and wringing my hands over the dear, old soul. And I really did shed many special tears when the doctor tell Mr. Charlie she can't stay home no more, he got to put her in the hospital.

"I am the first one he told before even Miss Joan or Miss Penny, his daughters them. They was not the kind a man could turn to in his times of trouble. I be the one he say am his friend through low time and high. Me and Pearlie, young as she were then. He say, 'You and me be true friends, Ella. I can count on you and your child to do what I need; and you can do the same with me. Now, ain't that what a body call friendship between white and colored?' "

After his wife was hospitalized, Mr. Charlie made a change in his domestic arrangements. He sent Ella into the field to pick cotton at $1.25 a day and hired Pearlie Mae to do the housework and cooking at $4.00 a week, a dollar less than Ella had been getting. He also arranged that Pearlie could pick cotton at the $1.25 rate whenever she found time from the home chores.

I asked Ella whether or not the new domestic and financial arrangement affected her feeling about the friendship between

Mr. Charlie and Pearlie and her. Did she believe his firing of her and hiring of Pearlie at a dollar less a week to be a sign of friendship?

She answered that, no, her feeling toward Mr. Charlie was not changed because he paid Pearlie less money than he had her. Pearlie was, after all, only fourteen and inexperienced. And as to his having fired Emanuela in the first place, well, understanding her mother's heart, he knew she would rather be in the field herself than to have Pearlie there, yes, of course.

"And, see, he shown his care, he show he was my friend when I first come to his house searching for my job. I remember how sweet he said to me, 'Ella, a lot of colored around here good enough to pick cotton in my field but ain't too many is good enough to work in my home.'

"So don't that show you something about the way he feel toward me? And the same to Pearlie Mae because he pick her, he think she be good enough to take care of his own wife?"

Bob and Stan hear this, too, at different times than I do. We all make a stab, of course . . . how could we not? . . . at pointing up to Ella the whole exploitative pattern. It's a small stab, though, and we discover upon talking it over, that all of us have withdrawn, stopped our explanations almost before we've begun them. And what has hurt us and made us stop was that mask of blankness, that guarded mask Ella showed us the moment we opened our mouths on the subject. She's as frightened of us here and now as she's always been of her angry colleagues on the board. They, and we, want to take from her, and she perceives it deep down, that unreality that alone makes her life more bearable. Listen, Bob and Stan and Sara, I'm something fine those "field niggers," with all their bigtime talk and accomplishments on the board, don't begin to realize. Mr. Charlie, though, he knew all right.

This is not logic speaking, it is naked need, it is terrible hurt, and you can't argue with it. At least Stan and Bob and I can't. And there are those who say, and we are the first to admit they may have a point, that white people like us who sometimes mask our thoughts as well as truth and reality for tactful reasons of compassion don't belong on such a project. The likes of Ella should be only with militant blacks who would never yield to the temptation to let her keep her dream for the time being, but would explode it at every chance.

Certainly, such black people as the ones our critics would replace us with never would have been able to bring themselves to listen—with sadness but no censure—to Ella's reminiscence of how "Pearlie come to be . . . how Mr. Charlie first gotten her.

"Well, it were a Saturday morning and Pearlie was off from the house and out in the field with me. It was maybe four in the morning and I never think Mr. Charlie be awake. He is, though, and say, 'Good morning, Ella and Pearlie Mae.' We said, 'Good morning, Mr. Charlie.' He say, 'It look like you gon' go somewheres, and where could it be, I wonder? Pearlie say, 'Oh, you be fooling with us, Mr. Charlie, because you know we are going to chop the cotton.'

"Then, he say to me, 'Ella, what you say if I told you I don't want Pearlie chopping no cotton today?' I knowed in my heart then, but still I was a-feared because we needed her dollar and a quarter pretty bad. So he read the impressions off of my face and say, 'Oh, you need that money Pearlie make, don't you?' And I say 'Yeh, Mr. Charlie.' So then he turn to Pearlie and say, 'You need that money, Pearlie Mae, honey?' And she say, 'We sure does, Mr. Charlie.'

"And he stand there looking at us and smiling pretty. Then he reach in his pocket and come out with a five-dollar bill wrap around his old finger. And he stand there smiling at Pearlie Mae and telling her, 'You can have this five dollar if'n you just want it with your heart.'

"And he put his hand on Pearlie's face and say, 'You is a sweet little baby and I like to have you, you know what I mean?'

"And Pearlie couldn't say, didn't at all know the right thing to say, so I done it for her. 'Oh, she know what you mean, all right, and she would love to, Mr. Charlie.' And they gon' on in the house."

Pearlie Mae's own version of this incident and her following relationship comprised pathology, sadism, all the little delights you can read about in any book about white masters and black slave women before the Civil War.

Ella, of course, knows all the details, every sickening, gory thing, and accepts it all in comfortable stride. No open resentment, no noticeable quality of despair, nothing but pride and joy in the fact that Mr. Charlie chose her daughter rather than someone else's.

Bob, Stan, and I, as I have said, heard this remembrance at different times, of course, and reacted in our quite varying ways. Bob merely listened to Ella, and didn't rap with her about the pride and joy. Since it is his unshakable belief that Ella's new world around the Agricultural Labor Project, her colleagues on the board and staff, will inevitably push her to change as he has seen so many others there do. In addition, the vocal young, like Emanuel Elias, who are bitterly ashamed of their mothers and grandmothers who were white men's mistresses, must force Ella to question her pride and joy in Pearlie's status with Mr. Charlie much more effectively than Bob can hope to do.

Stan agrees with Bob on the whole. But the fact is he's heard Ella's story of Pearlie and Mr. Charlie after several tense hours in the company of Emanuel Elias, of all people, and therefore feels impelled to try to interpret to Ella what would have to be Emanuel Elias's feelings of humiliation, debasement, and sheer hate if she told her story to him in the same mood she'd done with us.

I, for my part, am driven to talk woman to woman to Emanuela. As a mother who dearly loves her daughter, and also as a holy mother of the sanctified church ...

And Emanuela? I catch that expression of scheming, there's no other word for that thoughtful look with a trace of slyness, as Ella says, "Well, yes'm, Miss Sara, you is right about me doing my own child bad." Her voice is the high-pitched wail I often heard from her at the beginning of the project but hardly at all lately.

I've really worked hard to get Emanuela to stop calling me Miss Sara in that particular tone, and she hasn't for months. Now, though, she does it again at the same time as she tells me what she believes I want to hear. Or is it that? Is Emanuela once more gaming whitey or is the load of truth really on her shoulders? Does Emanuela know?

"My aunties," Emanuela says, "were as jealous as can be of Mr. Charlie picking my child first to work in his house and then to be a woman to him whilst theirs was also working for him, but only in his fields."

The lofty tone Emanuela uses, the condescending way she

explains how her aunts' children worked only in Mr. Charlie's fields while she and Pearlie were—wonderful accomplishment—in his house, stimulates many here and especially the young to a historic recall of slave days. They know, and discuss in angry detail, how "house niggers" such as Emanuela prides herself on having been, were rewarded for loyalty by being granted privileges over the "field niggers" and took identity, as Ella still does today, from the white masters.

No wonder Emanuel Elias reacts with such hate and blind fury whenever he overhears Emanuela comparing her and Pearlie's "house nigger" status to the rest of her lowly "field nigger" family.

"Dumb, dumb slave-timey nigger. We will be better off when she and her kind dies off, believe me."

"Well, the aunties them and their daughters," Emanuela continues her record of the family in relation to Pearlie Mae, ". . . sometime, my baby come in our cabin from Mr. Charlie's house and the aunts or cousins asking, 'Has you been with Mr. Charlie today, Pearlie?' And I tell the child to say nothing at all and try to keep the impressions off her face because I didn't want them knowing what she done or not with the man.

"And I don't want all of them to know what he given me and her, done for us two, neither. The thing be, he help us a whole lots by giving us all of his daughters' old clothes and all the meats we wanted out of his freezer, saying, 'Girls, take what you want and all that you want out of the freezers.'

"Well, my aunt was ailing by then and I would like for her to have fresh food. But we don't have nothing to keep our food in in our little house. Nowhere to keep us no cold water. So Mr. Charlie have a li'l ol' icebox and he given it to Pearlie for my auntie to use. We carry it on home, put our ice in it and we kept our food in there.

"And I remember when I got tired of the icebox and passed Mr. Artie's furniture store and in the window I seen he wanted fifty dollars for a secondhand refrigerator. And Mr. Charlie knew we wanted it so bad. And what he done so we could get it . . . he gotten me and Pearlie credit at Mr. Artie's. He tell him we was honest people. And then, anything we want, we could go in that store and charge with money or no money.

"And the best of all . . . it was a big bed in Mr. Artie's store with a real soft mattress and carved angels on all the four posts. Pearlie and me sure covet it for my auntie. So one day, Mr. Charlie say, 'Ella and Pearlie, stop in at Mr. Artie's and pick up the angel bed. It is my present to you.'

"And my uncle had him a little rattly-trap car and we taken that to Mr. Artie's store and load the bed. And I never will forget it when Aunt Bets seen it and we taken her off the straw mattress and put her on the soft one. She kind of getting deep breaths, you know, and say in a choky little voice, 'Praise the Lord.'

"And one Sunday morning . . . she lived about two months after we gotten the bed. The morning she dies, I never will forget it. I seen she didn't look right, didn't talk right. So I stayed with her. And I left a minute but I didn't get no place because the spirit tell me to peep in at her again. So I gon' right back to the room door where she was sleeping and I was peeping. Her eyes were shut and she had her two arms around the angels. But then they fell off and her head went to go back. She died smiling, and I know in my heart, she was glad account of the angel bed.

"And that is another reason I recognize Mr. Charlie. I honor him because he helped my aunt that raised me to die happy.

"Some people, when I tell them all Pearlie and I done for my aunt, they said some terrible mean things about us. They has talked about Pearlie selling her body to a white man. And me, they say I made her do it. And they call Pearlie Mae 'white man's whore' and me 'ol' slave-time granny whore.'

"The young race does that, Pearlie's kids and my own grandkids.

"And I say, 'Why, honey, why you want to say that bad word about me and Pearlie? I can't see that me nor Pearlie Mae did nothing wrong by getting my auntie a soft bed for her to die in.' And they say, 'These modern days you don't got to look up to no white man for nothing nor sell your daughter's body to him.' And they call me names, I can't even say it out loud, it be worse than anything. They say, 'What we don't like about you, mama, is you call up slaving time.' And, I say, 'Well, kids, I has made it through a pretty bad life and has helped you to make it youselfs. Yeh, me and Pearlie Mae.'

"And they says to me, 'Well, how you can say you make it when all of the time you sell your own child to a white man?'

"And I didn't sell nothing to nobody. I just try to treat white people in a way that they would help me when I needed it.

"And my grandkids say, 'You done what you done . . . you nor Pearlie didn't do nothing for your aunt, mama, but only because you honored Mr. Charlie as a white man.'

"Well, then, because I keep trying to please them, I says I didn't care nothing about his color. And the baby of them all, Lucy Ann, that is fifteen and all of the time being throwed out of school for fighting the white kids and not wanting to call the teachers 'yes ma'am' and 'yes sir' but instead saying 'yes' and 'no' to white people, she say, 'If you don't care about the color then how come you be so proud when you tell Mr. Charlie were white?'

"What I say to her then, I stop fooling with her and tell her real sincere from my heart that I am thankful to a white man reaching out to my color and giving me and my daughter things and teaching and enlightening us. It is more than any colored man like you kids' grandfather ever done.'

"Here they be six kids with three colored grandpas and they never done nothing. I ask all of my grandkids what did any or all of their grandpas or daddies ever do for me or their mama or them?

"I tell them kids, 'Well, y'all, here you telling me black men be beautiful and God hate white because they be ugly. And I say all your daddies and grandpas turn out to be just as mean and hateful as my Uncle George hisself. I had a rough life with them from the first to the last one."

Emanuela's first "boy," Pearlie Mae's daddy, was nineteen when she "done gon' with him. He had a kind of a fair complexion and that is why he were not all as mean and bad as my other men. He were nice, tall, handsome, and he never beat me.

"Well, when I first come to him, I didn't know about sex life and nothing about growing up life because I was thirteen and never had a man before. He taught me all that until I become pregnant. Well, then he become disinterested in me, and that sure messed me up 'cause I loved him and he hurted me.

"And seem like everybody was aginst me than. Uncle George, and even my Aunt Bets that loved me, got so upset about me being pregnant without marrying.

"Then the preacher of the church I been baptized in really put it on me. He preached right out in the open church about my sin and I better be saved, that I were going to die and go to hell. And when I cried and ask forgiveness, he say, 'Did you think you was sensible when you was doing all them things?'

"And me, it was something deep on my mind . . . well, really, I think to myself, I wonder what would have happen to me if I have a happy home. And I be trying to keep the impressions off my face to try to keep the preacher from knowing how I feel. I didn't think he should be so concerned into my affairs but just let me try to work it out with the Lord.

"And, see, I begun going around with this auntie. She were a drinker and often stayed in jail for drinking and fighting. And going around with her, it become a problem, and I begun to drink and that weren't good for me. My auntie, she tell me, 'You are too young to drink, a kid like you. You can go out and ball all right, but don't drink.' Then, sometime, she offer me a drink, and say, 'Drink and you forget your problems.' So I would get drunk. Well, I would feel all right while I were drunk but when I get sober I feel worse and got a hangover.

"Well, my second boy was named Joseph. He were the brother-in-law to the one sweet aunt I were crazy about, and that was Jennie. She married Limus, a older man, and he was not too light-skinned, right enough. But, still, he were good and kind as could be to her.

"So, when Pearlie were two years old, Auntie Jennie tell me I could take the kid and come to her and Limus's house. They like to help us out and all I got to do is help her around the house some."

Emanuela had lived with Jennie and Limus for four months or more, and little Pearlie Mae was thriving when Limus's brother, Joseph, "come down the house and he were dark skin but I don't worry about it because I figure he be a good old thing like Limus. He were a muckstepper, cut celery and pick beans, potatoes. They call them mucksteppers when you got to go down in the muck to pick.

"His wife had run off with another fellow and all he had at the time was Charlene and Annie Mae, the two children. Just three mouths to feed, him and Annie and Charlene. And he was pretty active picking, made seven dollar a day. And he have him a company house so there were no money needed for that excepting light and gas.

"Well, the first day I seen him he say he love me. So he couldn't marry me because there was no divorce, but he say because I have Pearlie I could come and live with him and not have to work. He say, 'You work when you feel like it, but, if it be in the summertime, I will always tell you to get out of the hot fields.'

"Well, because I had Pearlie so I needed a man. See, at the time I liked Joseph but I wasn't in love with him. My auntie, them, her and Limus, really, they say he were the ideal boy for me. Well, they was saying that I could grow to love him, so I did go to live with him.

"But it didn't work. He was mean and he was jealous. He couldn't stand for a man to look at me. That's the way he was, hollering all of the time. And he kicked me around and beat me. Then, too, he don't like work very much. Well, he done worked some the first months we was together, but not after I was with him for a year and got his baby, Elsie Lou. From then on, all he done was drink and gamble. That was his motto: cards and dice and whiskey. And I would have to go to work for food and also because we was living in the company house and they would put us off the place if nobody worked.

"And, you know, the first week I had Elsie, I was still too weak to work and Joseph have promise he would work till I got strong enough so we could keep the little house.

"Then he has a drink too many and he were on the highway with a carload, him and his mama and latest girlfriend. And he were shooting on the highway, shooting at nobody but just shooting. He didn't have no right and they put him in jail. I had just had Elsie maybe three, four days ago, my baby weren't a week old. Well, I didn't know he was in prison until in the morning. His mama come and tell me.

"And that day Mr. McKenzie, the foreman, done find out about him doing this and tell on us. And the next morning,

Mr. Gentry, he be the biggest bossman over all, come and say that since Joseph won't be working no more he want to take the li'l house back. We has to move by then and ain't got a place to go.

"So I beg to Mr. Gentry saying, 'Please to let us stay and I will work in the field so hard it will be like I am two people, me and Joseph both. He say okay, then, but if I am not in the field or work hard enough, they will surely take away our little house.

"So, here be me with that poor, little baby Elsie ain't a week old and I got to go and leave her with Miss Raney, the granny lady. And I carry Pearlie Mae at three down the field and taken along Annie and Charlene. Being eight and seven, they was able to help out good with the work, right enough.

"Other women help me see after Pearlie. And everybody were real nice to me, you know. See, I would sit Pearlie down on the end of the field I start working and tell her to stay there quiet and I would go on picking the row. And by the time I had got a little bit away some of them other women would be back at the end where Pearlie were. And they just kept track on her, you know. They had their own kids out there, too, all the kids was sitting down and playing with one another.

"And that was how me and the kids live till Joseph finished the jail time and beg me to have him back. He say he won't gamble no more and will leave the whiskey alone and never lay a hand on me nor the kids.

"Well, I never expect him quitting the gambling and drinking . . . I never think Joseph stop all of it, but at least some and I say, 'Look, man, I give you one more chance if you will be easy to mind and not make me too upset no more.

"But, oh, he upset me plenty because there be one thing I never allow, him hurting any of my babies. See, he have this hate for Pearlie Mae, little as she was, and he would sometime hit her till her teeny face had swole. And one time he done it and I can't take it no more.

"And so we start arguing and he knock me down and hit my head up against the wall. And I just tell him I hate him and didn't want him no more, you know. So he said he'll fix me. He were beating me, and the lady next door she come over and made him quit. So he left the little house.

"And I pack all mine and the babies' clothes and get on

ready to go from the place. And I also taken Charlene and Annie. They was Joseph's kids, not mine, but I knowed how they needed me and couldn't leave them behind."

Nineteen years old, and she took responsibility for two stepchildren as well as her own. For all of our impatience, and I can't deny all of us had it, with her bootlicking and nineteenth-century colored mentality that often held the program back, all of us black and white consultants had to admit to ourselves and each other, Saint Emanuela has great courage, even nobility. And if we can't reach her with our message, the fault may be more ours than hers.

Soon after she left Joseph, Emanuela and her children were recruited into a wandering migrant life by a crew leader named John Rote. "Mr. John," with thirty adult workers and perhaps three times that number of experienced child helpers, followed the crops—oranges, peaches, apples, celery, lettuce, onions, beans, cucumbers—from Florida to Georgia, Virginia, Delaware, New York, New Jersey, and Connecticut.

"Mr. John were a good man," Emanuela tells, "another sweet, white man I has to like. Well, I don't know what I would've did in the first place if he hadn't've come to me right after he hear about me walking out on Joseph. He didn't wait for me to go to him and say, 'So now what?'

"And I said I don't hardly know, that, maybe I go back to Virginia and my uncle's house, though I don't want my kids coming up like little dogs the way I done there.

"So Mr. John said, 'Well, Emanuela, my preach to you be that, now you be shed of that no-good nigger, don't mess up with no others. You be a fine worker, the way I see the thing. And I be proud if you join my crew. You do right by me and I promise I take care of you.'

Emanuela's wandering years are, in essence, very little different from those of other people here. There is a vast difference, though, in the nature and mood of her and their reminiscence. Johnnie Lou and Lincoln and Jesús, for instance, are reneging, now that they feel they can, on the decision they'd made during the days they had no choice, the decision to be satisfied with life's inequities. Now they are far from satisfied, and you know, in fact, they never were satisfied in the first place, but only resigned. And most of them are acrimonious in retrospect as they never dared to be in reality.

For us the true horror of hearing the details of Ella's life as a migrant when we did is that there was never a trace of horror in her recounting of it.

"The places we live in," she says, "well, some were pretty good and some rough. The worst ones, I guess, like we tell you at the sharing session, was the chicken coops. Some bossmen'd take the coops and make them larger for us. And I have to say that be kind of hard when you be a mother with four babies, And there was no toilets near the coops, oh, this one place in Virginia, well, in that one, there was no toilets at all. You just go out and squat and do your business that way. Many places had no outdoor toilets, and none we was at have indoor ones before this project began.

"In Delaware, we lived in coops the same as in Virginia, but they was fixed up a teeny better. Like the toilets, they had these ones with wooden seats. But they was out in like a forest or something. And in the nighttime so many times you hold youself in because me and the girls was afraid to go outside. Because you can't know what was there. My girls sometimes say they feel if they stick their heads out the door, somebody shoot it off, something like that. Them kids was funny and feel like there be wildcats around and would grab them.

"So I said, 'Don't worry about no wildcats but only watch out for the poisonous snakes, you know. If you looks out for them, you be okay.'

"Well, other places me and my kids lived in New York and New Jersey was in barns. All of the crew was living together there, men, women and children. Saints and sinners. And that were where it got too hard, Saints having to live with sinners. I mean if the Saints could only have been by ourselves. Oh, a lot of bad things, terrible things happen in the barn.

"Like this fellow, Preacher. His maiden name were Jones, but everybody called him Preacher because he use to have him this little sanctified church in Florida. Well, then, God and Jesus done condescend to have him come on to Mr. John's crew. And it were really uplifting to rise up in the morning to his little sermon, or the singing of 'I got a Key to the Kingdom.' It make you feel you can overcome for the rest of that day.

"But the sinners gets to Preacher and tells him, 'No more singing nor preaching, see what we mean?' And Preacher say all he care about be the Lord, he don't care what the sinners says, he gon' do all he can to make us Saints come through happy.

"And next thing the sinners have hit Preacher, slugged him, choked him till he nearly done pass out dead. And that be what them evil niggers—colored people—is like. They don't care if they kill you or not."

How to touch Emanuela and help her recognize the connection between the violence and the indignities imposed by the white power system upon her and the rest who lived in the chicken coops and barns. She counters all our arguments with this, How do we, who believe sinners are sinners because they're poor or black or trapped, explain the good, kind Saints out of the same situation.

"The saints were living in the barns and chicken coops as good as what the sinners done. Well, you know, that never done make the Saints unsaintly. They was still nice and didn't go around beating and hurting nobody. They showed their love toward people. They showed you they appreciated you. If you a holy person, it don't matter where you live at.

"And if you a sad person you gets your fits of crying, crying all the time. But if you are happy, even riding on the trucks from North to South, you going to be stomping and singing and carrying on in praise of the Lord because you knows you gon' to be in a better world someday so you can bear what you have to in this one.

"Even seeing you little kids, the babies, crying account of being hungry . . . Now that be something you never overcome in this world without'n you think about the next one. All that my kids could get on the road were what the bossman sell us, like potatoes, bread, and hash one night that was left over from the night before. Oh, the potato chips and soda pops they sell you in the field. And we all drunk a whole lots of soda pop, because, you know, they was not any water out in the field. And the heat makes you thirsty, especially the children.

"And only once in a while you got a teeny bit of money left over from buying that food so you could get a little treat for a kid. Like Elsie, being my baby and some on the sickly side, you like to please her if you can. And she always done covet candy. Well, one time a drummer man come around, and I buy a whole box of li'l chocolate-covered cherries for her. And I says, and this were my sin, I says, 'Elsie, you keep these for yourself. You hide them and eat them when you know nobody else can see you.'

"So, well, we all has our own little cots stretched on the floor and Elsie have her own little pillow and I has make this li'l coverlet for it. So she hidden her candy in between the pieces of straw inside of the cover.

"And these here kids . . . one of them kids from this real dark African family seen her. And she told all of her sisters and brothers. And they wait until me and all the kids but Elsie gone to the church and we hardly out the door when them kids shook and shook Elsie, and she kind of rised up and stretched. And they says to give up that candy. Well, she say, oh, no, she don't have none, denying it.

"And really, she don't have it because I didn't know but she give it to Pearlie and Charlene earlier on. So the kids drug her off the cot and begun punching and beating and holding her face against the fence. The poor baby, she got little scars where they cut it in two places on the barbed wire.

"Well, it were just lucky we decided not to go that night to the church or those mean black kids would have kill Elsie. And I wouldn't have saw . . . But Annie and Charlene happen to be running ahead with some other kids and Annie come back to me, saying, 'Mama, they killing our baby.'

"Well, I come running down there. And, in the meantime, Charlene knew where Preacher keep the gun he done buy after the sinners pounced him. And she taken it from under his cot and brung it to me. And I got the gun in behind them kids so I run them away."

But it sounds now, doesn't it, like Emanuela's "harping on the bad parts of the life for the kids. When all of the time there were also some good. Like Pearlie and Elsie, they sure done like going to school, especially in New Jersey and New York. Of course, they couldn't go when the weather were fine because, by now, they old enough to help out in the fields along with Charlene and Annie.

"Well, you know, them kids could hardly wait for the rain

to come. They look every night at the sky and say, 'You reckon it may rain tomorrow, mama?' And my heart sort of be tore when I hear them. I mean, if it rain and we don't work, we can't get pay. I tell them, 'Well, kids, if we don't get pay, how we gon' buy our food?' And I says, 'Better pray the weather be good so we will be able to work and have all we will want to eat.'

"So they says, oh, they rather go to school than to eat. I remember them telling, 'Oh, mama, it is so beautiful in the schoolroom and everybody has their own little desk and chair. It be only for you, and you be the only one allowed to sit in it. It *belong* to you, you know, the desk and chair.'

"And that lovely young white girl that were the teacher, she have some kind of way of making all of the kids feel good. Well, y'all knows how the stay-at-home kids would tease the ones like mine that'd have to hit the road. And when they done that, this teacher say, 'Listen, kids, Pearlie and Elsie, them kids knows a whole lots you stay-at-home children just never will.' And she say to the kids teasing mine, 'Well, yeah, how many you kids ever been to Florida in the winter time?' And she say, 'Pearlie and Elsie been there and seen the oranges growing on trees.' And Pearlie and Elsie says they not only seen it but has picked the fruit. And the other kids says, 'You mean you youself pick the oranges and grapefruits off of the trees? You be pretty lucky kids.'

"But, well, Charlene and Annie's teacher, they wasn't all as lucky as the babies. Well, all my kids has this bad body rash all of the time because we never known nothing about bathtubs and shower rooms, like that. Well, they was no way, you know . . . If you live in the camps like the barns and chicken coops, there weren't no way that you could get them a hot bath. They wash in the stream or the cold water from the pump outside. And sometime, like in New York or Jersey, it just be freezing.

"But some of the camps was much better, you know, like this'n in New York State where the babies love the school all that much. In that camp, you have your own little room with a gas stove in it, and could get the teeny tub and heat up the water for the bath. But it wasn't running water in any of the camps we lived before the project begun and you has to get your water out in the woods and you be scared of running into snakes and stuff.

"Well, about Charlene and Annie, they gets up on this morning crying and saying they got to have a bath because the other kids says they be dirty and the teacher say the skin rash be disgusting. And then, too, she say she don't want them around the clean white kids until they gets the rash off and gets bathed every day before school.

"Well, you know, a body got to laugh at that with having only the one teeny tub, and even if you was to go get the water it take a long time to heat up. And with two kids having to have a bath . . . so Charlene and Annie seen me laughing and get to crying because seem like the teacher tell them I be a bad mama and the rash is my fault because I don't see they get a bath every day, or something like that.

"So, when they gon' to crying and all, me being so dolgone tired gon' to hollering and roaring at them. And they crying, 'The teacher don't want us to school without us'ns has a bath. Don't you care about it?' And I be mad, too, by now. 'Well, baby, don't go to school, then, if you don't want to. I has got my own troubles, you know?'

"So, I always feel so bad about what happen then, Charlene and Annie quitting school in their hard feelings with me.

"Well, in the next week I says, 'You got to forgive and forget, kids, that be the only way to get on in the world. And if'n my roaring . . .' I says, 'Really, I be hurted if you was to stay out of school account of me because I loves y'all and wants your life to be a whole lots better'n mine.'

"So they says they knows I love them. But school . . . they make up they minds it be no good anyway, with'n the teachers and kids hassling them over everything. Beside, being in third grade, which is all they at, they feel pretty old for that, being twelve and thirteen, when the other kids is maybe eight.

"Then, too, the time be getting closer when we got to hit the road South again. So, the way that they see it, it be no use going back to school for just the couple days left.

"Well, then, Elsie and Pearlie get into it. The way them babies love the school and has lost track of time. And they start in to crying on and on about how they wants to stay in the school, they so sad, poor li'l ol' kids, you heart just got to go out to them. And not just me, but Charlene and Annie Mae, too, can't hardly stand to see them suffering so and carrying on. And so the big girls says to me:

" 'Mama, we has got a idea of how we all can keep our babies going to school the way they want to do so bad. We all go back to your uncle's house and take what we got to from him just so he let us stay. And you and us'n can find us some work around there and use the money for to keep the babies in school.'

"And that be what we done. And Pearlie and Elsie sometimes had a pretty rough way because their school were all colored and they didn't have no buses like they done to the white kids' school. So mine has to walk about five miles to get there in the first place. Raining and muddy, too, sometime.

"But, anyways, I thank God me and the big girls seen our dearest wish and was able to keep Elsie in school till tenth grade. And even Pearlie, she quitted in sixth grade when she were thirteen and first come to work with me at Mr. Charlie's house."

Not that Emanuela wanted or felt she deserved a reward for what she and the older girls had done for Elsie and Pearlie, but she knows of no other explanation for the extraordinary good fortune God heaped upon her during the early years after her return to Virginia.

First, of course, there had been the two, nearly three, affluent years she and Pearlie had had with Mr. Charlie. And after he had left town . . . It had, of course, been God's will and Ella never thought to question it.

She was never "unhappy" about Pearlie because she had "faith God and Jesus would bring her through this as so much else. And I use to carry her around to prayer meetings and all, praying she would find what she need in God's holy presence.

"And it done work out that, at this one revival, she find a certain happiness and I find mine through her."

This revival was the one occasion of the year when the well-off blacks mingled with the poor and the hoity-toity members of the African Methodist Episcopal and African Methodist Episcopal Zion Churches met collaboratively with Emanuela's own Church of God in Christ. During this one time the snobbish, better-off people, with their quiet worship services and contempt for the Holiness Church like Ella and her daughters, not only mixed freely with them but also responded to their leadership in the singing and dancing.

"Tonight you gon' see something among the proud peoples," Emanuela told Pearlie and all of her girls, "because, the Lord, you know, he going to bring them down to size."

She smiles with the quiet assurance she always takes on during discussions of religious matters, and says, "Well, the Lord done as I promised my child when he getting Columbus Feaver, the proudest of the proud, to call upon the name of Jesus and say the spirit of the Holy Ghost has overshadow him and he been like all full up with the sensation.

"Here that man ain't been inside of no church of God since he got grown. He drunk whiskey, smoked cigarettes, and gambled, flipped the cards. And his wife left with his kids . . . well, she wasn't really married to him, it were common law and she up and left him.

"And he come hurt and got worse than ever. And I do remember, even before I ever seen Columbus, Mother Feaver, his mama, and her and me work together in the church. And she asked us, but she always did love Pearlie best, so she asked her especial to pray for Columbus at the revival. She say, 'You, honey, who got the gift yourself, please take Columbus's hand and touch him and pray him to receive the gift.'

"And Pearlie taken his hand and said, 'Brother Feaver, come on and come through, just call upon the name Jesus.'

"And, oh, it were a sight, Columbus keep holding on to Pearlie's hand and drag her round the altar with him. The two of them stand at the altar, and there Columbus called the name of Jesus the way Pearlie said, and the Holy Ghost, this thing, come upon him. And something taken control of his tongue and he weren't talking like I be talking now. He were speaking Latin or Roman or something.

"Then he turned to talk English and say how the spirit done tell him he will be holy. And he say, 'The spirit be just a clean life. Jesus were clean. There ain't a spot on Him. And I can be clean, too. I can sacrifice this body, which is the temple, and make it like to Christ.'

"Pearlie was so proud because she were the one to help him through. And she stay proud a long time because Columbus done, he give up the tricky life, and come faithful to church, making so joyful a noise till he become a deacon. And always he say, 'It all be because of little Sister, Pearlie Mae.'

"Well, then, all the Sisters in the church without a man, they all set sights on Columbus. But he seem to like me the best, saying he like us to get married."

And now, here's Emanuela, at thirty, getting married both legally and within the church.

Her four daughters, paying her back somewhat for all she's done for them, give her a present, a bolt of beautiful, white voile she'll have made into a floating dress with a sweetheart neck and puffed sleeves. She is going to be a lovely bride. All four girls, supervising Granny Johnston, the seamstress, tell her that. They themselves will wear the same style dresses but made out of butter-yellow piqué. Also, everyone has new white shoes and eggshell silk stockings for the occasion.

Finally the wedding day dawned. Ella and her children, hair brushed back, stockings pulled tight . . . this family was up to snuff all right . . . walked together to the church.

The wedding was a time all right with flowers Emanuela's daughters, cousins, and aunts had picked, all over the church. Everone was happy and gay, even Emanuela's uncle, in his black suit Ella herself had pressed slick for the occasion.

And old Preacher Robinson, the same minister who had condemned Ella when she was pregnant with Pearlie, outdid himself at the ceremony. He presented this coming together of two Saints who had once been caught up in the evil world as a sample and example to gamblers, backsliders, and other sinners.

"And I got to say that the first couple years after we married was good years. We all work hard, Columbus and me and the four kids. We begun following the crops again, and it were never easy. And the money . . . seem like you can't save none no matter if one person or six peoples works.

"But there be some things that matters a whole lots more than money. Like if you has trust for one another inside of your own little family and no lying to one another. If you got liking and love in your family . . . well, the first years me and my kids have aplenty of all of that, and it be good, so good, living with Columbus."

Emanuela has talked to Bob, Stan, and me many times about her marriage, both separately and together. This is the first time, though, she's discussing it with all of us and also with Emanuel Elias and Pearlie Mae.

And the whole mood of her talk about Columbus is different than it's ever been before. Up till now she's interpreted him in the same sweeping way as she has all black men. They all, including Columbus, are betrayers and deceivers, bound to disappoint any woman foolish enough to become involved with them.

This is the first time she's admitted there were some decent facets to Columbus's character. And, it may—Emanuela's portrayal of at least one black man without her usual racist antipathy—just possibly be the beginning of a breakthrough between her and Emanuel Elias.

Emanuel evidently thought along the same lines because he grinned at Emanuela and said, "Now, cool it, mama, before you make us think there's something nice about the nigger. You ain't aiming to do that, are you?"

No, Emanuela's not, of course. Once more, as so often before, as always before and no matter what the stakes, Emanuel's good will in this case, she shows herself true to her nature, which means, above all, despising black men. "Oh, yeh, well, even if Columbus be nice in the first years, he change to his true, rotten self later.

"The way he showed himself up, you know it yourself, Emanuel, he were a devil to your own poor mama, Pearlie Mae."

There is something mean and nasty in Emanuel Elias's narrowed eyes as he says, speaking precisely, the way he sometimes does in anger, "And-how-did-my-own-poor-mama-Pearlie-Mae-show-herself-up-to-your-husband-mama?"

"None of it were Pearlie's fault." Emanuela's voice rises. "You know, Emanuel, you know yourself how she was rooted."

"Damn, dumb nigger bull," Emanuel says.

Emanuela glances at us, bright-eyed. "Well, these young people like Emanuel don't believe nothing until they maybe gets rooted theyselves like Pearlie were.

"But the old folks . . . they ain't nobody around here, well, very few anyways, who is as old as me, who ain't actually saw people barking like dogs on all fours. We all have seen people pulling out their hair, and hair falling out. And snakes crawling at the leg so it swell and burst, just all kinds of things because they was rooted."

"See," Emanuel says, "some of these black cats back in Virginia . . . What Pearlie done with Mr. Charlie didn't go down with them, nohow. So, you know, they could've zonked her in the head but decided to root her instead."

"They done rooted her, Emanuel," Emanuela declares, "that be the living truth no matter what you may say. It were three year after me and Columbus got married, and I begun to watch Pearlie. I knowed myself she begun to change. All she would do was sit and stare and would talk things.

"And then I would catch her doing different things that was harmful to her, you know. She would just do crazy things like trying to drink potash, lysol, anything deadly to her."

"And I would just act stupid or, you know, out of my mind," Pearlie adds. "I could walk a certain distance and my body would be itching like ants from my head to my feet. And the more I scratched, it would just be red with welts."

She reaches for Emanuela's hand. "I don't know what would have happened if mama didn't do so much to help get the spell off of me. Well, you see, I wouldn't even go to the root lady that would help me in the first place. See, the one that put the spell on me had it fixed so I wouldn't do nothing to help myself, no more than just sit and die.

"And mama had to go to the root lady for me. She went, ten, twelve times and it cost her fifty dollars."

"Excuse me," Emanuel says, "I need to go to the john and vomit." Instead of leaving, though, he lights up a cigar that smells up the cabin. "My people, all the bastards in the world ain't white, after all, are they?"

I ask Emanuela how she got her hands on the $50 in the first place and she explains she'd borrowed it from her crew chief, Mr. Al, during the ten-week period of the "cure" and then paid him back at $1.50 a week for almost five years.

It really looks, at this point, as though Emanuel Elias is going to have a heart attack. His face is taut and he's holding his voice back the way you do when you're making a tremendous effort to control yourself. "You tell me, Bob, Stan, Sara, anyone, how you make these dumb niggers know what's happening in their life?"

And Ella, speaking with such sincerity, almost lovingly, says, "See, when a body have to have fifty dollar becaust you daughter be destroyed . . . well, it weren't like it be today with us agricultural workers making good money where I could maybe put my own money down or else get it from the credit union and not have to pay no interest back. So I can't care at the time how much my crew chief charge in interest, I got to have the money because Pearlie was most important to me. And I knowed there was even worst could happen to her if we didn't get the witchcraft off'n her.

"So this root lady I pay all of this money to give me this muck, this mud, and tell me to rub it all over Pearlie's face. And the root lady draw me a picture of the one that hurt Pearlie and say that on the last week, the tenth one, we will rub the muck on the picture's face, taking the spell off of Pearlie and putting it on the woman that cursed her.

"So we done it and my child got cured."

"Cured, mama?" Emanuel asks. "Well, if she **was** all that cured and everything, how come . . . how do you explain all the things she did with Columbus? Go on and tell what she did with him, mama."

Emanuela is quiet.

"Tell them, mama, damnit."

She looks at him with despair. "I tell what be true and that is Columbus be to blame. Pearlie, what she done with Columbus . . . See, she got rooted again." She holds tight to Pearlie Mae's hand and keeps looking from Bob to me to Stan. "You see, people, the new spell was to make her go with men, her stepdaddy and others, too.

"It's one guy name George she had that were a musician, small, black, runty. And if there haven't be a spell on her, she never would have gone with him and got pregnant. He were really a homely man. Well, I only seen him one time, that was all. And I didn't know nothing was wrong with Pearlie at the time. He just brung her home one night and she introduced him to me and Columbus and we all got there sitting and talking over our life, how we came up and what church we belong to and everything.

"And, he tell me, he sung the blues in public, but he tell me and Columbus his mama be a member of Holiness and him, too, as a kid. And the songs he put words of the blues to was ourn out of the Holiness Church. So I says, 'Well,

George, do you think you doing the right thing by using the holy music in them dirty nightclubs?' He say, "Well, money be what I want.' And I say, 'Yeah, but your soul is what you want to save.' "

Emanuel's face closes up as Emanuela's has so often. I have never seen him sad before or heard the quiet voice in which he told us. "Here, the guy's gone and made her kid pregnant, and all she can talk about is the saving of his soul. Now, ain't that good old nigger for you?"

Emanuela, more in sorrow than anger toward Emanuel, says, "And that baby your mama have while she under the spell, maybe that be why you are so evil, Emanuel, because you was born of a man care more about money than Jesus."

There's a moment of hesitation as Emanuela stares strangely at Emanuel. It would seem that for one brief second she's seeing him as the enemy he's so often proclaimed himself. But he's her eldest grandson she raised from babyhood and there couldn't be unfriendliness between them. She turns to us and says, "Well, see Emanuel Elias be named for me. And, you know, my grandchildren, yes, I love all of them, I really do. But Emanuel Elias, I got a special love for him. And he, when he were a kid, was what we call 'old-fashioned.' He always had the sense of a old person. He never want to play ball or nothing but like being with me and Columbus. He call us his daddy and mama and Pearlie be like his sister."

Emanuel throws his cigar butt out the open door of the shack. "Yeah, I call Pearlie my sister all right. My sister, the prostitute."

He repeats the phrase again and again scornfully, spitefully, until Emanuela, flaring up for a change, and to his surprise, orders him to stop.

There are tears in Pearlie's eyes. She rubs them with her hand and I pass her a tissue. She nods thanks and asks, "Don't you got business in the bathroom?" I say yes, and Pearlie says, "Let me take you."

This is at a time when Emanuela's shack is one of the last six still standing, and, really, the bathroom's the only place we can achieve any degree of privacy.

Pearlie pulls down the toilet seat and wipes it with a soaped paper towel.

"Now you can sit, honey," she says in her warm fashion.

She holds out a pack of cigarettes and lights the one I take with a recently acquired silver-plated lighter.

And then she said something that truly shook me. It was so totally unexpected, what with everything she'd said in the shack about how only Emanuela's intervention with the root lady had saved her from the evil spirits. "Well, see, I never tell this to mama, but you know, I think sometime, talking to Emanuel and all like that, he say, you know, that my head, my soul be sick account of Mr. Charlie doing all of them things to me when I was just a kid. So what I want to tell y'all is that I ain't so sure as mama about the spirits and the rooting."

Back in the shack, Emanuela's telling Stan and Bob that "this time what the root people done were to give Pearlie a sexual spirit and make her oversexed. And there be a time when it had gotten to the extent, it seems like, maybe, we have to put her away. It was terrible, well, you know, she would just go with men, any men. They took the advantage of her and while she was under the spell, this was all she knew, she didn't know how to say no to them and they really take the advantage of her."

Emanuel Elias's voice sounds now as if a strangler were at his throat. "See, mama came in the house one day carrying me. She'd been picking and had me in the field with her because she couldn't trust any one else there to take care of me. We walked in the cabin. Oh yeah, Columbus and Pearlie were supposed to be deathly sick that day, so that's how come they weren't in the field. So anyways, we come in and find Pearlie and Columbus, well, you can guess for yourself how we found them. And now, dig this. Mama, though knowing all about what Pearlie'd been doing, never said a word to her, but just lit into Columbus, so he said, 'Who needs this?' and packed his duds and walked out of the damn house."

"And leave Pearlie with his baby inside of her," Emanuela says grimly. "And see, I known her to be pregnant at the time but I didn't know the father of it to be Columbus. I didn't know, and I say to Pearlie, 'Who the father of this one?' She tell me, 'I don't know, mama.' Because she don't want me hurted by knowing it be my own husband. But I get mad and say, 'Well, if you going to keep a-getting babies, bringing them in here, little Sister, you got to hit the door.

So, you my child and I don't want to put you out, but if you think enough of a man to do what you done, you should think enough to marry him.

"And Pearlie say, 'Well, you know I can't marry him, mama, because he be married already. And besides, he gone off and left us.' And she cry and say she loved me and didn't want to hurt me. And that if I put her out, then nobody loved her, nobody cared, nobody didn't care nothing about her, you know, even the men she gone with mistreated her. And she say, if I was through with her, she want to die, she don't want to live no more. She don't have nothing to live for so it just don't matter no more.

"Well, she try to take her life by stabbing herself with a butcher knife but Emanuel walk in and seen her so she give it up.

"Well, then I knowed I had to get the spell off her. I *had to*, and so I gone to the witch that is named Zeke and about eighty, ninety years old. His daddy and granddaddy been witches before him right down to where it were slavery time.

"So I knowed if anybody could come about taking Pearlie's spell off, the witch Zeke be the one. And he tell me the cost be a hundred dollar and I cannot work to pay it off, he need the money before he start working the spell.

"So what I done was gone to Mr. Al again. I gone to him and asked him for the hundred. He give it to me, I given it to Zeke and you can see for yourself how good and healthy Pearlie be today."

Emanuel mutters something sounding like bastards, heartless, hypocritical bastards and turns out to be talking not about the Mr. Als around here but rather Stan, Bob, and me, us "three so-called liberals." And he says so-called because, as he sees it, we are, typically, tools of the establishment, not only of the company that has us living in luxury but also of all of rich, white America. The white powers can live safe in their smiling knowledge that Bob, Stan, Sara, and the other consultants, with our special ability for disarming poor people, are around to do their dirty work for them.

Stan asks Emanuel exactly what he means by these names, and he answers that we are encouraging, deliberately, Emanuela's "nigger superstitions." The Coca-Cola Company, prime symbol of American white power, can feel fine about us because we're pretty clever operators.

Stan says we're not encouraging Emanuela's superstitions but only trying to understand them and her because the success of this program depends on such understanding. And Emanuel says he's had quite enough of white liberals' understanding that has always, and is still today, "holding my people down. Like so long as mama has . . . yeah, you three, sitting here and leading her on to talk about the root people and talk about them. And the way you keep smiling and yessing . . . Well, mama don't have to feel no pain while she's telling you about her root people. And what I'm saying is she ought to be feeling a pain in the heart every time the thought of them comes into her mind."

Then suddenly, quietly:

"Well, I bet you mama never did tell you too much about Lucy Ann being born or Elsie dying, did she? Well, Elsie wasn't one of mama's witches' successes like Pearlie. Now, I was there when she had Lucy Ann and saw the whole mess happen. See, mama never did know it, but, being a nosy little cat . . .

"Now, when Elsie started having her pains . . . it was very late, two, three o'clock in the morning. And, mama told me to get out of the cabin and far away. I started to go when this terrible screaming began . . .

"Well, so I went to peek inside at what was happening and, man, it was weird. Now, there wasn't electricity in the shack, and the candlelight . . . Mama held two candles in her two hands and Pearlie had two. And the root lady was rubbing Elsie's belly with her spell, whatever it was. And the granny lady had her hand inside of Elsie. I can't say for sure it was dirty but it looked that way to me.

"Well, Elsie was really a pretty girl, a gorgeous girl, but she was 'delicate,' as mama says, and the wonder to me, young as I was, was how come she could go on living with all that blood she lost, and . . ."

Emanuela breaks in:

"Well, and she done pull through fine after Lucy Ann. The borning leave her a little more sickly than she had been before but she would have not died.

"But her husband, Bill, he were the one. I blame him for my baby dying. See, he never listen to me when I told him she not be strong as other women. And he . . . if he care about his wife at all, he got to give up on staying with her and making her pregnant so she will likely to die. And he say, 'Old lady, you mind your business, and me and Elsie will mind ours.'

"And so I gone to Annabel, her being the same root lady pull Elsie through with Lucy Ann, and say, 'Put the spell on Bill, now, and drive the sex spirit out of him. Make him satisfy to be a brother to my child and not want no other woman for the sex either, because that will make Elsie jealous and then she will go with the man although it is so bad for her.'

"So that," she declares "were this mother's way of overcoming the problem of Elsie's health and keeping her alive."

Listening to this unique solution to Elsie's problem, told in Emanuela's sincere and gentle way, we have to empathize with Emanuel's cynicism toward our tolerance of her and her witches and root ladies.

He studies us awhile, then smiles and says that for all our seeming belief in the efficacy of the witches and root people, he's sure we won't be too surprised to hear that Annabel's spell was a failure. Bill wanted a relationship with his wife and Elsie became pregnant again.

"Well, then, mama, if it hadn't've been for her faith in the damn witches and root people, dig, might, just might, have tried to get Elsie to a hospital to have her baby and then, who knows, she might be alive today to tell you about it."

And during another rare and uncharacteristic outburst, Emanuela gives it to Emanuel, quite literally tells him off.

Does Emanuel believe that if Emanuela had been offered the option, she would have chosen Annabel or any root lady over a qualified medical doctor for Elsie?

And does he think, besides, that if she'd had her choice of whether Elsie should have her baby in a hospital or the cabin, she would have picked the cabin? Does he really?

Emanuel said, "Well, mama, you know yourself, you never even tried taking Elsie to a hospital."

"Because I knowed she couldn't get in one, was why." She glares at Emanuel Elias and says, "Now that we has the fine medical program this company have give us, and when a woman come pregnant, as soon as, she can go to the doctors and nurses for help, it be as good as if she white since we got this project.

"And I am thinking if we had nurses and doctors then, Lawd, dear Lawd, Elsie might be alive today. Y'all better hear me now, Emanuel Elias. And remember it any time y'all want to talk bad about this company. Remember it."

⇜ Johnnie Lou Atherton

"If you think of me today, as I know you do, as a hell-raising lady, baby, how I wished you had knowed the men in my family, my daddy and my brother, Bobby. Man, my daddy, in the first place, he always say, 'Anybody, colored, white, anything hurts my family . . . I ain't gon' stay quiet and just let it happen. I gon' protect my family.'

"And he done his best to do it, too. But at the time, and being a migrant worker like he was, well, he would have to fight for our rights and often get in trouble. Like, if anybody, colored *or* white ever try to hurt my mama or one of us kids, and he was to know it, well . . . He be quick to fight whoever done any of us wrong, and never think what will happen to him if he was to fight a 'bossman,' especially if he was to be white.

"Like I told y'all about the first time our family was picking in Virginia, and this bed with the straw and bugs in it, and me waking up sick and screaming and the bossman smacking me. But I never told you what happen afterward when mama and daddy come home and see how I has got beat up. And daddy asked who have swole my face up like that. And when I said the bossman . . . So he just didn't say nothing more excepting to tell mama to stay in the room with me and Bobby the whilst he gon' off to do what he has got to do.

"And mama said, 'Oh, Jimmy, I know where you be going. And it ain't no good, darling. So supposing you do beat the bossman up? What good can that do excepting to get you put in jail as you been so many times. And what gon' happen to the family then? You only gon' hurt us more than we be already.'

"And she put her hand on daddy's face and stroke him like, oh, man, they was so much in love then, and said,

'Leave us compromise it, my sweetheart.' And daddy kissed her and hold her close in his arms for a while, and say how he love her so much. And I guess she thought she have got it made, he will *really* compromise it. But then, all of a sudden he begun yelling, so loud it scare me and Bobby and Mama. 'Compromise it, you say? Compromise the man that hurted our baby so bad? I just can't do it, honey.'

"And off he gon'. Well, that whole night almost, Bobby and me gon' on asking mama, 'Where our daddy at? Where he be?' Oh, we asked even though we knowed in our hearts that he was in jail. Well, me and Bobby knew all about jails by then, we has already seen a whole lots of migrant peoples arrested for all kind of things.

"And mama told us, she didn't try to fool us but say our daddy be in jail, but leave us hope and pray he will come back as soon as day come in. So I sat all night and watched for day. 'Day, please come, day.' So morning finally came. But no, our daddy didn't come.

"Me and Bobby wait a couple days . . . we wouldn't leave the room and our bed because we did believe daddy would come and not know where any of us was at. And we tell mama we wouldn't leave the place till our daddy come. And she say, 'Well, now, kids, I ain't gon' on foolin' you no more. You got to accept the thing that he ain't going to come for a long time.'

"So we raised so much hell and say, 'Well, you promised us, mama, and we accept your word.' And she got plenty other troubles, too. Now y'all know how pretty my mama is, still to this day. Well, she were even prettier then in her young years. But, also, she was never strong. And working . . . Well, she could work okay when side by side with daddy, helping him out. But when it ain't nobody to do the picking except for her . . . Bobby and me was still too little at the time to be of much help. She hardly could make any money.

"Then, too, the bossman come and say we ain't doing enough to even be worth our little space in the camp, we got to give it up. So where was we gon' go at then? No food and no place to sleep, that be a scary thing.

"Well, we don't know this at the time but I has heard the story since I got grown enough to understand it. Seem like the crew chief have always had eyes for mama—all the men did—and he have this here li'l house away off from where the camp was at and he tells mama that if she come and be his woman, well, we can all live in the little house and all she need do be to stay home and cook. Everything gon' be fine for us all.

"Now, mama and daddy was not sinners like me. They wasn't exactly Saints either, but was very religious people all the same. And like I say before, if there was ever two people in love it was my mama and daddy. So mama cry her eyes out, but then, because she can't see no other way out, no other way to take care of us, she accept the crew chief's offer and we all gon' to live with him. We was eating pretty good all of the time we was staying there.

"But then my daddy gets out of prison and come on back to the camp and find out what have been going on. And mama, she cry before him and try to tell him why she done it all. But daddy were tough and just could not forgive her. And he say he gon' to go off and leave her. And so that mean he gon' off from me and Bobby, too.

"And I begun crying and begging him to not leave us. And, like he were really beautiful. I seen tears in his eyes and he grab me up, held me tight, and don't need to say nothing for me to know he wouldn't ever leave me could he help it. Then he done the same with Bobby.

"But he tell mama, 'Since you be living this life of sin, well, I think the kids got to be with me where they can have the holy life. And mama, I guess she, well, the way she would tell y'all today, she were ashamed of what she have did and couldn't bring herself to tell daddy no, we have to stay with her. So, although it broke her heart, she say to daddy that, okay, he can take me and Bobby with him.

"Oh, how I done miss her in them early days, but at least me and Bobby did have our daddy, which was more than a whole lots of other migrant kids has. And, at the time, I can still remember him teaching me all different kind of prayers. He done a lot of praying, whew, and I done the same in them long-gone days, done enough praying then to make up for all I don't do today. And I use never to go to bed at night without my daddy listening to my prayers. To me he were the most, even though he done become a Saint, and I don't know, I never did like the Holiness way ever since I were a kid. It sort of struck me bad to see folks crying and carrying on, and especially when my father were among them.

"Then, too, this other thing he done make me feel awful bad, although, today, I does understand. Well, with him and mama not being together and he being so lonesome, he got hisself a woman, the one he call his wife. She were a Holiness person herself. And daddy think it be a good thing for me and Bobby, that she will teach us good and bring us up nice. And him and me and Bobby gone to live with her and her two boys and three girls. So there was seven of us kids altogether, and us all eleven living in the little migrant sheds.

"Well, my daddy never known it because me and Bobby didn't tell him nothing about it. But my stepmother was pretty mean. Oh, I would try to do everything to please her. Like, I will get up in the morning early. And I will go knocking on doors. 'Does you need someone to clean the house?' And if I get a little money, whatsoever the people would give me I would bring it to her. This were before I got old enough so my daddy let me start working in agriculture.

"But nothing I done made her like me better. This were because I was my mama's child, and my stepmother were allus jealous of her; well, she taken it out on me. And, too, she didn't like me for myself neither. Because, as long ago as that was, I were a fighter even then like my daddy hisself. She beat me up, and, baby, I just hit her back as hard as I could do it.

"And what I start in to doing at this time, I used to run away every night almost. But I never done stay away, because Bobby come looking for me and he would find me, no matter how far I had got. And I turned back when he say to because I knowed how much I would miss being away from him especial, but also my daddy."

Johnnie's brother was "the wonderfullest," doubtless the most important person in her world, more important, even, than her father. His power and strength seemed so great to her, she still thrills today when she talks about it, as she often does.

"Well the way I feel about Bobby, I feel there wasn't nothing my beautiful, big brother want to do that he couldn't. He were so good-looking that everybody known him say, 'That boy be the best-looking kid in the whole country.'"

Bobby laughed all the time "and made jokes, and done imitations of all the grown-ups and especially our minister. See, he get all the kids together, me and my stepbrothers and sisters. They was all older than me and him, but after we was together awhile, they all become his followers. And he made believe he was the minister of the church and preaching the sermon. And he were a better actor than even Robert Redford is today. He would put on this voice just like the minister, he were screaming and hollering just like the preacher done.

"And he done this other joke, like pointing to my stepsister, Jane Mary, and said, 'You be washed pure and clean of sin, the purest and the cleanest Saint of all. And so, when you done with this sad life on earth, you know where you going at then, Saint Jane Mary?' And, see, like Jane Mary known she was supposed to say, 'Well, I think I go to heaven, Reverend.' And then Bobby get this mean tone, like the minister do sometime when he bawl out backsliders and sinners, and say, 'Heaven. Look who think she going to get to heaven. Well, ain't you heard yet that heaven and hell be upside down now? Because heaven be for the sinners, now. And hell be for the Saints.'

"Then, too, before Christmas, one way we celebrate Christmas were that my daddy bought a sackful of flour for my stepmother to bake pies and cakes. But Bobby steal some of that flour, and us kids put it on our faces and made believe we was white.

"And one time in the church, we each taken our little bags of flour and when the Saints begun their hollering and jumping and about forget us kids on the children's bench was even there, why, we dip the flour all over our faces and tell the other kids the Lord have turned us to white folks now."

She hesitates a long moment, and says, "It is a funny thing thinking today whilst on the project that make us know how black be beautiful, it be a funny thing to think back on that time when we all thought black were very ugly, you know. And a person got to be careful to tell the true story of life as it was back then and not the way it be for us today. Like, you know, I would enjoy to tell you, us kids was showoffy, nothing more, about making believe we was white. But the truth be, we was far from being *just* showoffy. What I for one was really doing, was dreaming I were what I wanted to be. Because, my biggest wish in the world at the time were to have my black, nappy hair turn straight and blonde. And I want to have blue china-doll eyes instead of my own brown ones.

"Well, see, I thank God this here project come in time to save the kids around here from all of that. They see the truth about black being really beautiful, too. And I am so proud when I see the little ones coloring the faces in their coloring books black instead of white like I would have did when I were small. I gets so *proud* I can hardly hold it in.

"But coming back to me and Bobby as kids, or rather, coming back to Bobby, him and the church. I remember we had been living with my stepmother and her family about four years by then and gon' to the same church we started in when we come there first. So Bobby and me was on the children's bench with about thirty, forty other kids. And like we could sing and shout along with the grown-ups when the time come for it. But when the preacher get on his long sermon, baby, I tell you, there better be no sound from us except like to tell him to 'Preach loud this morning,' or to put in the 'Amens' where they belong.

"So, on this day, me and Bobby were chock in the middle of the children's bench. And Bobby have this little way of talking out of the corner of his mouth. So he whispered that he be a person who has got the spirit there in the church for the first time. And he just looked at everybody strange and crossed his eyes and say how the spirit have hit him hard.

"Well, the kids fall out laughing. I mean fall out. And the people come to see what be doing and some mean, little tattletale tell about Bobby saying he is now a person with the spirit. And my brother gets this real serious look on his face and say, 'Why, sure I tell them kids I has got the spirit because I has got it.' And the way he say it and gone up to the altar to be saved and all the folks talking about 'the sweet, young brother looking like an angel.' And, you know, he did look like a angel, and I said to myself, 'Oh, my, Bobby gon' to be a Saint now, and that be too bad for me because all of that fun we been having will be out from now on, I guess.'

"So, then, walking home from church, I tell Bobby the same thing and he say, 'Gal, you must have cotton stuffed in you head where the brain should be. Well, see, to talk about being saved and telling the people you be saved, to talk about the spirit . . . Well, I just talk about it, Johnnie, and that is all. I ain't no more saved than you, youself.'

"And when I say, 'Well, why say you is then?' he say, 'It strike me funny and I think to myself that maybe it gon' make you laugh, too, Johnnie Lou.'

"And he were all of the time bugging my stepmother because he was so mad at her for always picking on me like she done. Like he tell her, 'Oh, Miz Ollie, you must be one of the Lord's favored.' And she say, 'Well, how come, what do you mean by that, boy?' He answer her, 'Oh, you be so good to kids ain't even yourn, like me and especially Johnnie Lou. Well, a person got to get her reward in heaven for being good like that.' And she don't know what he mean by it, if he be fooling or not. Well, she knowed she weren't good to me—or him—but, listening to him, looking in his eyes and listening to that soft voice, it were hard to believe he wasn't talking sincere and straight from the heart."

Johnnie would grit her teeth when Bobby talked this way to her stepmother and hold her laugh. Later, out of hearing of her stepmother, she and Bobby would laugh and laugh.

For many years, until he died at seventeen, Johnnie's "beautiful, wonderful big brother," with his combination of animal vitality, raw courage, and brilliance, his inordinate sense of life, served as both a lifeline for her bitter present and her prime hope for a better future.

"Well, you know, Bobby always have a dream. It don't take no project like this to have him think and say . . . a lots of peoples here has their dreams since the project begun . . . but Bobby, you know, have his dream a long time before that. Well, when he was about eight and me six, I remember him saying, 'Little sister, I know what I want in my life . . . everybody got a dream. And none of us poor people can never know what be the rich man's dream. Now the rich man, with all that money, he may still be unhappy and has a dream how to make hisself and family feel better. I don't know about the rich man's dream,' Bobby say. 'But the dream of the poor man, Johnnie, he may just be dreaming of a nice home, money, a nice car. And, I ain't going to say that won't make him happy if he ever got it, though I don't see how he can do it without no schooling, not knowing something of reading, numbers, and like that.

" 'So, my dream is to get that schooling and for y'all to get it, too.' And then he explain how, if we once got education, we could get out of our rotten life. We can beat it.

"Now, it was real hard at the time . . . even if you was a white kid in these parts, it were very, very hard to get you any schooling to mean anything. Because it were strawberries needing to be picked in wintertime. Bossman want all of the kids out working with the grown-ups. So the schools was closed all of the winter and only open during the summer months. Those be the white schools.

"Now for the black kids, there were just nothing except when it rain, summer *or* winter. And sometime, even on rainy days, that brokendown teacher they give the colored school don't show.

"And even when he do show, well, he don't have too much education hisself. Bobby could read as good as him, learning by hisself. I swear! So he told me one time, he say, 'Hey, Johnnie, I am gon' to figure out something so we have a chance to learn how to read more than this here dumb teacher can learn us.'

"Then, next thing he gon' over to this Catholic school, Sisters of the Poor Catholic School. It were where they had a center and a station, but that been only for white kids. And Bobby speaks to the nuns at the white center about how much some of us colored kids want to learn to read and couldn't they please come over our way and have a school there for black children as well as the one they was running for the whites. So they opened one up and lots of black kids left the regular colored school and come to the nuns' school. Most still had to go out and work with their folks all the good days and only gon' to school on rainy days. But my daddy say that if my stepmother don't like it she can lump it. Me and Bobby was gon' go to school everyday.

"Well, the nuns really cared for us and we liked them, too, because, mostly, they was very good to us. But, also, they was strict on you and really want you to learn. And most kids . . . oh, some didn't have no daddies and some, like us, had no mamas. So, she, Sister Ann Marie say—it be sort of like a dream now, but I think I remember her saying away back then—'There be a lie people put out about black kids never learning so good as white.' She say way back then what all of us say today: 'Black can learn every bit as good as white do if they will be given the chance to do it.'

"And then, getting back to the kids without mamas or daddies, she will tell them, 'Now, see, child, just because you don't have a mama nor daddy, it don't mean . . . See, I ain't gon' to tell you, poor little orphan, you don't have a mama or daddy, so I can't learn you that two and two be four. What I will say to you instead, be, that, listen, child, just because you don't have a mama or daddy, me and you is gon' to learn very good that two and two is four. You got to have all the learning you can, because only you will help you.' She were a lovely sister, really."

"That be why there is one time I just hate to remember even today, that me and Bobby made her so mad. Well, some of us was having a game and I were like doing a striptease. I mean, I didn't take nothing off, but I made these faces I think a stripteaser would do. And, like I get in front of Bobby . . . All of the kids was making all kinds of cracks like saying, 'C'mon, Johnnie, show us what you got.'

" 'Old Johnnie got plenty,' somebody else say. And then Bobby got in the act. 'C'mon, baby, c'mon.'

"I reel, rock, and wiggle. And next thing I know, here is Sister Ann Marie looking mean at all of the kids, but mostly Bobby and me. And she say something, I can't remember the words now, but it were sort of hinting around, you know. Oh, she started in asking Bobby if me and him sleeps in the same bed. And Bobby said something like, 'What y'all care where me and Johnnie sleeps at? It ain't none of your business, Sister.' Then she say something about my brother being lowdown and has got a evil spirit, though she never would think that of him before. She use allus to love him before this time because he were the smartest kid in the school, and everyone knowed it.

"All the same when she say Bobby got a evil spirit, you know I be getting into it then and say, 'Sister, what in hell you mean? You gon' start any funny stuff about Bobby, well, it ain't gon' be so good for you then. She slapped me and I gon' wild and beat her up. So me and Bobby got expelled from the school.

"Then my stepmother done talked my daddy into having us work like her kids was, and only go to school, the regular colored one, on rainy days. So after that, I stop all of trying to learn, seem like I just couldn' care no more, but Bobby never would stop trying. And even though we was both working a lots of the time in the tomato fields and squash and cucumber, he still taken time to learn on his own. That was Bobby for you.

"Well, me and him got up early, four o'clock in the morning, and it were cold sometime so you got to build a fire to dress. And in the tomato fields and picking the cucumbers and squash, this was hard work, a whole lots harder than picking oranges. And if we pick by the piece, we would make ten cent a bucket on the tomatoes. And we pick beans and corn. We was getting like six cent a box for the corn. And I always hated picking corn, I could never pick corn good. And when it was cold, I couldn't hardly bear it.

"Well, my cousin, Sam Snooker, being about twelve when me and Bobby begun working full time, he have been working two, three years picking tomatoes, and we gon' to work alongside of him. Wheresoever he would pick to go work, me and Bobby gon' along. And all of the three of us being tall and young and strong we was the 'special niggers' of the bossmen and crew chiefs. They all wanted us working for them, young as we was. Well, being a special nigger in them days was plenty better than to be a 'dropshot,' well, what you call a dropshot or 'poor joke," just say, 'poor gal' or 'poor boy.' Somebody don't weigh much, look sickly, don't look healthy, so no crew chief wouldn't want them on his crew, that was a dropshot.

"Well, I try today—again since the project begun—to remember back how you would feel to be a special nigger because it is sort of like to be a special dog or cat, I would say. But in them days, all the blacks try to pull himself up ahead of the next one. Because, back before this project, all of the bossmen I worked for in my life, a agricultural worker or migrant be one of two things to him—a special nigger he can make money off, or a dropshot he can't. And like you can imagine, he maybe show *a little* respect for the special nigger, but none at all for the dropshot.

"I get so ashamed today to remember how I sort of puffed myself up around the dropshots, making them know I was better than them because the bossman and crew chief done tell me so.

"Well, I wasn't a very serious mind in them days. None of us was, I reckon, excepting my brother. Being in the fields all day, I don't think any of the pickers, excepting Bobby, give much thought to anything but just 'how much money can I make today, and how many bushels of tomatoes or whatsoever can I pick?'

"And us special niggers was allus changing jobs. Because, like a crew chief would come along and say, 'You can make more money off of my job than the one you are on. And, us, we believe him, and go on to his job. And hardly ever make no more money than on the job we was before. And sometimes even make less. All of the crew chiefs was liars; it seem we ought to know that, but didn't, because, see, we want to believe things gon' be better for us someplace else than they was where we were. If you don't believe that, then you got no more reason for hope than the dropshot do. And once you let youself know that, well, what be the use of living then?

"And them crew chiefs get you on some scary jobs sometimes, though you don't know that when you go. Like one time me and Bobby and Sam Snooker gon' to pick peppers for this man were suppose to pay so good, givè you everything be coming to you.

"Well, the way it turns out, he was nothing like the crew chief say. In fact, he locked the gate after the trucks was in, and walked around with a whip to keep you scared and working like he wanted.

"Me, Bobby, and Sam only stayed there this one day. And all the time I wondered what would I do if he ever put the whip on me or my cousin or brother.

"Well, I seen him use the whip on people two time during that one day. Once it were on a man didn't have too much sense, he were a poor, raggedy dropshot. I wanted to jump him then and beat him back for that dropshot's sake, 'cause I knowed he never could—nor would—do it hisself. But you know how it were. Although wanting to, I didn't do nothing at the time such as I would do today in a minute.

"The second time I seen him use the whip, sometime I still hates myself for letting him whip this old lady beside me that have just stopped her work for a minute so she could look to see was there any rattlesnakes. Now this farm was on the rain line, so, over there, you had to always look for snakes. There was rattlesnakes all over, and they always was crawling around somebody's legs.

"So, when that bossman whip the old one just for stopping to look for a snake, whew, I got evil then. And if he hadn't've rode off so fast and Bobby and Sam hadn't've come up and take, each one, a-holt of my arm so I was not able to move and run after him . . ."

Two weeks after Johnnie left that "slave-time job" a strange man came to her shack to tell the family that Bobby had been killed when the truck he was riding to a job that was supposed to be better than any other around hit a pole while going at thirty, thirty-five miles an hour. Seventeen years old. Johnnie is the last to hear the news. Her father, sobbing, tells her.

It's the worst thing that's ever happened to Johnnie, worse even than having lost her mother. It releases in her a helpless but savage hostility and belligerence at "the mean, miserable bossmen and crew chiefs send my people out in the beat-up trucks they wouldn't put their cows in, you know, because the cows be worth money to them.

"Well, Bobby's, Sam's, and my crew chief when Bobby were killed, he was Jim, a black man hisself. And he don't care no more about us black agricultural workers than if he have been white. And that damn truck of his, see, I could've been on it along with Bobby and Sammy if I hadn't've been sick. And I'd've knowed what have happened even if Sam Snooker wasn't there to tell me. Sam were hurt, too, shook up, and don't want to talk about what happen at first, not even to me. But, after a while, he tell me what have been and the reason for the truck going off the road. See, the driver couldn't steer the wheel. He keep on and on trying to move it the right way. But it broken off anyways, the steering arm just broken the hell off.

"Well, all the migrants known the steering in that beat-up truck was loose. It have been hard to steer from the time we first begun riding in it two weeks before. Hell, it never gon' straight on the road like it ought to, never, from day one we begun riding it. And all of the time, you know, me and Bobby and Sammy and all of us would tell to Jim that there gon' be a accident because the steering were so loose. And we were all the time saying, 'Please have someone take the truck to the shop, Jim.' And he says, 'Yeah, sure I do that.' But then he never done it.

"Well, see he never ride in that truck hisself, him nor his wife nor kids. They got their new Cadillac every year, and that what they go in. And that Cadillac was kept serviced up to date, believe me.

"I seen him one time after Bobby died, Jim, I mean. And I told him, 'Man, you was the one killed my beautiful brother by not taking the truck in the shop when you should. You got all of these people riding and don't even care enough to check out the truck they going in.' So, he tell me, he said, 'Well, it be a question of time, you know. How can I check out anything when the truck got to start out every day of the week at six o'clock in the morning, and don't get back till seven or eight at night. You know yourself the shop be closed by then.' So I say, 'Well, why don't you just *take* the time, like, you know, ain't my brother's and other people's life worth a hour or two in the whole seven days of the week?'

"And Jim said, 'Well, you can't blame me. If I don't get all his work done in the time he want it, the bossman gon' fire me and our whole crew. So I were afraid to take the time to have the truck fixed.' He were telling the truth; I known it myself. So the fault belonged to the bossman, really. And he were a white man, damnit."

Johnnie Lou tells how her now eternally young dead brother's presence kept her company for a long time, condemning her, at first, to a state of inner raging, ending in self-hatred at her frustration and impotence. And changing, little by little, into a hostility not only toward the system in which the agricultural workers were caught but also toward white people . . . "any or all white people," as she put it very often during our talks.

"Well, first of all I remember then, and get so mad at it all, I feel I can bust inside, I think, to myself, you know, how many, many times my stepmother use to teach my stepbrothers and Bobby . . . the main thing she use to tell all the boys was, don't they ever speak out to a white woman. She tell them that day by day. And don't ever speak out to no white man either. And when Bobby or one of my stepbrothers may seem like they ain't listening to her, she will say, 'You just better listen to me, you has to believe me 'cause that the way it be, that the way. If a colored man was to smile at a white lady or speak against a white man, he may as well be dead 'cause they gon' to kill him!'

"And my stepbrothers listen to her, but Bobby sometime tell her in return, he said, 'Well, then, better no white man smile or speak out at Johnnie Lou or any other colored girl I happen to care about. Or might be I kill him, you know.' And my stepmother say, 'You plain crazy, boy.'

"And then, one time, not too long after Bobby died, me and my stepsister was walking downtown and passed this mean-looking gang of white men, and they say . . . I would be about sixteen and my stepsister a year older . . . and they called us prostitutes and asked us to go with them for the money, though we don't be too pretty so they are not willing to pay us too much.

"And ain't no sense making believe, me and my stepsister both known we was very pretty. But that ain't the point. The point be, my stepsister say to me at the time, 'I just thinking that if Bobby was alive today and heard them men calling us whores, especially you, Johnnie, well, he would fight them. And maybe, like mama always say, they would kill him for that. So, you know, a hell-raising kid like him, I don't think he could have a long life anyways.'

"And I think about what she say then, and known she were right. If he hadn't've died on the bus, he would sure have been killed for standing up for our rights. Because it were much worse in Florida then than now. Like begging time, it was. Me and Bobby and a whole lots of peoples on the project today knowing or learning we are as good as any people and has got our rights the same as anybody has grown up in a real begging time when you didn't . . . Like, if you was downtown and I don't care if you have taken castor oil, you could not go in a bathroom that the sign didn't say 'colored.' You could not sit down and get you a sandwich.

"And I remember all of the things about hitting the road, and thinking about it all, I has to say, 'Why and how can such things be?' Like you must ask of the Lord, if you have got religion, 'Well, how come, Lord, our family leave Florida, go up North to work in, say, the apples and cherries, and in so many places, so many states you can't use the bathroom even if you was to bust?' It be this way then in all of the service stations along the road. It was exactly the same as in the Florida stores downtown. Only the whole thing was even worse in the service stations upon thinking it over. Because, see, in the Florida downtown places, at least you ain't spend up all your money in those. But when we stop at a service station to fill up with gas, they taken your money for the gas all right, but you could not use the rest room, if the colored one was, what they say 'out of commission,' and usually it were, you know.

"And after Bobby dying, I don't know, but all of the little stuff and big things never used to bother me all of that much begun to get to me then. And I become, little by little, I become what some white folks around here still call a 'smart nigger.' Like, even till today, if you in line and a white lady in back of you get out of her place you supposed to let her get in front of you. Up until today, and since the time Bobby die till today, I just wish some white woman even tries that with me.

"Well, the first time they seen me to be a smart nigger, this white man shoot my dog about turning over a garbage can. And I always loved that dog and even called him Bobby after my brother died. And I gon' down there to that man's house, and I say, 'Mr. Johnson, why did you shoot my dog?'

"He said, 'Because the police told me that if the dog turn over my garbage can, I could shoot him.' So I say, 'Mr. Johnson, if you ever get a dog, I am gonna shoot *him*.'

"I wouldn't have shot him, I would never shoot any dog, because I love animals too much. But he shot my dog and I was hurt. So I said, 'If you ever get a dog, I gon' kill him.' His wife were listening and she called the cops, saying, well, I heard her telling them, 'Well, this mean nigger threatening at my husband, and say if we ever get a dog she gon' shoot him. I want her in jail for saying she gon' shoot our dog.'

"Well, the policemen don't put me in jail, not at the time. But they given me a talking to, they come to the house and call me out and say, 'You know what could happen to smart niggers around here, they goes to jail for talking bad to a white man. And if you was to shoot the man's dog on him, why you can be killed youself for shooting a white man's dog.' So I say, 'Well, how in the world could I shoot that white man's dog when he don't even own any dog?' Then one of the cops smacks me in the face and says, 'Keep it up, nigger, if y'all want to be a dead nigger. See, us policemen be watching you from now on. It be our pleasure to stick you in jail and let you rot there.'

"Well, then a couple weeks later, I done make it to jail just like that cop say I would. I go uptown to buy a blouse and get in a argument with one of the salesladies has shown me a blouse I liked. Long and then, if you were black, you would pick out what you want. And they has dressing rooms for the white ladies to try on things, but not for black. Not only can't you use the white dressing room, but, like they don't have no colored one either. So I say to the saleslady about why don't they have some place where black, or I say colored at that time, why don't they have some place where colored women can also try on something before buying it?

"And I can tell it make her hot, but she don't at the time say nothing in answer. But what she done, well, the way it work, you pick out what you want and point it out to the saleslady. And you can't hold or touch it, but she will hold it in front of you for you to make up your mind. Only after you decide you take it was you allowed to touch it, to put a hand on it. And then you got to take it because you have touched it. See, you got to give the saleslady the money for whatever it cost. She will write out the ticket for it, and the lady behind the counter would take the money and give you your change.

"This blouse were a dollar ninety-nine and I give her two dollars. So she write up the ticket and instead of giving me my penny change, she tell me to pay her another two dollars. 'I given you the money.' 'Oh, no, you hasn't,' she say. 'Oh, yeh, I did.' And so we was standing there and this lady who sell me, well, I knew she have seen me give my money to the other one at the cash register, but she said, 'Will you give her the two dollars?' She say, 'You has not give it to her.' And I say, 'Well, you was standing right there and seen me give it to her.' She say, 'You better give her that money, nigger, because she say you didn't.' And I said, 'Well, I don't give a damn what she say or what you say, I know I given it to her and I ain't gon' give her no more.

"So that really burned her and she called me every name you heard of and kept yelling I was a 'bad nigger' but would soon be a good one, because what they gon' to do, if there be menfolks around, they would kill me for talking this way to white ladies. And they said how everyone know that 'the only good nigger is a dead nigger.' And she start from behind the counter to hit me, and I said, 'Well, you hit me and I gon' hit you right back.' So she called the police.

"Well, I gone home and they come to my house to arrest me. By now, I has been in jail many a time and all over the country. A jail don't scare me no more, but then . . . I never will forget when they slammed that cell door on me. I screamed. The jail had four sections, a 'white men's,' a 'white women's' and 'nigger men's' and 'nigger women's,' as they called it. And in the white womens' section, and even the white men's, they got like cots and a toilet. But in what they calls the 'nigger women's section' you sleeps on the stone cold floor with nothing but buckets to use when you needs to go. Two big buckets and all five of us has to use them. And the woman keeper come around once in a while and screw up her nose. Like she say, 'Oh, this nigger smell. Even in the jail the white criminals don't smell like the nigger ones.'

"Calling us criminals, well, I don't know what the white ones was there for, but us black ones, well, first of all, there be me. And I am the one they say is the worst of the whole lot, because I am a smart nigger and talk back to the white folks, and it is the same in their eyes, as being a robber or killer. But the other four, nobody can call them smart niggers. Three of them was real dropshot ladies, old and sick. They was in for drunk and disorderly, poor old dropshots, your heart has to go out to them.

"And the last one, you would've cry to see her. Annie Jean Little. She look to be thirteen or fourteen years old, but were really fifteen and a half. That's how tiny the poor little soul were for her age. And even her being fifteen and a half . . . they wasn't supposed to send anybody her age to jail in the first place. She didn't have no mama nor daddy, and had been a couple years in a juvenile home in Miami. Till her old grandma come up from Georgia, somewhere, and taken her out. Well, then, her luck, the grandmother died, too. So here be poor little Annie Jean Little hitting the streets because what else could she do? And she were in jail for that. Also she was pregnant, and most feared she would have the baby in the jail.

"So, I says, 'What be the difference in or out of jail?' And she say that, well, if she be out, she have her a young doctor, this fat, jolly, doctor named Anderson, come out to the juvenile home when she were there. He were really beautiful, she say, although a white man. And one time she overhear him tell the matron that taken care of the pregnant girls' section, he tell her that, like, any of the girls that need him, she could call him down to the hospital he work at and he will take care of them any time of the day or night.

"I don't believe Annie, because to me, at that time, I has never met any white person that you could say has *any* care about the blacks.

"And I say to Annie she is a fool if she think any white man, doctor or not, will do something for nothing for any of us. Now, sure, if she were still in the juvenile home and pregnant, the charity be the one to pay for the borning. I know that much, because gals I known in the juvenile home has their babies under a doctor's care. And a lots of them try to get in juvenile for just this reason when they come pregnant.

"Well, then we left the jail, me after three weeks waiting for my trial, and Annie, too, although she have been in two weeks before I got there, also waiting her trial. She were there five weeks altogether. And the judge say to me, I was first to come up before him, and he says, 'Are you guilty or not guilty?' And I says, 'Guilty of what?' So he say, 'Oh, I see you be a smart nigger still, talking to me this way, and I could put you back in jail for a year just for being so smart. But instead I will put you on probation. And in case you don't know what that mean, well, it mean the next time you act smart to white people you gon' go to the pen for a *long stay*.'

"Then, when Annie's turn come to go before him, she just tell him how she have nobody in the world to help her out and has come pregnant and so please, could she go back to the juvenile home till her baby come. I mean, she was the right age for the home, still a juvenile, you know.

"But the judge tell her no, and send her back out in the street. Once we was outside, Annie, she say, 'I don't care about not going back to the home, because Dr. Anderson help me anyways. I be very sure of that.' And then she say, 'Johnnie, if you ain't believe he do this, you call him up on the telephone.' So I done it. And just talking to him . . . Well, see, me getting to know Dr. Anderson have come at a time when I just done *hate* everybody having a white skin. But how in the hell can I hate any who say, 'Remember little Annie? I sure does. Will I take care of her? You bet I will, if you or her just call me up so I can make the arrangements in my hospital.' And he ask, 'Well, where at she gon' to stay till the baby come?' I say, 'Oh, at my house.' I knowed my daddy would want for me to help her out even if my stepmother wouldn't.

"So, Annie Jean live with us three and a half weeks and, on this morning, at four in the morning, see, I has given up my own place in the bed to her, and were sleeping on the floor . . . well, she got out of bed and stood over me and she call me: 'Johnnie Lou, I has a whole lot of pain, worse than ever before, and think it be the baby trying to make its way out.' I said, 'Oh, honey, couldn't you pick a better time?' But I got up and gon' all of the way to Sam Snooker's house and get him and his old rattly-trap car to drive us to Miami to Dr. Anderson's hospital.

"That was the first time I ever set foot in a place like that, and I were surprised when we got there, people being really nice, the aides and nurses and all. And they say I could go on upstairs to the ward with Annie. They have about eleven or twelve women there waiting for their time to come. There was, maybe, twenty babies already in the nursery, and so many women and young girls waiting, you couldn't hardly move.

"At the end, seem like I were having that baby myself. I like to have a heart attack, because Annie grabbed my hand and wouldn't let me go. 'Don't leave me, you know, please don't leave me. Hold my hand, rub my stomach.' And this was the first time I have seen anybody about to give birth, and it made you worry when the person giving birth be a poor little dropshot kid like Annie and you love her a whole lot. I just think I can't stand to see her, I just want to faint because I knew the pain she were going through. And it was nothing I could do but stand there helpless. So they finally took her out to what you call it, the borning room, or whatever.

"And she say, 'I got two favors to ask you, Johnnie. The first is that you stay here, no matter how late, until I has my baby.' So I says, 'Well, I couldn't leave no way until I know, for sure, the baby is born and you are fine. What is the second favor you want?' So she say, 'Johnnie, maybe I can't tell Dr. Anderson, when he come to take the baby, where at will I get words to tell him how good he be, and how much such a man mean? Y'all tell him for me, Johnnie.'

"So, after one of the nurses come down and tell me Annie had a little girl, 'Johnnie Lou, you can go home now and get a little rest,' I says, 'Well, before I goes, I got to see Dr. Anderson because I promised Annie.' And the nurse said, 'Well, you know how busy the man be, you seen youself all the ladies in labor. But I show you his office, and his own nurse happens to be there at the moment—you can leave the message with her.' So I did. I tell the girl, the nurse, Annie's feelings and mine, too. I say I want for the Doc to know I be out of agriculture, a whole family of agricultural workers. And none of us ever dream to have our babies in a hospital before he come into Annie's life. I also say, 'Please to tell the Doc I got a hate on all white people before, but not no more, since he have done what he did. I can't no more, hate all white people since knowing he be in the world, a white man like that.'

The next day I gon' back to visit Annie and see the baby. And Doc Anderson has told the nurse for me to call him. When I do, he asked me to come to his office and we talked. He say he be a Quaker. Well, by now, I know there are many wonderful peoples like him in that group, because I has met some Quakers during my travels and they all been good people. And in other groups, too, there be good white people.

"Doc Anderson say he be interested in my people, and us getting to hospitals like anybody else. In two months, on his vacation, he say he will come down to see for hisself, and try to work something out to help the agricultural people." She adds, in her wriest tone, "Well, he never come. I never gon' looking for him either, as I know I would have did today. Instead of that I tell myself, 'Well, what you expect of a white man? Yeah, he give you the good word, but, when it come to action . . .' And, see, I just put out of my mind all that he had did for Annie. Well, that were action, wasn't it, but, see, I put it out of my mind, and told myself, 'Oh, well, he be just another white man is all."

"And never change my mind about white people till this project begun and I come to know the people at the company, the big men like Luke Smith and Don Keough and Bill Kelly. And also y'all from HRI. Now, since this project, I would never again think the worst of a white man like Dr. Anderson or any of y'all.

"But him having seem to let me down or if any of y'all was to seem to let me down, I would think since this project, something must've happen in their life, something bad to keep them from carrying out their promises. And I would come looking for Doc Anderson or anybody in the company or HRI to find out what have happened and can I help out if it was something bad."

PART III

Nine Years
after the Beginning

Saturday, March 26, 1977, was bright, a tranquil and happy day for Bob, Arnold, and me. The people of the Agricultural Labor Project, many of whom we'd kept on keeping in touch with over the years, caring about with the same passion and hope for their futures as we'd ever felt while on our jobs, had invited us to their annual meeting and a ribbon-cutting ceremony for a new building, housing the personnel for both another regional project (there are now four projects covering twenty-one counties) and the administrators for the combined projects, incorporated as ALPI, the Agricultural Labor Project Incorporated.

This new headquarters is a wonderful thing, a culmination of everyone's hopes and dreams, the people's, the company's, and ours from HRI. For the project's move out of the company's offices and into its own headquarters signified yet again that it had grown up, after nine years of existence, to be a people's program, a people's movement in the truest sense of the word. The company does not any longer have to serve as its Big Daddy, its only funding agent. The project boards and staff, themselves, are able now to devise service programs and write such effective proposals describing them that they elicit large sums of operating money from the government and other agencies. It makes them know for a fact that the company, though it never did, is now not even in a position to give them orders, at least no more than any funding agency is.

It's still early for the ceremony, and huge numbers of people dressed in their best (nobody would laugh at how they look now, as they often laughed in our day) are milling around outside the building. Many are, predictably, unknown to us. Since the two years or so ago when we last visited the project, it had not only expanded tremendously but also achieved the concept we'd always hoped—but sometimes doubted—it would do someday. Membership, as well as use of all the services and facilities—medical centers, child development centers, one-to-one tutoring, legal services and education, housing advice, and much, much more—has become open to all the poor people in the twenty-one counties making up the project areas, including the migrants who are working for other citrus growers. ALPI is not serving itself alone any longer, but has assumed a role of definite, recognized leadership in all the communities of which it is a part.

We are telling each other how glad and proud we are, when I hear my name called by Lily's warm voice. I turn around and there she is, my old, familiar friend with whom I had spent so much time, talking, planning, laughing, joking. But I can't either forget the times, when things had gone wrong on the project, when people's feelings had been hurt because, not always knowing what made them tick from our own experience, we and, sometimes, even she, herself, had said or done something to pain them, and she'd sat silent, tears of frustration rolling down her face. Now she cried again as she embraced us, but the tears were happy because she'd missed us over the years as we had her. And although I had seen her both strict and tenacious when a situation warranted, I'd always known her to be a sentimentalist at heart.

Once we, all of us, let each other go, and stood apart, looking one another up and down, I had to tell her she wasn't *quite* my familiar Lily after all. I'd never imagined her so elegant as she looked in her well-cut smart pants suit. I reminded her of the time soon after she'd come to Florida, her status as a welfare mother still very much on her mind (as it is, in fact, today), and I'd felt compelled to say to her, "I'm sure glad I like that brown dress, Lily, since it's all you ever wear."

Until I and others shamed her into it, she hadn't wanted to take any time off the job she worked at seven days a week and almost as many nights just to shop for clothes.

She's the program director now, though, elected by the board as are all major staff, and "realizes looking decent has also got to be a part of my job." (Since this visit Lily has been selected acting director.)

I say, "Well, you sure must be succeeding since I heard about that fact in New York."

Bill Kelly told me three or so years ago when we met in New York that Lily was doing marvelously on the job. He also talked about her noticeable dignity as well as that of other people on the project in whom he knew I was interested.

"About Lily," he said, "she's always had dignity, you'd have to be a fool not to notice that, but it was an inner sort of dignity. Now it's outer as well. I think she realizes, from the pride all of us take in her, she's got reason to be proud of herself." He hesitated. "I wonder if her clothes would indicate . . . she's certainly dressing *well* these days."

Lily looked away from me, and down at the ground, shuffled her left foot back and forth, and said something like, "Oh, yeh, oh, sure." Embarrassed as hell because she had to know I was telling the truth, and compliments always were—and are still—hard for her to take.

Bob tactfully changes the subject, and tells Lily we can't seem to find our other old friends, the early staff and board members, in this crowd of new faces.

"I'll bet Johnnie Lou's the one you want to see most," Lily says, and all of us say that of course we do.

"Listen," Johnnie says as soon as Lily's found her, and we've greeted one another and exchanged embraces, "my kid's in college now. And his grades, man, he's getting straight A's and B's. Well, I got to give the project all of the credit for that. Without the project, I still would be picking fruit and living in the old shack. And Billy, what would he have to look forward to except being a fruit picker, a migrant himself? Now he can be a doctor, a lawyer, a engineer, a teacher, you name it."

"A doctor or a lawyer," she repeats, and adds, with one of those do-I-have-something-to-tell-you looks and her arms folded against her chest, "Do y'all know two of our kids, no, young people they are now . . . well, one of them is finishing up in medical school and the other is a senior in law. Besides, we have got forty-five kids in college now. And two of our people are teaching in the public schools."

Lily says, "Listen, I got to tell you, Johnnie Lou's come kind of a long way herself."

Johnnie shrugs her shoulders. "I have come to be a regional director is all."

"A regional director with a huge staff working with her," Lily says, and adds, "She raises a lot of funding for their salaries from such agencies as CETA [Comprehensive Employment Training Act,] the Department of Community Services, colleges in the area, the Home Extension Service—I could go on and on. But the big point is, Johnnie Lou thought up the programs these agencies are supporting and giving her staff for, and wrote the proposals for them with only a little help from the other staff."

"First, she went to see the agency executives and impressed them so much. Well, you know Johnnie Lou. She admitted she didn't write so well, but when she started talking and describing the programs she'd thought up, everyone flipped and knocked himself out to help her. Then, when the agency officials went down to her area, and watched her operate with the people there, all of them said she was the one to administer the programs; they'd never met anyone more dedicated or real or loving toward the people, even those she ruled with her 'iron hand.'"

"Look who's talking about ruling with an iron hand," Johnnie says. "Lily Haskins, of all the people on this project, is talking about ruling with an iron hand. After what she did to rule me—making me go to school and all that. She knocked me out about going to school every time she saw me. Her and Arnold both would keep saying, 'You got so much on the ball, Johnnie, you got to go to school!' I was hearing those words in my sleep. 'Go to school.' Bob, Sara, remember how Lily, Arnie, and me used to fight over the business of me going to school. There were times when I hated both of their guts."

She turns to Arnold. "Much as I hated y'all for that 'go to school, go to school' business, I really loved you for learning—teaching—me about getting government loot for our projects. Listen, remember the times you took me along wherever you had to go to work out your proposals for all the centers we got now. Man, I sure listened to all you said to them people controlling the money, and watched y'all like a hawk. The way you stroked (that means compliment in your language, man, in case you don't know it) them people, instead of blurting out what you had to say like I would have done in your place. Yet, all the time you didn't pull punches neither. You told them how if we got them facilities, we were gon' to use them to do so much good for all the poor people.

"And now, Arnie, I couldn't believe it when you said, 'Someday, Johnnie, if you'll only put your mind to it, and, oh yeh, go to school, too, the funding people are going to listen to you as good as or better than they do to me. Because, Johnnie, you know your people's life, their sufferings, and all they need from your own experience. It means you can make the funding people know it better than I ever could. They have got to listen to you, if you only learn to get with them, swing with them.'

"Well, I never thought, in my whole life, I could do anything as good as, and sure not better than any of y'all at HRI. But . . ."

Arnold says, "But without going to school, as Lily and I were always preaching at you to do, Johnnie . . ."

Johnnie smiles, a mysterious smile that is full of wisdom, love of life, and certainly pain. "Well, what I told you about going to school in the old days still stands, Arnie. I never, in this life, would have go to school with other people because of the shame of them knowing all I didn't know. Oh, I wanted to go very much, because I knew what y'all were saying, and you Lily, was right. I never would be able to help my people the way I wanted to without me going to school. But, like I said, I was *so* ashamed for them knowing the little I knew.

"But then, with the tutoring, one to one, just my teacher and me, I saw there wasn't a reason in the world, anymore, to be ashamed. And I said to myself, 'Johnnie, if you don't get into one-to-one tutoring, then shame has got nothing to do with it. You are just a lazy, good-for-nothing, and don't really care a damn about helping your people like you always saying you do.' So I did it, got into one-to-one tutoring. And now there is just my teacher and me and we get together in my house. And I must say I am learning more every day."

Lily speaks up and says, "Johnnie's English is improving a good deal though she'd be the first to say she's still got a lot to learn. But her numbers, her arithmetic, her accounting techniques . . . See, she works out her own budget, and it's big, believe me. She manages it perfectly. And she's going to be getting her GED [High School General Equivalency Diploma] very soon, if I'm not mistaken."

"Well, my teacher is a big help to me getting my GED . . . when I ever do, *if* I ever do. And Ed Rouse was a big help when it came to teaching me about numbers and how to keep a budget."

Ed Rouse is the former accountant for the Agricultural Labor Project who came at about the time we consultants were leaving, not only to keep the records but also to teach the board treasurer, aides, and other responsible members to keep their own accounts.

"But that one-to-one tutoring," Johnnie Lou says, "it is the thing that helped not just me but also people from seven to seventy and older ones, too. All of the people in the program are so proud of what they are learning. And the real old ones are proudest of all."

And as though to prove her point by sample and example, here comes squat, whimsical old Granny May Lolly. "I'm so glad to see you folks," she says. "I supposing you thought to youselfs, 'Old Granny May is dead by now.' But, she ain't. She is alive and kicking!" She smiles broadly, and self-consciously, obviously showing off her set of gleaming false teeth; she had a few rotted front teeth when I saw her last.

"How you like these new teeth I got in my old age?" she asks me. "Ain't they just beautiful?"

"Beautiful," I say.

"That sweet li'l ol' dentist in the medical center, he get these teeth for me, and it be hard to believe, but I needed to pay him very little money for something that pleasure me so much as these teeth do. Sometime I can hardly wait to get up in the morning and put my new teeth in my mouth. I smile and laugh all the time now so people can see my pretty teeth."

She stays silent awhile just smiling to herself first, and then at each one of us. Finally, she says, "I got me more wonderful things happening, too. I got me a teacher come to my house and shown me how to spell my name, write and spell it out loud if I want to. M-A-Y. That be the way y'all spells May. L-O-L-L-Y. That how you spell Lolly." And then Granny May added, "I ain't satisfy no more with only be able to spell my name. See, I ain't never gon' be satisfy till I am able to read the Bible, the Good Book, by myself."

"Miss May," Bob asks, "would you say you're the oldest student in the tutorial program?"

Granny May Lolly smiles again, holding the smile long enough to show the false teeth to their greatest advantage, and says, "Oh, no, I sure ain't. Well, we has got a man of ninety, and one that *say* he be going on a hundred year old. He may be telling a little lie about being nigh on a hundred, but well, why not? You see him, you believe youself he be ninety-five, ninety-six year old. And all them years he been like me, having to sign things with a cross because he don't know how to write his own name. Now he do know how to, though, and I swan he be the proudest person in the world about that. *The proudest.*"

Now, we go into the new ALPI headquarters, and if I'm not mistaken plenty of delicious food prepared by the catering committee, headed, Johnnie says, by our old friend, Mother Bets.

The new headquarters has been designed by the company's Glen Rauth, after consultation with the boards and administrative staff. The offices are simple, painted an off-white, yet possessed, somehow, of a certain individuality. A picture here, a poster there, a program chart in Lily's office, the rooms reflect the people they're housing. There is also a very modern kitchen where Mother Bets, looking better than I've ever thought she could (I can't help but recall our early board meeting at the motel where the tourists laughed or were angered by the sight of her), is presiding over a crew of volunteer caterers who are preparing finger sandwiches, cake and punch.

I take a bite of a sandwich Mother Bets has been sampling, and she says, "Oh, you ain't changed a bit, baby. Taking bites off of other people's food instead of getting your own." (I'd always had to laugh in order to keep myself from weeping and railing when I realized, as I did very early on the job, how flattered, even thrilled, not only Mother Bets but also a close friend like Johnnie Lou, were at the notion of me, a white woman, deigning to eat food they had touched.) She turns to the other women, most of whom are new and unknown to me, and says, with pleasure "See, Sara was here for nigh on two years and me and her has lunch or supper together on many a time. Well, she always was on a diet or say she were, and ordered herself up some dinky-looking salad or something like that. Now, me, I didn't care in them days if I was fat or skinny or what. I mean I just didn't care then how I looked, because the way I seen things, what was there to look forward to, even if I was to look *good*?

"So, here is Sara with that little salad make me sick to look at it, and here is me with my big plate of barbecued ribs, french-fried potatoes. Man, my food look good to me. And must look the same to Sara. Because, first thing she saying is, 'You know, I am on this diet, Bets, but could I have *one* of your barbecue ribs? The littlest one you got.' So I says, "Well, please, honey, help youself.' So next thing you know she got her hand in my plate, and breaking off a rib. Only it ain't the littlest like she say; the biggest be what she take. Then she start picking on that little salad, and I say, 'How about a french-fried potato?' Well, she taken four or five potatoes, and a other rib to boot. Them was some funny meals her and me use to have. Ain't it Sara?"

I nod yes, and say, "Not to change the subject Bets, but you said something I want to hear more about."

"All you got to do is ask me, hon."

"Well, you said you didn't care about your appearance, the way you looked, in those early days of the project. Does that mean you do care now?"

Bets nods vigorously.

"How come you changed that way?"

"Lawd, I got the money to help me make myself look good now, buy me nice new clothes that I never believed in my life I would have money for clothes. See, last year, working on the oranges I make near seven thousand dollars."

Mother Bets is not the only company worker to have such an altered self-image since our early days together. The new economic security they had never dreamed they would experience in this life has given the majority a new feeling about who they are. (As well it might; they are the highest paid agricultural workers in not only the U.S.A. but in the world today. Harvesting employees of The Coca-Cola Company Foods Division are paid 21 percent more per box of oranges than the average picker. Nearly 40 percent of grove and harvesting employees now work year round as regular company employees, which gives them the fringe benefits and seniority rights other kinds of employees traditionally enjoy.)

And as Paul Austin and Luke Smith realized even before the project began, rather than finding this program on the debit side, the company has found that by treating its migrant workers with dignity and concern, it has benefited all concerned. Before the change, it was necessary to process five thousand people through the payroll annually to maintain a work force of twelve hundred. Today this has stabilized—a relatively unchanging force of nine hundred harvesters perform roughly the same work as the twelve hundred who previously dropped in and out, and to keep the workers at this level requires processing less than seventeen hundred people.

"Well, who wouldn't want to work for this company now," Mother Bets's eldest son asks when I discuss the new conditions with him. No longer picking, a foreman on his way to becoming a supervisor, he explains, "Was a day before this project, when no black man like me could hope to be a supervisor. Now, though, you do a good job and you get what's coming to you no matter what your color is."

One of the first matters of business at the annual meeting was the installation of four new officers to the board of directors, the policy board composed of twenty-five people elected by the advisory councils of all the regional councils, northern, central, southern, and eastern. This board combination was undertaken, after much deliberation and discussion on the people's parts, because they came to realize that unity meant power and would be an aid in obtaining operating funds from local, state, and federal agencies. It might also serve as one more step toward the achievement of independence from the company which had, after all, funded the people's activities before anyone else came to believe in them, to the tune of some five million dollars.

Rudy Maxwell, project manager for the past few years, and now manager of Corporate Personnel, The Coca-Cola Company, is here to install the new board people. He's young, attractive, well spoken, well dressed, a model for the several aspiring executives in the room today who'd never before believed they could make it because of the color of their skin.

Solemnly, Rudy told the board members, "You are taking a very large step in becoming a member of this board. Not only must you follow the bylaws and articles of incorporation governing what is now your board but also you are under oath to go out into the community and find the people who might not themselves seek our your organization and ask for the help they need. You are going to have to go out and find the disadvantaged, the poor people, the ones who, like you yourselves may have done at one time, have lost faith and trust in a society which has so mistreated them.

"Now, it's going to be your place, to some extent, to restore their faith and trust. You must wrack your brains to introduce and carry out programs to touch these people's lives and make them know the winds of change are blowing as well for them, as they did for you . . ."

Now come the reports of the deputy directors and coordinators. Lily, as deputy director of program tells, impressively, of programs in all four regions consisting of one-to-one tutoring, GED instruction, cultural enrichment, consumer education, youth group activities (summer and winter), child development, voter education, adult vocational education, prevocational education, Spanish as a second language, basic legal rights, English for the foreign born, job development counseling and placement, college information counseling and placement, housing counseling, health information, counseling and referral, emergency assistance, remedial reading.

She's especially happy, actually vain, of ALPI's outreach program funded by the CETA office of the Manpower Services for the past two years. The ALPI outreach staff are paraprofessionals, selected from the target population, and given intensive preparation for interpreting the services and programs ALPI offers to the kinds of people Rudy talked of earlier. They have knowledge also of all other service-providing organizations, agencies, and institutions. They receive ongoing instruction in housing, counseling, nutrition, basic legal rights, education, preventive medicine, home health care and detection of illness, realty law, and housing code enforcement. Then they go into the community, into migrant camps and the homes of people who need individualized services and have no notion of how to get them. They help many people who may well be unknown to any other agency in their various communities.

We were told, not just by ALPI members but also Manpower officials that the ALPI outreach program, like the one of child development, is the most competent one in the state.

The next report is made by Ed Clarke. He has taken Ed Rouse's place, and is assisted by three former migrants Ed Rouse has trained in accounting techniques. Unlike Rouse, a large, black man, he is small, slender, and in many ways an archetype of white middle-class America. Very blonde, and white-toothed, as Granny May, who's sitting directly in front of me, turns round to point out, "Ain't that boy got just the purtiest teeth?"

Ed Clarke's report is short and sweet. "Nineteen seventy-seven has got to be a good year for ALPI. Our net operating budget will be $752,849.82. If you add the rural health service money, it is $1,152,849." (Lily told me, in a recent telephone conversation, that ALPI will soon be receiving, from both federal and local agencies, an additional $750,000 both to start new programs, and be enabled to activate ongoing ones; the outreach program, for instance, is receiving $200,-000 this year in recognition of its past accomplishments.)

Now Bill Kelly, quiet-spoken as always, tells of the project's beginnings and his own constantly changing reactions during the years he'd spent administering it.

"I'd seen poor people before," he told, "but never people caught in such a cycle of hopelessness decreeing that "This is your life, and it will be your children's life, and their children's life as well.' I didn't see, at the beginning, how you could change your situation, no matter how much help we could give. But watching you, working with you, I felt better every day. And, today, well, it's a wonderful day in my life as well as yours."

Listening to Bill now, I can't help but be reminded of my many friends and acquaintances who, when I told them about the project, as I, myself (prejudiced as *I* was at the beginning) was seeing it operate, succeed, change people's lives . . . I can't help but to think of the ones who said time and again:

"Damn, Sara, it's hard to believe you're so naïve. Don't you know *why* that company is doing all of the things it is? Just to keep Chavez and the union out, that's all."

The answer to what they went on saying, though, is that I was still around the groves when the company, true to its promises of worker self-determination, raised no questions about the conducting of union elections and signed a contract for worker representation with Cesar Chavez's United Farmworkers' organizing committee. Incidentally, Bill Kelly, at the union's request, was made a trustee of the Martin Luther King Farmworker's Fund. He resigned in May of 1976.

Bill continues his talk. "I recall so many incidents during my years here, but two I will always remember. One's very funny, very humorous, and I've told it often. A wonderful lady who's been remarkable on the project but doesn't want her name mentioned . . . Well, I'd brought a lot of big shots down from Atlanta and Houston, and we, all of us, including the staff, the deputy directors, the child development coordinator and some other ALPI staff, were sitting around and sort of getting acquainted. Somehow, we got to the question of what colleges we had gone to. And all of us told our colleges. Then, when it came this lady's turn, she said, 'Me, I am so-and-so, and I went to the University of Cloud Grove.'

"Then, later, one of our executives said to me, 'Bill, you know I've heard of all the colleges the people at our meeting mentioned . . . except one—the 'University of Cloud Grove.' Where's that?"

Whoops and giggles spread around the room, for everyone in the room knows Cloud Grove is an orange-picking area around Fort Pierce.

After the laughter died down, Bill continued, "There's one more story I've got to tell you about another lady who doesn't want her name mentioned. This one was heartrending, hurtful to me until I started thinking it over and realizing the point she was making. It was late one night, and I'd been to a meeting, oh, a lot of meetings, and looked into a lot of faces as I was doing at this meeting I am talking about, and always had to wonder to myself: 'Are the people hearing what I say? Can they possibly be believing what they hear from *me*? Why *should* they believe *me* anyway?'

"And as these thoughts were running through my mind, this lady I'm talking about came up to me, and said, 'Mr. Kelly, I don't know whether what we're, all of us, trying to do, is really going to help improve my life. It may be too late for me, but one thing I got to tell you, Bill Kelly, is that it's going to help my children and grandchildren, for sure. Now I'm not saying that my children or grandchildren won't be picking fruit for a living, because we're going to make this a better job. And it may be good enough so they'll *choose* to pick fruit. But, at least, they'll have the opportunity with the education and all of that they're getting now to be anything else they may want to be. It'll be their choice, where, for me, you know, there never was a choice. I had to be a fruit picker, a migrant, and that was all there was to that.' "

Tom Cleveland, who has replaced Bill as the adviser to the project when it requests advice, speaks next. He says first that it seems to him that the lady who said "she was a graduate of Cloud Grove College has not only her bachelor's degree, but also her master's. What she has contributed to the project, due to all she experienced in a lifetime of migrancy, coupled with a natural intelligence and feeling for other people, is immeasurable. And," he continues, "there are so many here like her, I feel privileged to know them. You know, all the time I listened to your recital of the Lord's Prayer, your moving and beautiful spiritual singing I kept thinking over and over:

"You people, the way you have pulled yourselves up by your bootstraps and now are helping other people to do the same is excitingly significant of a benediction the minister of my church used to say, following his Sunday morning sermons: 'Only one life, 'twill soon be past,/only what's done for Christ will last.'

"To me this means that when you do something for yourself it doesn't count a lot, but when you do something for someone else it has a lasting meaning. I am sure that a lot of what you're doing here, in this program, will have meaning for a long time."

Of course there have been some failures among the people on the project since we left. A few old-timers have even left it for, basically, two reasons. Either they were so white-oriented, so authority-oriented, that they were not able to adjust to the fact the company people like Bill and Gerry, as well as we consultants, were gone. They were not able, as many like Emanuela were, to accept the leadership, excellent as it is today, of their own people. Or they were, like Mack Milton, the first vice-president of the project and one of its most ardent advocates in the early days, angered by the new professionalization, for reasons he explains.

"See, the project is so different from when I were vice-president, well, y'all know. In them days, we were trying to bring out the people, small people, that have just about given up hope about them or their lives, right, Sara, Arnie? We opened several doors to such people, said to them, 'You come out and say what you want because that is what matters on this program.' And some of these here same people turned into leaders as you know. *Leaders* could hire and fire staff. And it make them feel good about themselfs, and they come out to things, and work hard. Now that it is so different, though—well, they taken all of the board's power away, since y'all gone, so why waste time being on it?"

He is referring to the project's reorganization as ALPI, and to the fact that though the policy board chooses the administrative staff and program coordinators, they, not the board leaders, are responsible for hiring and firing other staff. He regards this as a usurpation of the "people power" principle on which the project was founded.

It is easy to see, of course, why Mack would feel the way he does. And when we come down to it, we consultants have to realize that at least some of the blame rests with us. After all, being who he was, Mack had never thought of the abolition of migrancy as a cause, or himself as a leader toward its abolition. Then we came along and persuaded him he was. But we never realized the importance of helping him know how leadership in the early days was one thing, and is another in the highly successful days the people are presently experiencing. In other words, we had neglected to prepare Mack—and others—for rising in the world as rapidly as they have. He is still—and God knows, with good reason—fearful for and defensive of himself, his leadership abilities. It seems to him—again with reason—that others are replacing him.

But, wonderfully, there are infinitely more Johnnie Lous and Emanuelas than Macks. Their lives have changed immeasurably in the past nine years. The "I-am-a-nigger" guilt has disappeared from the majority of their characters. The company employees, especially, have reason for feeling themselves community benefactors instead of, as they'd used to characterize themselves, "pairs of hands" and "lowest of the low." So many necessary facilities are due to their hard work and willing sacrifice for those who have less than they do. The Rural Health Centers, for instance. They have three doctors in two clinics covered six days a week; there are also two full-time dentists. Migrants and other poor people, sometimes as many as two thousand a month, know that they finally have a place to come when they are ill, whether or not they can afford to pay. And that they will be treated with the same care, the same respect, given the same welcome as the counties' middle- and upper-class folks.

The clinics' functions include not only disease prevention but also minor surgery and diagnostic work-ups. If patients come with serious problems that are beyond the clinics' ability to handle, they locate specialists with whom they review the cases and to whom they send their own summaries. Some patients, of course, need hospitalization, and the clinics arrange for their admission. If the patient has insurance or other resources, it is brought to the attention of the hospital or specialist. If he has neither insurance nor resources, as is most often the case, the clinics pay the hospitals or specialists, on a Medicaid basis where it is acceptable.

After the patient leaves or is discharged from specialist care, the Rural Health Service does follow-up work with him, as long as its necessary.

Also, the Rural Health Centers employ, in addition to the doctors and dentists, registered nurses, licensed public health nurses, X-ray technicians, nursing aides and out reach workers. They were discovered in the target populations and include not only former company employees but also other rural poor who had given up any hope of "counting for something in life," as one young nurse in training, a former orange picker from another company, says.

Interestingly, less than 10 percent of company employees come to the clinics. Their income and insurance enables them to go to private doctors and hospitals. Presently, the clinical patient load, according to Administrative Director Dudley Higgins, is composed of about 60 percent migrant workers, the vast majority coming from other companies than Coca-Cola, about 35 percent of rural poor, living full-time in the areas, and about 5 percent of Medicare- or Medicaid-covered people. The racial proportion of dental patients is (and I never would have believed, when we first conceived a dental clinic, this could have happened in central Florida) 30 percent black, 30 percent Chicano, and 40 percent white.

Arnold and I spent a week in Florida visiting the various areas, talking to their administrators and people both on and off the advisory councils. We also sought to discover the feelings and opinions of outsiders, people from other agencies, some of whom had resented the project very much at its beginning and had sneered at it as "Coke's nigger project." We were especially eager, of course, to contact the public school teachers who had children out of our child development centers in their classrooms.

Having accomplished it all and seen and heard what we did at first hand, I'm almost afraid to write the truths we discovered. I have this nagging thought that some readers won't believe what we saw and heard about the program. And, especially, the way the people, the former migrants and their sons and daughters, have taken over and, with some professional help they themselves have chosen, are making it work so well.

First, we see Yvonne Patterson, the new, smart, and well-trained coordinator for child development. She stares at us in astonishment when we describe to her the conflicts between the Saints and sinners in the centers that had been a problem from the day we arrived until we left. Today's employees, still chosen from among migrants (although not necessarily Coke pickers) and the rural poor, still ardent Saints and sinners, seem, finally, to have gotten over seeing each other as strange, suspicious, dangerous, due, to a good degree to the weekly training sessions they have with their directors, as well as Lily's attitudinal training. The important thing they have in common is their concern over the welfare of the babies and children in their care.

Remembering the days when Mickey Roberts urged the aides who worked in the infant rooms to talk to the babies because it was the way *they* would learn to talk, and their overt hostility to the whole idea ("*What,* me talk to a baby that cain't, nohow, understand a word I be saying? That white lady, that Mickey, have got to be out of her head!") . . . Remembering those days when Arnold and I spent much time in the centers' infant rooms, we now had to stare at one another, awed and altogether incapable of explaining to ourselves or one another what had happened to the teacher aides who now talked, with ease, to the babies. And why it had happened as it had. They seemed, as they hadn't in our day, to see their work as a mysterious and exciting adventure, one that made them as happy as they were managing to make the babies. Nobody who didn't know the project would have believed they'd come from where they had, and weren't specially trained infant teachers.

Where were the ones we had known, who chatted together or looked bored because the infants weren't really all that interesting to them? What has totally disappeared from the atmosphere of the infant rooms, as we knew them, is the every-woman-for-herself aspect we deplored, but had to understand when we were working on the project.

Naturally, Rudy, the last project manager, was one we talked to at length about all the changes we'd noticed.

"Yeh," he said, "things are going great, aren't they? The way the people have picked things up, their professionalism has got to be startling to anybody who knew their backgrounds. You know, Johnnie Lou, when she employs a new staff member, she'll tell him:

" 'Look, if you're applying for this job just because you don't like what you've been doing like picking oranges, you don't like getting your hands dirty . . . if that's the reason you're applying here, you better forget the whole thing and be on your way. Because *the people* are what matter on this project, not those of us who've sort of made our way a little bit, but the ones who haven't yet. You're going to have to get out there in the fields and *work*. This project's not large enough for you, me, or anybody to set ourselves up as executives, and if I got anything to say about it, it's never going to be, no matter how many people we get to join us, no matter if we get every damn body in all of these twenty-one counties. And this is our aim.

" 'You come join us, you got to put a lot of time and patience into the people that need it from you. You got to be willing to work day and night so we can stand on our own feet and help all the people do the same. See, Coke did so much for us, and HRI helped alot, too, but now we're at a point (and the most of the work in getting there was done by us people) where we are independent. That means everything in the world to us.'

"This project has really changed me, too," continues Rudy. "Remember how I used to be concerned with being only a vice-president of Coke? And now I'm sad, in spite of a big promotion, that I'm not here anymore. The people on the project gave me something I know now I'd never had before, idealism and faith in people, if they're given half a chance."

It's what the people on the project gave me, too, though *I* thought I'd had it all my life.

"Listen, Rudy," I ask, "would you say, from where you're sitting now, there have been any real program failures on the project?"

"Yes, I'd say we have had some failures. The worst one was in housing. In the last two years there have been better than twenty-five houses in Lakeview Park that have gone through foreclosure." He shakes his head. "The mortgage companies, though, are more to blame for it than the people. Formerly, if you were forty-five days behind in your mortgage payments, you were contacted, warned, in effect. Also you were put on a delinquent list so the housing committee would know you were having problems and could help out. The companies don't do that anymore, don't warn you or put you on a delinquent list, but rather foreclose without a reminder of any kind. Their money is guaranteed by the federal government, so they have nothing to lose and everything to gain if they can manage to get the houses returned to them. Then, they can loan out the mortgage money at a much higher interest rate than they did to us at the time the project was first begun."

And hear this, Rudy says: There is a game played by some mortgagors known as "Ginnie May" and "Fanny May," by which a person's mortgage is sold to another company at auction. "Say I've been making my payments to the Southeast Mortgage Company. I send two months of payments there, and it's returned with a letter reading, 'We're returning your money as of now. You'll be notified where to send it in the near future.' Well, you aren't notified for sixty days or longer. You've got money in hand, there's a chance you'll spend it, right? All of a sudden, another company, called Colonial, to whom Southeast has sold your mortgage, is calling you. 'You owe me three months, four, six months back mortgage. Pay me or give up your house.' "

"But, see," Rudy says, "I'm not blaming everything on the mortgage companies either. Some of what happened was our fault, the fault of the Homeowners' Association. We didn't explain to the people all we ought to have done. Take the matter of mortgage recertification, for one thing. When a man first bought his house he may have had to pay a seventy-five-dollar monthly mortgage because of his low earnings at the time. Well, then, his income increased . . . considerably. So, therefore, did his mortgage. And he didn't connect that increase with the fact his mortgage also increased. Dura Mae, having been a migrant herself, explains the connection between income and mortgage payment to the homeowners in the simplest way she can. But maybe it's too late for explanations, and some wouldn't understand her even if it weren't. Anyway, some people got teed off, figured they had been exploited, promises had been reneged on, all of that. And off they went, leaving their houses vacant.

"Then, there were two or three people who didn't understand what home ownership meant, though the association had tried its damndest to make it clear. Anyway, they left both house and job after the season was done. And there were two men, alcoholics, one of whom walked away from his house, while the other drank up his payments. But the association is in the process of getting his house back now; he's kicked the habit.

"And Sara, Arnold, you'll be so proud of especially Lily, but also Mr. Ocea, Johnnie Lou, Dura Mae, and other members of the homeowners' association when you learn how hard they're fighting to keep the people's houses under their ownership as had been originally planned. Take this matter as an example. The Farmers' Home Mortgage Company offered the Lake Wales Housing Authority the opportunity of purchasing the twenty-five vacant houses at Lakeview Park and using them for rental purposes. Lily, Johnnie Lou, Mr. Ocea, and several members of the Lakeview Park Homeowners' Association went to the Lakeview housing authorities and persuaded them not to purchase the houses."

I ask Johnny Lou how she, Lily, and the others managed this. Her smile, as she relates the story, tries to be cynical, but her pride isn't, as she tells me what Lily said. "See, when these houses were built, the whole idea behind the thing was for poor people to be in a position to own their homes in a place where everybody owned their homes, too. I mean, that was the whole reason behind Coke's giving us the seventy acres on Lake Clinch and putting $145,000 into a water-treatment and sewage system. And, now, here come Farmers' Home, and wants to make rentals out of houses should belong to poor people, be *their own*.

"Then she said, 'The housing authority is supposed to *help* poor people, not hurt them.' 'Yeh, right,' they say. So she says, 'Well, if you rent those twenty-five homes, you are going to be hurting all the other of the Lakeview homeowners.' She asked them please not to buy the houses and let us see can we sell them instead. Well, they said, 'Okay, let's try it out awhile and see what can happen.' Only it wasn't as easy as I make it sound. Lily gave them *hell* in her way."

Then suddenly, quietly:

"You may find this hard to believe, but we, by ourselves, are . . . Well, there is fifteen houses we believe is going to be sold. Fifteen! Lily got bulletins about them houses in churches, stores, anyplace people get together. And we keep getting more applications all the time."

The ALPI staff and board have been able to set up homeowners' associations in other areas, including Fort Pierce and Indiantown, too.

"And the associations in those places are *powerful*," Lily says. "Their houses were built by private contractors who took the worst kind of advantage of them. I mean the kitchens and bathrooms were shambles. They were, literally, falling apart after a few years. And when the people themselves contacted the contractors, and asked, begged them to do something, you can imagine the answers they got. But when the homeowners' association got after them, and Judge Ralph Flowers, our lawyer, threatened legal action, they did a double take. They replaced broken-down kitchen and bathroom facilities and just made those homes livable. Now, Ralph's conducting courses for the Fort Pierce and Indiantown associations about their responsibilities and rights as homeowners. And the people are . . . well, overwhelmed and joyful, are the only words that come to me when I try to describe them. They're beginning to realize the importance of people power from the contact they're having with our people.

"Among the things they arranged, in order to prevent their community from deterioration, was police protection; the area is carefully controlled now. Also, many of the young people have become volunteer policemen, and very adequate ones."

The people in all the twenty-one counties have also begun to organize themselves for ways out of seasonal work. At the project's beginning, Disneyland, at Lily's behest, began training and employing company employees during the off season in the groves, for many jobs in the recreation complex. The trainers were patient, the employees eager, and the program a success for both Disneyland management and company migrants, who acquired through that work still more of a sense of independence, both as individuals and as participants in the project.

In line with the value they began to place on their own increased self-reliance, members of the regional advisory councils have appointed a task force for working out not only a repetition of the effectual Disneyland program but also other money-earning programs to help the people on an individual basis, and pay for programs the boards consider important, even though outside funding is not available for them. Recently, the task force went to North Carolina to meet with the National Sharecroppers, who are experimenting with a new kind of organic farming. Mr. Ocea, our first board chairman, explains the principles of organic farming. "Well, in that kind of farming, you dump all kinds of seeds together when you are planting them, okra, onions, tomatoes and all. Then what happens when they grow out . . . They grow out separate, but each plant depend on the other to help it. Like onions planted organically will keep insects away not just from themself, but the other plants, too. Then you got taller crops to help shade littler ones from the sun.

"Another thing the sharecroppers going to do is to work with us on a new way of growing potatoes that been used in Tuskegee, the agricultural college, for desert areas. It, like Disneyland work, is something our people could do in the off-time of picking."

The task force also plans to teach not just migrants out of all the central Florida companies but also any rural poor who want to learn such service occupations as guard service, maid service, and lawn maintenance.

"The idea that intrigues me most," Lily says, "is one I believe originated with Mr. Ocea. You see, there are few, if any, proper cemeteries for black people here in the South. We want to learn how to make headstones and vaults so we can develop and operate a decent black cemetery."

The councils are considering new ideas for working in horticulture as well as agriculture. They are thinking of opening a garment factory. The project wouldn't require much capital outlay as they conceive it. Also, Lily's got an idea for "making Coke hats. You know how old Coke bottles, and mugs with Coca-Cola written on them, and Coke shirts and such sell. Well, why shouldn't Coke hats sell, too? So we've gone to the company and asked them to contribute their used cans to us, and also to give us a contract for making the hats."

The regional boards intend to go to other citrus growers in their areas, small growers who can neither afford group insurance or are thinking of providing it for their workers, and telling their officers, according to Johnnie Lou, "We know you can't give group insurance to your workers, and we ain't blaming you for that. But, see, we can help you out so you can do what is right about it. We can take your workers into our group insurance plan. They will pay so much, you will pay so much, and we will help out by giving you all the services you couldn't get for yourself. Like, for instance, we could do all your accounting for you, at a lot less than you could get it any other place. And your workers could become a part of our credit union, too."

She laughs. "Well, see, in that way, we don't need to tell them what is in it for them if they go along with our plans. Like, they would know such a thing could help them keep their workers instead of having the big turnover they got all the time. And the nicest thing of all is we can help the workers out of other companies that some of them don't even know about group insurance and credit unions, and help ourselves, too. I think the small growers may be ready to go for our idea, and, when I think about it, well, Sara, don't it make you feel *good* when you think about us, that nine years ago we felt we were nothing, and today, I and plenty of others think *we* can maybe change the whole thing of migrant people's life around here in Florida."

She hesitates, and I see there are tears in her eyes. "You know what is in my head on some days when everything seems to be going right with ALPI? It is that maybe, someday, all the growers in American that they got migrants working they gon' take a lesson from how good we are doing, and know migrants are people as good as anybody else and can do as good a job . . . for *them*. See, we got to make all the growers know what is the truth, that the company ain't lost money because they helped us at the beginning when we needed help. If you ask me, we workers are giving them back as good as we got. I mean, we work hard and as faithful as anybody else. And we ain't always quitting the job like other pickers in other companies.

"Sara," she asks, "do you think I am off of my head, or is there really a chance other migrant people (and the growers, too) could take a lesson from what has happened here in the company groves and try doing the same for theyselves and maybe making it like we are beginning to?"

Bob and I, when we first conceived this book, had thought to include a chapter addressed to social scientists and others concerned with the problems of social change about the behavioral science concepts and principles that first inspired the people with their own faith and belief in change. About the Normative Systems Model, based on the assumption that people, even those as hopeless, defeated and downtrodden as most we met during our early days in Florida, do not need to passively adjust to what exists but are capable of redesigning the cultures of which they are a part.

Then, on our last trip to Florida, we talked to Johnnie Lou about what we meant to do, and she challenged us. "I bet I could tell you, because I have thought about it often, some of the things you done to help us do what we did." She told us, of course, and listening to her, we realized that not only had she grasped the whole significance of the Normative Systems approach but that her interpretation is as effective, and maybe more in its way, as any we can hope to give. We ask her, therefore, to allow us to record and publish it in her words.

"See," Johnnie Lou says, "HRI were the first people to tell us what the word 'culture' means. It means that when people like us come together or when the big shots, the 'bossmen' do, when *any people* come together, they form what you call a culture. And that that culture may be the most important thing in your life. Because it make you believe that you, and the other people in it with you . . . you all are a certain kind of people, and all that happens to you is for that reason. You got nothing to do with your own terrible life if you are a migrant like us. You just live that life the happiest way you can, *if* you can, and don't try doing anything to change it because it won't do any good, anyhow.

"Like all I, and all the others in my culture, would hear from the time we were babies, the time we was born almost, was, 'Well, a dumb migrant is what you are, and all you'll ever have the brains to be. You ain't good for anything but picking the bossmen's oranges or pears or plums or whatsoever. School? What you need to go to school for? You are too dumb to learn anything in school anyway, as was your ma and pa before you. And their ma and pa before them. So why bother about even *thinking* of going to school?

"Well, I and all the people in my culture, being told this from early on, being seen like this from early on, how would you expect we gon' to see ourselves, feel about ourselves; what you expect we gon' do about ourselves? Well . . . *nothing*. Why? Because, if everybody think of us this evil way, we come to think of ourselves that way, too. And can't believe we have it in us to change our life, and certainly not the life of other people in our culture. We live by, you know, the 'norms of our culture,' what everybody told us was the normal way for migrants to live.

"Like if I, as a migrant, go out and spend my bread on getting drunk because I hate my life so much and want to forget it as near as I can and as often . . . If I, as a migrant, get drunk instead of saving to buy me a house or for my kids' education, and everybody I meet tells me or lets me know in some other way, 'Well, you poor dumb migrant, you are just a natural drunk, is all, and don't ever think about tomorrow or your kids. You are a *bad* person and *deserve* your lousy life.

"Let me tell you, you get told that often enough and treated like you don't deserve any better than you're getting because you are who you are, you start to believe it youself, it is you 'culture norm.'

"So, what happen then is you don't do nothing to try to change your life, or your kids' lives, because, like I say, you don't believe you have it in you.

"But if you learn you do have it in you, you are no more

dumb than anybody else but just kept down by other people who been telling *lies* about you and your people not being as smart or good as anybody else, well, then you know you can change your life. You know it, and your people know it, and you get together, like we did at ALPI, and you do change your and your kids' lives. You get education, you give it to your kids, and you find out, it's doing you a lot of good. And your kids . . . Well, they can learn as good as any other kids if they're given a chance to.

"Well, sure, at first, you need help. And I myself always will be grateful to the company and HRI for giving us that help when we needed it, helping us believe in ourselves. That were, was, I mean, one of the most important things they and y'all done for us. Then, letting *us* decide what we needed to make our life what we want it. You feel important, like other people, when you see you know what you want and can help get it for yourself, you and your people. Knowing that brought a change in our norms, our 'cultural norms.' The minute you say, '*I* am in a position to make my life what I want it to be, *I got it in me, and my people got it in them,* even if we was born migrants, to be other things if we want . . .' Well, it is like you are born again. Your whole life changes when you *know* you are as good as everybody else.

"And our kids, the little ones especially, the way I see it, they gon' know they are as good as anybody because that is what the rest of us are working for, the kids' having everything."

"By everything, Johnnie, do you mean every advantage?" I ask.

"Yeh, sure. The child development center will start them off. And they go on from there, to regular school and high school and college. Maybe even medical and law school, like I tell you two of our kids are doing right now. Because the children are what matters most to us in the world. And I believe we matter a whole lot to them. They know in their hearts all we are doing, as the outsiders also do. I mean, the ones who didn't care or believe we had anything on the ball when you was first here to help us become what we are today. You know, all the social agencies that used to make fun of us, and call us 'Coke's nigger project,' well, I just wish you hear what they say about us today."

Following Johnnie's lead, Arnold and I went to visit area agencies, and hear, at first hand, their attitudes toward ALPI. Here is what they told us.

Vernon Lee—Community Action Agency: "ALPI works hard to assure tenants' rights. They are among the best when it comes to dealing with eviction problems and such. They have been the reason why more people have been enabled to stay in their homes, when they would have been put out, than you can imagine."

Maynard Clayton—Food Stamps Agency: "ALPI helps our applicants more than anyone else. For instance, they assist them in filling out applications and providing collateral contacts, references, you know. And their Rural Legal Services are invaluable in helping us resolve migrants' complaints against grove owners and crew chiefs."

Edward Ellsworth—Health and Rehabilitative Services, State of Florida, and president of the Council of Social Agencies: "We have a purchase of service contract with ALPI's child development centers. And we are delighted to have our children going there. Really, the child development centers are the best in the state. They work with us very actively. Incidentally, no, that's the wrong word—excitingly. Their members, children's parents as well as those who don't have kids, are very active in working with the Council of Social Agencies. And they are creative in their work with us. Having been migrants themselves, we look to them to develop 'creative ideas,' 'realistic ideas' we couldn't possibly come up with in helping other migrants. They are so *sensitive* to the people's needs, it sometimes makes us shudder to realize how much we don't know by comparison to them.

"During the 'seventy-six freeze here, all the agencies were terrified over what might happen to the migrants. ALPI, being what it is, may have been most scared of all of us. God knows, they'd have reason to be.

"Well, you know what most people do when they become scared. They freeze like the weather did. Not ALPI, though. They called all the social agencies together and said, 'What can *you* do about "Operation Freeze?' They developed the name Operation Freeze, by the way. 'What *will* you do?' And got us all thinking as we hadn't done before. They themselves offered overnight housing and cooking facilities both in their headquarters and members' homes. We couldn't have done that, obviously. I'm sorry to admit our members couldn't conceive of that kind of generosity. Besides, ALPI didn't have to cope with the red tape we did. You know, people needed bed and board, they provided it. Period. They work from the heart, which is not to say they don't use their heads, and all of the social agencies in the areas appreciate that."

At last Arnold and I are at the point of visiting the schools the children out of our child development centers attend . . . an activity we've been lusting after since we arrived in Florida. Here is what we heard about the children from their teachers in the Fair Lawn School, attended by all the kindergartners and first-graders in the town, white, black, chicano, rural poor, migrant, middle class, and even occasionally upper class.

"Deane Fillmore . . . I surely enjoy that child. He has a fine sense of humor and good personality. He is above average socially, a quality I ascribe to his years at the ALPI Child Development Center. I also ascribe his affectionate nature—the first thing he wants in the morning is a hug—to his years at the ALPI center. And he is mature, far more mature, than the rest of the group."

"Gerald Mahoney [a first-grader] is in the top group of his class. And very well adjusted to school. I attribute that to his time at the child development center. Also, the fact he is looked up to as a leader in the classroom."

Of course, there are children in the school, as there are adults in ALPI, who are slow learners. Their IQs, according to their teachers (and I can't be entirely sure the teachers are right because I don't know their prejudices), are low, and they can't learn on a level with the other children, no matter what you do to influence them.

But, then, there is Tyrone, Bob's, Arnold's, and my favorite since he was eight months old and summoned us to his crib with his eyes and smile. His teacher says, "Tyrone's at the top of his class. I mean, he's at the top level of the top group. He came into the kindergarten class knowing numbers, colors, all the letters of the alphabet. None of our privileged kids had what he did at the very beginning of the semester. That child development center has got to be great. But the way I see it, Tyrone's Tyrone, and has managed a lot on his own. Here, in my class, he works totally independently. His sight vocabulary's terrific. Man! Children like him, I could teach one hundred of them at a time. I swear, my prayer for Tyrone is that he'll become president of the U.S. one day."

It is Bob's and my prayer, too.

INDEX

A

Abell, Gerald, xi, 66, 109, 111-13, 116, 124, 126
Agricultural Labor Project, Inc. (ALPI), xiii, xvi
  accomplishments of, 257-65, 269-76
  criticisms and failures of, 261-62, 266-68
  headquarters building for, 249-50, 255
  Smith on, 68
Aides, *see* Community aides
Alpine Quarters, 15-21
Auburndale (Fla.), xiii
Austin, J. Paul, xi, xvi, 257
Avon Park–Frostproof–Wachula Community Development Corporation, *see* Community Development Corporation

B

Babies
  talking to, 264
  See also Child care; Child development
Barbecue, 106-8
Bars, 33-42
Belle Glade (Fla.), 113-16
Black power, 64
Board of directors, regional, 257-61
Board of trustees, 96, 102-8, 124-28, 177-80
Bossmen, *see* Supervisors

Bourgeois ("boojie") blacks, 110, 117
Budget, 124-28, 259
Burning crosses, 39, 90

C

Califano, Joseph, 58, 62-65
Catholic school, 233-34
Cemeteries for blacks, 269-70
Central Region Child Development Center, *see* Child development program
CETA (Comprehensive Employment Training Act), 252, 258
Chavez, Cesar, 55, 71, 259
Chicanos as "whites," 48-49
Child care
  original lack of, 6-7
  proposed, 52
  See also Child development program
Child care center, 106, 117
Child development program, xiv, 100, 164-80, 274
  budget for, 127-28
  finding director for, 118-24
  plans for, 117-18
Child labor laws, violation of, 6
Christmas, 230
Churches, 25-32, 44, 135, 194-97, 214-16, 230-32
  See also Sinners
Clark, Ed, xi, 259
Clarke, Kaye, xi, 106, 135-55, 175-76, 178
Clayton, Maynard, xi, 274

279

Cleveland, Tom, xi, 261
Coca-Cola Company
   benefits to, from program, 257
   employees' attitudes to, xiii-xiv, 11-12, 47, 222
   idealism and commitment of, xiii, xvi, 128, 134, 170
   local attitude toward, 23, 26
   long-term program of, 61
   meeting between workers and officers of, 58-65
   officers of, xi
   projects sponsored by, 181, 249
Coca-Cola hats, 270
Community Action Agency, xi, 274
Community aides
   hiring of, 43-45
   meeting between Coca-Cola officials and, 58-63
   preparation for visits to people by, 96-106
Community Development Corporation, board of trustees of, 96, 102-8, 124-28, 177-80
Council of Social Agencies, xi, 274
County health clinics, 154-56
County health director, 181-83
Cultural norms, nature of, 271-73

D

Disneyland, 269
Drinking, 16, 54, 90-91

E

Earnings of agricultural workers, 6, 256
Eating customs, 83, 85, 185-86
Ellsworth, Edward, xi, 274

El Paso (Tex.), Spanish forbidden in school in, 75-77
Epstein, Dr., xi, 142, 144-45, 151-53
Everett, Dura Mae, 110, 111, 116, 121, 123, 267

F

Fair Lawn School, 275-76
Farmers' Home Mortgage Company, 267-68
FHA (Farmers Home Administration), 102
"Field niggers," 202
Field-work students, 122-24, 134
Fires, 16-17
Fitting rooms, lack of, 240-41
Flirting by southern belles, 111
Florida Health and Rehabilitation Services, 160, 274
Flowers, Ralph, 268
Food Stamps Agency, xi, 274
Free things, lack of appreciation for, 3-4
Freeze of 'seventy-six, 274
Fringe benefits of employees, xiv, 256

G

Garbage pickup, installation of, 51
GED (High School General Equivalency Diploma), 254, 258
Guns, collection of, 85-86

H

Harris, Arnold, xi, 118-21, 153-63
Haskins, Lily, xi, 110, 111, 116, 122, 123, 179, 182-83, 186-87

on black schools, 120-21
as program director, 250-55, 258, 267, 269-70
at sharing session, 131-32
Health care
exceptional case of, 242-45
original lack of, 5, 19-24, 50, 157-60
regional organization of, 262-63
Health centers (clinics), xiv, 100-1, 106-7, 262-63
aides for, 135-41
dentists of, 101, 160-63, 254, 262
funds supplied for, 160
Health interviews, 141-56
Health Education and Welfare, *see* United States Department of Health, Education and Welfare
Higgins, Dudley, xi, 263
Home Extension Service, 252
Hospitals, *see* Health care
Hotel Naples sessions, 66-81, 83-84, 112
"House niggers," 202
Housing
foreclosures on, 266-68
new low-income, xiv, 101-2, 184-86, 266-69
original, 14-21, 45
Human Resources Institutes, 109
authors as members of, xiii

I

Intelligence of blacks, 97-99

J

Jail, personal story of, 240-43
Jews, 97
workers' attitude toward, 10-11

Johnson, Lyndon B., 62
Jokes, racial, 69-70

K

Kennedy, Robert F., 92
Kelly, William M., xi, 59, 66-67, 72, 92, 97, 106, 109-10, 116, 122, 251
on ALPI's beginnings, 259-61
background of, 53
Keough, Donald, xi, 58-65, 66, 92, 97
Klan, *see* United Klans of America

L

Labor unions
Smith on, 71
See also United Farmworkers' Union
Ladders to pick oranges, 4
Leaders, 191
criticism of power of, 262
search for, 33, 39, 43
Lee, Vernon, xi, 274
Library, living-learning, 117, 126-27
Life histories of two women, 191-246
Lighting, installation of, 51, 107
Lunch program, 173
Lynch, Rev. Charles Conley, 89

M

Managers, training session for, 66-81, 83-84
Manpower Services, 258
Marriage
black-black, 216-18
black-white, 35-38, 92-93
Martin Luther King Farmworkers' Fund, 260
Maxcy Quarters, 14

Maxwell, Rudy, xi, 257, 258, 265-67
Medical association, local, 160-62
Medicaid, 263
Medical care, *see* Health care
Miami Beach (Fla.), 115
Midwife, 15-20
Migrancy
  Coca-Cola program as example of what can be done vs., 62, 270-71
  decline of, xiv, 257
  how to overcome, 56
  personal stories of, 208-14, 226-27, 234-37
Migrant Health Funds, 160
Migrant Health Service, 156
Minute Maid, *see* Coca-Cola Company
Mortgages, foreclosures on, 266-68

N

National Health Service Corps, 160-63
National Sharecroppers, 269
New York City, as Sin City, 9, 29-31
"Nigger"
  "field" vs. "house," 202
  use of term, 68-70, 77, 80, 83-84
"Nigger meat," 83
Normative Systems Model, 67-68, 271

O

Operation Freeze, 274

P

Patterson, Yvonne, xi, 264
Pepsi Cola, 58-59

Pheasant, Dr. Tom, 156, 160-62
Poetry, 44-45

R

Regional board of directors, 257-61
Regional Medical Program, 160
Religion, *see* Churches; Sinners
Roberts, Mickey, xi, 119-24, 166-71, 173-78, 264
Rogge, Ed, 156, 160
Root people, 218-19, 221-24
Rouse, Ed, xi, 254, 259
Rural Health Centers, 262-63

S

Schools
  Catholic, 233-34
  Fair Lawn, 275-76
  original lack of attendance at, 5-6
  Spanish forbidden in, 75-77
  See also Child development program
Seniority rights of employees, xiv, 256
Sexual relations
  black-black, 29-31, 204-6, 220
  black-white, 197-204
  See also Marriage
Sharing sessions, 74-81, 83-84, 128-34
Silverzweig, Stanley, xi, 125, 128-31
  as Jew, 10-11, 97
Sinners, 102-5, 165-66, 175-80, 228, 264
Slavery, 14, 193, 202
Smith, C. Lucian, xi, xvi, 46-47, 51-53, 57, 92, 97, 107, 257
  meeting between workers and, 58-65

at training sessions, 66-73, 77, 83-84, 112-13
Social change, 271
Soul, 123
Spanish language forbidden in school, 75-77
Spanish newspapers, 159-60
Starnes, Tom, 110, 113, 119
Supervisors
  changing attitudes of, xv
  example of home life of, 85-95
  example of original attitudes of, 3-9
  loans by, 86-87
  training sessions for, 66-81, 83-84
  See also Worker-management meetings

T

Tocqueville, Alexis de, 162
Toilets
  in buses, 107
  lack of, 7-8, 12-13, 24, 48, 239-40
  new, 51, 107
Tuskegee Institute, 269

U

United Farmworkers' Union, 55, 71, 259-60
United Klans of America (U.K.A.), 34, 36-37, 39-42, 67
  supervisor's defense of, 89-92, 95

United States Department of Health, Education and Welfare
  health center and, xiv, 160
  lunch-program records for, 173
United Way, 163
"University of Cloud Grove," 260, 261
University of South Florida, field-work students from, 122-24, 134

V

Violence, 16, 33, 45-46
  by United Klans, 39

W

Wages of agricultural workers, 6, 256
Whipping by crew chief, 236-37
Whores, 29-31, 33, 90, 239
Wilmington (Del.), 83
Witches, 15, 135, 136, 141, 172, 218-19, 221-24
Women, life histories of two, 191-246
Women's club, local, 35
Worker-management meetings, xv
  proposed, 51
Worms, 21-24

Y

Yaeger, Dr. Howard, 156-60